ELEANOR ROOSEVELT

MODERN FIRST LADIES

Lewis L. Gould, Editor

TITLES IN THE SERIES

Helen Taft: Our Musical First Lady, Lewis L. Gould

Ellen and Edith: Woodrow Wilson's First Ladies, Kristie Miller

First Lady Florence Harding: Behind the Tragedy and Controversy, Katherine A. S. Sibley

Grace Coolidge: The People's Lady in Silent Cal's White House, Robert H. Ferrell

Lou Henry Hoover: Activist First Lady, Nancy Beck Young

Bess Wallace Truman: Harry's White House "Boss," Sara L. Sale

Mamie Doud Eisenhower: The General's First Lady, Marilyn Irvin Holt

Jacqueline Kennedy: First Lady of the New Frontier, Barbara A. Perry

Lady Bird Johnson: Our Environmental First Lady, Lewis L. Gould

Betty Ford: Candor and Courage in the White House, John Robert Greene

Rosalynn Carter: Equal Partner in the White House, Scott Kaufman

Nancy Reagan: On the White House Stage, James G. Benze Jr.

Barbara Bush: Presidential Matriarch, Myra G. Gutin

Hillary Rodham Clinton: Polarizing First Lady, Gil Troy

ELEANOR ROOSEVELT

TRANSFORMATIVE FIRST LADY

MAURINE H. BEASLEY

UNIVERSITY PRESS OF KANSAS

Published by the University Press of Kansas (Lawrence, Kansas 66045), which was organized by the Kansas Board of Regents and is operated and funded by Emporia State University, Fort Hays State University, Kansas State University, Pittsburg State University, the University of Kansas, and Wichita State University

ISBN 978-0-7006-1727-2

Printed in the United States of America

Book Club Edition

CONTENTS

EDITOR'S FOREWORD

Eleanor Roosevelt occupies a singular place in the history of modern first ladies. During her twelve-year tenure in the White House, she changed the expectations and standards of performance for wives of the presidents. Activist and controversial, Mrs. Roosevelt served both as a surrogate for the president and as an independent political operator pursuing her own agenda of good causes. The range of what first ladies could do experienced permanent expansion after Eleanor Roosevelt's abundant energies had been applied to her position.

Though she has been the subject of numerous important biographies and specialized studies, Eleanor Roosevelt as first lady from 1933 to 1945 has not been the focus of a single analytic narrative. Maurine Beasley, a scholar with a rich background in the life and times of Eleanor Roosevelt, has now crafted a book that provides just such a detailed examination of this innovative and important first lady. From the ways in which Eleanor Roosevelt earned a living to the domestic arrangements in the White House, Beasley is an insightful and informed guide to the historical issues surrounding Mrs. Roosevelt's performance. No major question about Eleanor Roosevelt is ignored, and fresh light is provided on her relations with her husband, the people around her, and the causes she championed.

The result is a book that will both reward general readers interested in Eleanor Roosevelt's historical importance and inform specialists looking for judicious appraisals of the controversies surrounding this first lady. Beasley has infused her story with the accumulated wisdom and sound judgments of a historian who has immersed herself in the literature and sources on her subject. Anyone interested in the enigma that was Eleanor Roosevelt will discover in Beasley's work the essential information for understanding how this dynamic and troubled woman succeeded in transforming the institution of the first lady during a dozen years of activism and commitment.

—*Lewis L. Gould*

PREFACE

Biographers of Eleanor Roosevelt work in quicksand. They try to capture her essence, only to discover that what seemed apparent at one phase of her life vanishes at another. She presents a maze of contradictions: an idealist who inspired the world yet carried on a moneymaking career in the White House that depended on her position, a conventional-appearing wife and mother who found emotional succor mainly from intense relationships outside her family, a feminist heroine who nevertheless opposed the Equal Rights Amendment for most of her life, the first president's wife to openly court the press at the same time she insisted that her personal life be off the public record. Was she sincerely intent on good works or, as political opponents charged, a busybody who traveled incessantly in a quest for personal fulfillment if not aggrandizement? Collective memory has rendered a verdict for the former, but questions remain regarding Eleanor Roosevelt's role as first lady.

How much did she influence the administration of her husband, Franklin D. Roosevelt, the only individual to have been elected president of the United States four times? What did she actually accomplish in the White House during two pivotal eras in United States life—first, the Great Depression, and second, World War II? How did it happen that a woman whose physical appearance and speaking voice engendered scathing criticism and ridicule became one of the leaders of an evolving media age? Eleanor Roosevelt remains a conundrum. Writing during his mother's lifetime, her eldest son, James, described her as a bundle of contradictions, "wise and naïve, rational and impulsive, determined and uncertain, compassionate and occasionally misguided."[1] He called her life "full and fascinating," adjectives with which it would be hard to disagree, but which do not boil down to a simple statement.[2]

My personal fascination with Eleanor Roosevelt stems from her influence on my mother, a housewife in a small Missouri town who read Roosevelt's syndicated newspaper column, "My Day," to me when I was a small child. Rock-solid Republicans, my parents detested Franklin Roosevelt, convinced that big-city bosses who formed part of the New Deal coalition corruptly influenced American life. Yet, my mother relished "My Day," which described Eleanor's White House activities, and insisted, "I am sure that *she* is better than *he* is." Years later, as a journalism historian, I wondered how Eleanor Roosevelt made her life as first lady speak to my mother and many other women with such force and meaning. This book is in part an effort to find out.

ACKNOWLEDGMENTS

First, I want to thank Lewis L. Gould for his help through the years as I have studied Eleanor Roosevelt and tried to assess her significance as a public figure. Because my own background is in journalism, I initially concentrated on her as a communicator. Prof. Gould, however, urged me to think more broadly about her as a political leader as well as role model for her successors. I am grateful for his excellent insights and encouragement.

Many individuals have graciously allowed me to interview them about their personal recollections of Eleanor Roosevelt. Among them are Max Desfor and Eleanor Zartman. I am appreciative of help from members of the American Newswomen's Club, to which Roosevelt belonged when that organization was called the American Newspaper Women's Club.

Special thanks go to the many archivists who have cataloged Roosevelt's multitudinous papers and generously given me their time and expertise. They include Robert Clark, supervising archivist, and Karen Anson, Mark Renovitch, Kirsten Carter, Alycia Vivona, and other members of the staff of the Franklin D. Roosevelt Library at Hyde Park, New York, which holds a large part of Eleanor Roosevelt's papers. I have benefited from the aid of archivists at the Eric Friedheim Library of the National Press Club, Washington, D.C., and staff members at the Manuscript Division, Library of Congress, Washington, D.C. Librarians at the Washingtonian Collection of the Martin Luther King Jr. Memorial Library of the District of Columbia have readily located some of Eleanor Roosevelt's press coverage during her White House years. I am grateful for the professional expertise of these individuals.

I wish to express appreciation to Fred Woodward and his staff at the University Press of Kansas, with whom working has been a pleasure. Prof. Barbara Perry, who kindly reviewed the manuscript in detail, offered concrete suggestions for improvement. I am in her debt.

In particular, I want to thank my husband, Henry R. Beasley, who has encouraged me in this endeavor, provided computer expertise, and generally proven to be my strong right arm. Without his love and support this book would not exist.

ELEANOR ROOSEVELT

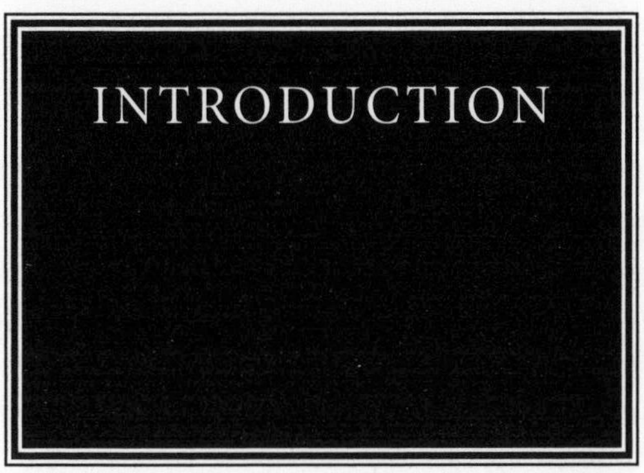

INTRODUCTION

Politics was a family affair for Eleanor Roosevelt, who found her own place in it, both symbolically and practically, after years of struggle. As an orphaned adolescent in an English boarding school, she knew that her favorite uncle, Theodore Roosevelt, had become president of the United States. As a shy young wife, she helped her husband, Franklin D. Roosevelt, follow in Uncle Ted's footsteps. As a widow and novice diplomat, she surprised her peers by serving as the guiding spirit behind the United Nations Declaration of Human Rights, one of the pivotal documents of contemporary times. When she refused to run for the U.S. Senate from New York, an office she easily could have won, she said she did not want to interfere with the political aspirations of her children.[1] She lived to see two of her sons elected to the United States House of Representatives, but far more importantly, she herself personified the liberal wing of the Democratic Party.

At the time of her death in 1962, she assumed almost mythic proportions, revered by millions as the embodiment of humanitarianism. A widely reprinted cartoon by Bill Mauldin showed a group of cherubs peering through the clouds and exclaiming, "It's her."[2] Yet, as the noted historian Arthur M. Schlesinger Jr. wrote in his diary, she was both less and more than a symbol. He called her a "tough and salty old lady," a political pro who devastated opponents like President Harry S Truman, with whom she differed at the 1956

Democratic convention by pushing Adlai Stevenson's presidential candidacy over Truman's opposition.[3] Schlesinger saw her as a woman whose emotional needs colored her personal and political interactions. "I was never close to Mrs. Roosevelt—those really close to her were those she could do something for, and I did not fit into that pattern," he wrote, adding that he "valued her counsel."[4]

To her grandson, Curtis, known as "Buzzie," when he and his sister, "Sistie," whose real name was Eleanor, lived in the White House as small children, "Grandmere" remained a paradox throughout her life. While her "lasting reputation rests upon the broad concern she evinced for others . . . empathy eluded my grandmother when it came to family members," he noted in a memoir.[5] "She was much more at ease with people who were simply her friends, and she was even less inhibited with strangers."[6]

Gender, family, and life experience, tempered by personal anxiety, served as defining elements for Eleanor's own involvement in politics, which she believed could be used for social good. As her career evolved, she mastered political skills that made her both an idealist and a pragmatist. She reached this point after years as the nation's first lady. As "Mrs. Roosevelt," the way almost everyone outside the family referred to her except Lorena Hickok, a journalist and close confidante who used her first name, Eleanor transformed herself into a political icon.[7]

Presiding in the White House from 1933 to 1945, Eleanor developed what had been a supporting role into one that personified the growing efforts of American women to achieve in their own right during the middle of the twentieth century. Biographers initially portrayed her as a submissive wife who turned into an unconventional political partner by acting as her disabled husband's surrogate. Joseph P. Lash, a close friend, won a Pulitzer Prize for a book that added to this narrative by revealing that Eleanor launched her own career after agreeing to remain in her marriage following discovery of Franklin's romance with her social secretary.[8] Newer scholarship has uncovered other important areas of her life: these include erotic elements in her relationship with Hickok, a lesbian; the strength Roosevelt drew from networks of women; her contribution to civil rights after leaving the White House; and the importance of her work on human rights at the United Nations.[9]

Relatively little work has identified the specific ways she made the White House her stage for twelve years to perform an unusual role as first lady. Reinforcing her husband's administration, she moved continuously, traveling the globe, speaking, writing, meeting people, but always keeping in sight goals that she believed represented the right kind of political action. Today, when large segments of the public distrust politics and politicians—and candidates routinely run opposing the "Washington establishment"—it is easy to forget that Eleanor, known for her devotion to the downtrodden, was herself a consummate practitioner of politics.

Eleanor left an indelible impression on her successors. Hillary Rodham Clinton, after the failure of her health care plan in 1995, even held sessions in the White House with a psychic philosopher who persuaded her to enact inspirational conversations with Eleanor Roosevelt and Mahatma Gandhi.[10] For years presidential spouses have been described as either activists in the Eleanor Roosevelt mold or traditionalists who do not follow her example. Eleanor widened the concept of the first lady from being a minor player to a key supporting actress in the drama of the presidency itself. As she grew in her position, she used it for self-expression, writing a daily newspaper column, magazine articles, and books and giving paid radio addresses and lectures. In her public communication she demonstrated extraordinary ability to reach out to ordinary citizens, gaining respect and recognition from many, but by no means all, Americans.

Nevertheless, Eleanor displayed ambivalence as an advocate for complete equality of women. If there was a superficial aspect to her activities, as critics contended, it stemmed from her own position in a male-dominated political world. Superficiality masked such issues as the ill-defined parameters of the first lady role, conflicts among women in politics, and her own inner need for personal accomplishment. While Eleanor worked to make the political process more accessible to women and other groups left on the margins of power, she recognized that white males held the upper hand and that women had little choice except to adjust to their rules.

In one of her early magazine articles, "Women Must Learn to Play the Game as Men Do," published in 1928, the year her husband won election as governor of New York, she urged women to emulate male politicians.[11] In her own political dealings she emphasized her role as wife and, later, widow of Franklin D. Roosevelt, the only individual to have been elected president four times. Eleanor appealed to women by stressing that political involvement enabled them to broaden their traditional concerns for home and family to a wider community. Her own interests embraced traditional feminine concerns—such as maternal and child health, aid to the downtrodden, education and jobs for youth, loyalty to family and friends—which she laid out on a broad White House canvass.

Although Eleanor modified her opposition late in her life, she never was a strong supporter of the proposed Equal Rights Amendment and worked against it while in the White House. She believed in a form of feminism that took into account gender differences and needs.[12] Individual, more than group, achievement by women characterized her view of women's participation in the public world. She presented herself as a wife and mother in politics, not as a politician, although she made her White House years an opportunity to stride forth as a political figure.

To some she cannot be counted as a full-scale feminist because she did not acknowledge the overall effects of gender on society. She did not look for discrimination or try to analyze causes for societal assumptions of female inferiority. She did not peer at the world through a gendered lens.[13] What she did do fit the spirit of her times. She used her access to the emerging power of the mass media to present herself as a model of political womanhood for the mid-twentieth century.

This book tells the story of how she operated, both in and out of public view, to advance the causes in which she believed by participating in the political process. In various degrees previous first ladies had acted as their husbands' helpmates, hostesses, and unofficial advisors. Eleanor took the ambiguous position of first lady and transformed it into an institution of the American political system, dramatizing her actions through constant exposure via newspapers, magazines, radio, and motion pictures. Her concept of the role of the first lady was not revolutionary, except in terms of making the president's wife far more visible than previously as a political celebrity. Her abundant energy did not translate into a coherent political program, in part because she lacked any direct way to sponsor one, although elements of a program can be seen in the legislation she was known to favor.[14] Conscious that she was not an elected official, she had to mute herself, yet her ability to project herself as a symbol of compassion for the poor, minorities, women, young people, and refugees gave her credibility that greatly enhanced Franklin D. Roosevelt's administration.

Eleanor was not a plaster saint, but an individual in whom insecurities and personal misfortunes created her own ego needs to be loved and recognized. At the same time she served as a symbol of caring for multitudes of Americans beset first by the strains of the Depression and then by World War II, she pursued a personal money-making career. While in the White House, she earned income as a journalist, author, and commentator, using it to validate her own self-worth.[15] Analysis of the strengths and weaknesses of her performance as first lady must begin with her relationship to her own family and to those she drew into her orbit, making them a part of her extended family.

Personal relationships, not abstract theories, gave Eleanor the emotional and intellectual ballast she needed to mobilize her own resources in the context of her unique circumstances. She networked through women's organizations, just as she involved herself in the Democratic Party. She saw politics as a means for initiating governmental action to help millions better their lives, although she marshaled whatever political capital she possessed as first lady in idiosyncratic, not always effective, ways.

Generally known to be more liberal than her husband, to whom she did not hesitate to state her opinions privately, in public Roosevelt did not disagree with him. When he ordered Japanese Americans sent to internment camps, she stopped making public statements opposing this policy. Her White House career grew out of her involvement with her family and associates, which remained the nucleus of her political world. During the course of her political development her thinking moved beyond her girlhood concept of Victorian charity to bold affirmations of human rights, from individual family matters to concern about humanity throughout the world. She experienced intense friendships with individuals outside her social class. Still, years after the death of her husband, she remained proud to be called "Mrs. Franklin D. Roosevelt," a symbol of being a wife and mother, as well as "Eleanor Roosevelt," a symbol of an independent woman. This book explores how personal relationships led her to hone skills that resulted in the evolution of the position of the first lady from relative passivity to active political leadership.

CHAPTER 1

FINDING A PLACE

"I think I was a curious mixture of extreme innocence and unworldliness with a great deal of knowledge of some of the less agreeable sides of life."
Eleanor Roosevelt in 1903, from her autobiography

During the winters of 1903 and 1904 a shy, willowy woman, secretly engaged although she was only nineteen years old, paid occasional afternoon visits to the White House. Eleanor Roosevelt sipped tea and made polite conversation in its historic parlors, which had been newly refurbished under the direction of her patrician aunt Edith and exuberant uncle Ted, the elder brother of her deceased father, Elliott Roosevelt. But she did not feel at home, turning down an invitation to spend a night in its storied atmosphere and describing herself "as always awed by the White House."[1] In 1905 she declined the opportunity to be married there to her debonair distant cousin, Franklin D. Roosevelt, preferring a quieter setting in the adjoining Manhattan townhouses of her maternal relatives.

For the young Eleanor Roosevelt, who had lost both parents before the age of ten and lacked a real home of her own, the White House meant the formidable residence of part of her extended family, but not a place in which she felt comfortable. It symbolized power and politics, which meant little to her at the time, although, as she was to learn, they meant a great deal to Franklin, a handsome Harvard student intent on wooing Eleanor in spite of the objections of his domineering widowed mother, Sara Delano Roosevelt. Historians have speculated for years on what drew Franklin, considered charming but shallow, to the serious-minded Eleanor, his fifth cousin once removed.[2] Nicknamed "feather duster" by Theodore's acid-tongued daughter Alice, and other young women in her social set, as a takeoff on his initials F.D., perhaps Franklin sensed that Eleanor could help him realize his potential.[3]

According to an intimate friend, Eleanor once confided that Franklin had proposed saying, "with your help" he would make something of himself and that she had answered, "I am plain. I have little to bring you."[4] Not dissuaded, Franklin continued to press his suit, and Eleanor accepted, explaining, "I had a great curiosity about life and a desire to participate in every experience that might be the lot of women."[5] Unlike many other debutantes, Eleanor could discuss books and ideas and appealed to Franklin's intellect. More to the point, perhaps, she was the favorite niece of Theodore Roosevelt, the president of the United States. Franklin admired Theodore and wanted to follow in his footsteps.[6] The editor of the Harvard *Crimson*, Franklin had aspirations that extended beyond living the life of a Hudson Valley country squire at the family estate in Hyde Park, New York.

But, if calculation figured into his ardor, so did cupid. Franklin fell in love with Eleanor, writing in his diary, "E. is an Angel."[7] The couple became engaged in the fall of 1903, but postponed their marriage for more than a year because Sara hoped that Franklin would change his mind. Eleanor herself feared that he might. A cousin discovered her weeping: "I shall never be able to hold him," she cried. "He is so attractive."[8]

When Sara finally consented to the engagement, Theodore expressed his delight. He wrote Franklin that he was "as fond of Eleanor as if she were my daughter."[9] As a girl, Eleanor, who lived mainly with her strict maternal grandmother, had made occasional trips to Sagamore Hill, Theodore Roosevelt's home at Oyster Bay, New York, joining in boisterous family games. Uncle Ted's wife, Edith Carow Roosevelt, pitied the unprepossessing Eleanor, an ungainly child with protruding teeth, but still saw promise in the "poor little soul," noting presciently in a letter, "Her mouth and teeth seem to have no future, but . . . the ugly duckling may turn out to be a swan."[10] Although they were the same age, prim Eleanor was no match for her sophisticated cousin, Alice, called "Princess Alice" during Theodore's presidency. A celebrity who shocked Washington society by smoking cigarettes, Alice, unlike Eleanor during her formative years, liked the limelight, a taste that Eleanor acquired in middle age. Alice's elaborate White House wedding in 1906 to playboy congressman Nicholas Longworth took place before 1,000 guests.

On visits to Washington, Eleanor much preferred the comfortable townhouse of her aunt, Anna "Bamie" Roosevelt Cowles, Theodore's sister, also known as Bye, to the formality of the White House. Married to an admiral, William Sheffield Cowles, Bamie lived at 1733 N Street NW, just blocks from the president's mansion. Her home served as the temporary headquarters for Theodore, when he unexpectedly became president following the assassination of William McKinley. Bamie's conversational and social skills transformed her house into a salon where leading political and intellectual figures met to advise Theodore during his administration.

As a teenager Eleanor had taken only passing notice of Uncle Ted's political fortunes. Away in England at Allenswood, an elite boarding school for young ladies, she had paid little attention to his election as vice president in 1900 or his succession to the presidency in 1901. After her return to the United States, she dismayed her relatives by walking out of the New Year's Day reception at the White House in 1903 and showing no interest in an admiral's reception, apparently dismissing the capital's social and political scene.[11] She claimed she barely noticed Uncle Ted's election campaign for president in 1904, writing in her autobiography, "I lived in a totally nonpolitical atmosphere."[12]

Yet, family contacts gave Eleanor glimpses of the political arena, even when she was preoccupied by her romance with Franklin. Bamie, who played a crucial role in the Roosevelt family, kept a close watch on politics as they affected Theodore's career. Extremely close to her ambitious brother, Bamie had taken charge of Alice, after the death of Theodore's first wife, Alice Lee Roosevelt, following Alice's birth. She cared for her until Theodore married Edith when Alice was three years old. In spite of having a deformed spine, Bamie possessed a genuine interest in other people, and in keeping with her vibrant personality displayed a motherly affection for both Alice and Eleanor.

While Bamie ridiculed the idea of woman suffrage, Eleanor could not help but notice that Bamie, along with her sister, Corinne Roosevelt Robinson, who became a noted lecturer and writer, and Edith, acted as Theodore's unofficial advisors. The three women provided more positive role models for Eleanor than the maternal relatives with whom she lived. Aware that Theodore would slip away from the White House to confer with Bamie about the appointment of officials, Eleanor recalled later that he never made an important decision without talking it over with his sister.[13] In years to come Eleanor would follow Bamie's example by advising another Roosevelt as president.

Eleanor also recognized the necessary role that Edith played as first lady, performing confidently as a hostess although devoting herself mainly to her own family of five children plus Alice.[14] When she became first lady herself, Eleanor rejected the narrowness of her aunt's approach to the position. Yet her aunt's example acted as a starting point for her own years of official entertaining in the White House.

Politics held little interest for Eleanor before her marriage except as a spectacle. Both Franklin and Eleanor, sitting on the steps of the Capitol just behind the presidential family, watched excitedly as Uncle Ted, affectionately known as TR to millions, was inaugurated as president on 4 March 1905. Eleanor wrote later that she had "no recollection of what he said" and "never expected to see another inauguration in the family."[15] Nevertheless, she was struck by the forcefulness of his delivery.[16] Perhaps it made her aware of the importance of the White House as a political stage, although her own years in its limelight lay far in the future.

Eleanor had a good reason to be preoccupied that inauguration day, since her own wedding was less than two weeks away. It took place on 17 March 1905, a date picked to suit Theodore, who was scheduled to be in New York that day to review the annual St. Patrick's Day parade. After completing his ceremonial stint, he arrived for the ceremony at the Seventy-sixth Street townhouses of

Eleanor's cousin, Susie Parrish, and great-aunt, Elizabeth Ludlow, with whom Eleanor had lived after returning from Allenswood. The noisy parade blocked the street outside so guests had trouble entering. Once inside they showed more interest in the president than in the newlyweds, although the willowy Eleanor, her blue eyes glowing, wore pearls and diamonds that ornamented a satin and lace wedding dress with a train.[17]

Uncle Ted performed the perfunctory role of giving the bride away. Immediately after the couple exchanged vows, he kissed Eleanor and announced to Franklin, "There's nothing like keeping the name in the family," before making his way to the refreshment table.[18] The twenty-year-old bride and twenty-three-year-old groom, then a law student at Columbia University, were left standing alone as the guests followed Theodore. Eleanor, whose early life had been marked by disappointment in general, remarked in her autobiography that she was not "particularly surprised at this."[19] Few would have predicted that the upstaged couple would develop a flair for showmanship that rivaled Uncle Ted's fame as a reform-minded, trust-busting politician.

How much exposure to Theodore and his family influenced Eleanor's eventual political career remains a matter of conjecture. According to Theodore's daughter, Alice, who was Eleanor's first cousin, "Politics were always being talked about at Sagamore. Eleanor Roosevelt would have heard [about] politics there."[20]

Well-known for her biting wit, Alice may not have been a reliable source regarding Eleanor. Alice referred to her cousin as a "Trojan mare" when she was first lady, a barbed reference to Eleanor's lack of beauty as well as being a popular symbol of social welfare legislation Alice disliked.[21] Yet, Alice thought Eleanor dramatized herself in her writings as more of an isolated ugly ducking than she actually had been as a girl. "Many aspects of Eleanor's childhood were, indeed, very unhappy but she had a tendency, especially later in life, to make out that she was unattractive and rejected as a child, which just wasn't true," Alice recalled. "She claimed that nobody liked her. Well, we all liked her."[22]

While Eleanor spent relatively little time at Oyster Bay, it is likely Theodore and his family had some impact on her later development. According to Eleanor's grandson, David Roosevelt, Bamie introduced Eleanor to the correlation between poverty in New York City and Theodore's efforts to attack predatory business practices, "invaluable lessons to the life she was, unknowingly, about to embrace." He added, "Although it was not apparent to Eleanor, I think TR became the role model she had missed in her own father, instilling in her the deeply ingrained characteristics of social obligation and caring so prevalent in generations of Roosevelts."[23]

Eleanor herself denied that her uncle and his family provided her with an early introduction into politics. To the contrary, in a 1932 magazine article published a month before Franklin's first election as president, she pictured herself as "totally ignorant" of political matters until after her marriage, saying she had been "the typical old-fashioned girl," whose grandmother had brought her up to believe that women inhabited a separate sphere from men. "It might be thought that, as a niece of President Roosevelt, I must have lived in an atmosphere of political excitement and grown up with a profound political penetration," she commented. "This was far from being the case."[24]

At this point Eleanor may have been reluctant to admit that she had received any political education from the Oyster Bay Roosevelts. When it became obvious that Franklin, not Theodore's sons, seemed destined to follow in TR's footsteps, partisan political loyalties split the Roosevelt clan. Following Theodore's death in 1919, ill will developed between Eleanor and her cousins that lasted for decades. Franklin clearly modeled himself after Theodore, taking the same path he had cleared to the White House, serving first as assistant secretary of the navy and then as governor of New York before winning the presidency, to the irritation of Theodore's own offspring, who thought they should be his political heirs. One glaring difference separated Theodore and Franklin. Unlike the Oyster Bay Roosevelts, Franklin was a Democrat.

The Roosevelt family had been Democrats before the Civil War, but it had sided with abolitionists during that conflict and changed to the Republican Party. Franklin's branch, which lived the life of country squires at Hyde Park, New York, soon reverted to being Democrats, an allegiance kept in spite of Theodore's rise to the presidency. When Corinne Robinson, Theodore's sister, preceded Eleanor as the first Roosevelt woman to speak in public about politics, she delivered a speech at the Republican, not the Democratic, convention. In 1920, the year women first won the right to vote, Corinne became the first woman in history to give a presidential nominating speech at a major political party convention.[25] Her action was a slap in the face to Franklin, who made an unsuccessful bid for the vice presidency that same year on the Democratic ticket. Further enraging Franklin and Eleanor during the campaign, Theodore Roosevelt Jr. said of Franklin, "He does not have the brand of our family."[26]

Franklin's candidacy led Eleanor to make a public declaration of allegiance to the Democratic Party in spite of her roots as an Oyster Bay Republican. In one of her early contacts with the news media, she told a newspaper reporter she championed the Democrats, "for I believe they are the most progressive."[27] Presenting herself as a modest and traditional wife, she prefaced her remark by saying, "I haven't been active in politics in any way, and so you see there isn't much of a story to be found in me."[28]

While Eleanor pictured herself as a political innocent, the fact that Uncle Ted took a progressive stand on social justice issues during his presidency from 1901 to 1909 played a part in her subsequent emergence as a political figure. Reflecting on his death in her autobiography, she wrote, "The loss of his influence and example was what I seemed to feel most keenly."[29] Theodore's ideas on progressive reforms reinforced her own activities before her marriage, when she participated in the settlement house movement in New York in common with other wealthy women interested in social betterment. Led by Jane Addams in Chicago, women who spearheaded settlements believed in social services to ameliorate harsh conditions confronting the poor in urban areas.

Biographers generally have credited Eleanor's involvement in the settlement movement to an outgrowth of precepts instilled by Marie Souvestre, who was her beloved teacher at Allenswood. At the urging of Bamie, who also had studied under Souvestre, an intellectual with a sense of social responsibility, Eleanor's grandmother had sent her to the exclusive finishing school from 1899 to 1902. Yet, Eleanor's interest in helping the less fortunate also stemmed from her family background.

As a Roosevelt, Eleanor belonged to a New York family of wealth and privilege with fortunes made as merchants and investors. Like others in their rigid social world, the family practiced the concept of noblesse oblige. Eleanor wrote in her autobiography, "In that society you were kind to the poor, you did not neglect your philanthropic duties, you assisted the hospitals and did something for the needy."[30] Social convention called for benevolent behavior.

Eleanor cherished a childhood memory of accompanying her father, Elliott, when he served Thanksgiving dinner at a clubhouse for newsboys, often homeless children hawking newspapers on the streets to eke out a meager existence. Aid for newsboys had been just one of the many charities of her grandfather, Theodore Roosevelt Sr. Known as "Greatheart" for his philanthropy in New York City, he helped found the Metropolitan Museum of Art, the Museum of Natural History, and the Children's Aid Society.

The younger of Greatheart's two sons, Eleanor's father, Elliott, sophisticated and congenial, disgraced the family during Eleanor's formative years. Addicted to alcohol and drugs and suffering from depression, he betrayed his wife, Anna Hall Roosevelt, in a series of affairs, including the seduction of a servant, who bore a child believed to be his. His conduct brought shame and grief to Anna, Eleanor's beautiful mother, one of the most admired debutantes in New York before her marriage in 1883. Members of the most exclusive social group in New York, called the "Four Hundred," because that was the number that could fit into Mrs. John J. Astor's ballroom, Elliott and Anna had personified the carefree lifestyle of the rich and wellborn until Elliott's instability ruined their marriage.

Recalling years later warm memories of her father that she loved to share, Eleanor buried a darker side of her childhood. No more than eight years old, for example, she had held Elliott's dogs on a leash, as he had told her to do, for six hours outside the Knickerbocker Club in Manhattan while he drank himself into a stupor. Even after he was carried out unconscious, Eleanor kept waiting for him to return until a doorman finally took her home.[31]

When Elliott's increasingly erratic behavior and sexual misconduct resulted in his separation from his family, he penned tender letters to Eleanor that she read and reread for years to come. They lovingly admonished her to develop qualities that would make her a good person. Perhaps aimed at her efforts to stop biting her nails, he wrote, "I am glad you are taking such good care of those cunning

A four-year-old Eleanor, dressed in her best, cuddles up to her beloved father, Elliott Roosevelt, in this photographic portrait made in New York City on 30 April 1889. Courtesy of the Franklin D. Roosevelt Library, Hyde Park, New York.

wee hands that Father loves so to be petted by, all those little things will make my dear Girl so much more attractive if she attends them, not forgetting the big ones. Unselfishness, generosity, loving tenderness and cheerfulness."[32]

Her father expressed his love in words, if not in actions. He saw little Eleanor as lovable, whereas her mother appeared to Eleanor as a remote, distant figure dissatisfied with her daughter's looks and manner. Of her father Eleanor wrote, "He dominated my life as long as he lived, and was the love of my life for many years after he died."[33] Delusional and violent, Elliott died after jumping out of a window at the home of his mistress two months before Eleanor had her tenth birthday in 1894. By this time she also had lost her mother and one of her two little brothers, but these deaths had far less impact on her.

Anna Hall Roosevelt died from diphtheria when Eleanor was eight years old, leaving the little girl strangely unmoved. She stated bluntly in her autobiography, "I can remember standing by a window when Cousin Susie told me that my mother was dead. This was on December 7, 1892. Death meant nothing to me, and one fact wiped out everything else. My father was back and I would see him soon."[34]

The dissolute Elliott, who had not been allowed to see his wife on her deathbed, could not take care of Eleanor and her two little brothers. Although he fantasized with Eleanor that they would go away together and live happily, this was not to be. Her idealized view of her father, repressing a realistic view of his actual behavior, became part of her psychic makeup. It led her to misjudge people in later life, coldly sulking in silence, if those she trusted failed her.[35]

In contrast to her father, Eleanor's mother exhibited disapproval of her daughter, or at least so Eleanor thought. Basing her earliest recollections on the fact that she did not measure up to her mother's standard, Eleanor started her autobiography by noting, "My mother was one of the most beautiful women I have ever seen."[36] She pictured herself as a pitiful infant except in her father's eyes: "from all accounts I must have been a more wrinkled and less attractive baby than the average—but to him I was a miracle from Heaven."[37] Her mother, she observed, "troubled by my lack of beauty tried hard to bring me up well so that my manners would compensate for my looks, but her efforts only made me more keenly conscious of my shortcomings."[38] If her solemn little daughter could not be a belle, Anna insisted she at least could be a model of deportment. From early childhood on, Eleanor was taught that exemplary conduct coupled with good works provided an alternative route for a woman to gain recognition. Not surprisingly, she sought to do good during the rest of her life, although her definition of good changed markedly over the years.

Anna left custody of the three children to her widowed mother,

Mary Ludlow Hall, a member of New York's illustrious Livingston family, which included a signer of the Declaration of Independence. Grandmother Hall willingly took in the motherless children, but she turned them over to servants as was customary among the upper classes. Eleanor and her brothers experienced little conventional mothering in the Hall household. Two rebellious sons and two emotional daughters made it resemble the setting for a melodramatic Gothic novel, rather than a proper Victorian home populated with upright men, demure women, and well-behaved children.

The Victorian social code prescribed strict attention to morality, which Grandmother Hall could not enforce in her own family in spite of her stern exterior. As Eleanor grew up, Valentine and Edward Hall, her uncles, increasingly lost their self-control in drunken sprees. These included random shootings in the neighborhood around Oak Hill, the Hudson Valley estate where the family lived when not occupying its gloomy brownstone in Manhattan. Meanwhile, Eleanor's aunts, Edith "Pussie" and Maude Hall, indulged in temperamental outbursts over their frequent romances.

Although she required family members and servants to attend prayer services twice a day, Grandmother Hall spent much time alone in her darkened bedroom, unable to deal effectively with her own offspring or to show much affection to her grandchildren. Elliott Jr., who was five years younger than Eleanor, died the year following his mother's death. This left Eleanor with a strong sense of responsibility for her baby brother Hall, who was not yet two years old when their mother died. Having been told by her father to look after Hall, Eleanor tried to do so for the rest of her life, although, like Elliott, Hall became an alcoholic. As an adult he had difficulty holding jobs and distressed Eleanor many times, according to his daughter, giving Eleanor "yet one more reason to turn to her own work in an effort to ease the ache in her heart."[39]

Fearing that she had been too lenient with her own children, Grandmother Hall disciplined Eleanor strictly, dressing her in outfits too short for the tall girl, and inculcating religious precepts. She devoted Sundays to churchgoing, a practice that Eleanor continued throughout her own life. Perhaps, as a result of her upbringing, in the last decades of her life, Eleanor took her grandchildren and house guests to the Episcopalian churches that she herself faithfully attended. She affirmed her own belief in God as "my greatest source of strength" in a book written for young people the year before her death.[40]

Although less known than the Roosevelts for their benevolence, the Halls, in spite of family strains, practiced the rituals of good works expected of the Victorian upper classes. Eleanor went with Grandmother Hall to decorate Christmas trees in children's hospital wards and accompanied Uncle "Vallie" on holiday visits to children in Hell's Kitchen, one of New York's worst slums. She joined Pussie and Maude in singing at the Bowery Mission, commenting in her autobiography, "I was not in ignorance that there were sharp contrasts, even though our lives were blessed with plenty."[41]

In her eventual career, Eleanor translated the family idea of noblesse oblige into public service that included politics. In his memoir of his grandmother, David Roosevelt referred to Eleanor's heritage of social consciousness: "Although not universally, the majority of my family has been raised with a sense of duty and obligation, whether to serve our nation in some governmental or political capacity, or merely through civic responsibility and voluntarism."[42] Yet, an enormous gulf existed, particularly for women, between acts of charity and the smoke-filled rooms associated with political parties in Eleanor's day. Much of her subsequent evolution as a public figure would depend on her ability to bridge that gap.

Eleanor's interest in social justice deepened when Grandmother Hall sent her to school at Allenswood outside of London, where she spent three happy years from the ages of fifteen to eighteen. Her grandmother acted partly to keep Eleanor away from the undesirable behavior of her uncles, who may have made sexual advances, but also because the sons and daughters of upper-class Americans typically traveled to England and the Continent, learning to be at home on both sides of the Atlantic. As a six-year-old, Eleanor had accompanied her parents to Europe and experienced an unhappy stay in a French convent. When she started private classes in New York, she had continued to study French. Her ability to speak it facilitated her adjustment to Allenswood, where French was the language of conversation and instruction.

Run by the seventy-year-old Marie Souvestre, the independent-minded daughter of a well-known French philosopher, Allenswood

Eleanor, second from left in the second row, wearing a hat, poses with her classmates at Allenswood, her boarding school located near London at Southfield in Surrey (about 1900). Courtesy of the Franklin D. Roosevelt Library, Hyde Park, New York.

enrolled some thirty-five young women from wealthy American and European backgrounds. Souvestre took a maternal interest in the bright but gawky, shy, and self-conscious Eleanor. She helped her acquire a more stylish wardrobe and chose her as a traveling companion for trips abroad. Under Souvestre's tutelage the insecure adolescent, who had been given to fibs in a desire to please others, blossomed into a self-confident young woman.

Travel broadened Eleanor, as did her association with Souvestre, a liberal-minded atheist whose lack of faith disturbed the religious Eleanor, although she eventually concluded Souvestre's views did not harm her and "shocked me into thinking."[43] Souvestre also was a lesbian, but there is no record that Eleanor was aware of this facet of her life. Her school gave Eleanor an appreciation of European culture that provided invaluable background for her unforeseen diplomatic career a half-century later.

Allenswood enlarged Eleanor's understanding of social and political issues. Souvestre, an advocate of trade unions, preached to her young charges the moral necessity of broadening their horizons beyond their own class to uplift society. This was a lesson that Eleanor carried with her as she left Allenswood in 1902 to make the

New York debut required by her family. Feeling like a failure compared to her mother and aunts, Eleanor pictured her debut, which took place at New York's famed Assembly Ball, as an unhappy experience: "I knew I was the first girl in my mother's family who was not a belle and . . . I was deeply ashamed."[44] Still, she was invited to important social events, including those where she renewed her acquaintance with her distant cousin Franklin.

As a debutante Eleanor automatically became a member of the Junior League, an organization of wealthy young women who volunteered to assist in the settlement house movement. Eleanor chose to do more than simply lend her name to a good cause. During the winter of 1903–1904 she taught calisthenics and dancing to immigrant girls at the Rivington Street settlement on New York's Lower East Side. She arranged for Franklin to meet her there, introducing him to slum conditions that he had never imagined existed. After taking an ill girl home to a squalid tenement, he told Eleanor, "My God, I didn't know anyone lived like that."[45]

Eleanor also was drawn to the National Consumers' League, part of a network of reform-minded women's organizations, which played important roles in her eventual political development. As a youthful investigator for the league, Eleanor gained firsthand knowledge of sweatshop conditions. Through the league she witnessed women working together to effectively publicize local conditions with the aim of correcting them through political initiatives.[46] In years to come she used this knowledge, relating women's reform efforts to party politics. She formed political alliances with women she had met in the settlement movement who later became members of such organizations as the League of Women Voters and the Women's Trade Union League. But at the time of her marriage, no one—least of all Eleanor—would have predicted her own political involvement. Neither Franklin nor Eleanor considered her volunteer work a serious commitment that would be continued after her marriage.

As a young wife Eleanor was preoccupied with motherhood and managing her growing household, although her own upbringing had given her little preparation for successful parenting. While she soon learned that marriage to the jaunty, gregarious Franklin did not offer her the emotional intensity that she craved, she assented to his desire to have a large family like Uncle Ted's. Between the years of

1906 and 1916, she gave birth to six children, one of whom died in infancy, or as she put it, "For ten years I was always just getting over having a baby or about to have one, and so my occupations were considerably restricted during this period."[47] In common with other upper-class women of the day, she left most of the actual care of the children to servants.

Eleanor's only daughter, Anna, was born in 1906. James arrived in 1907 (to her great relief because she had feared she would be unable to produce the son that both her husband and mother-in-law wanted).[48] The first Franklin Jr. was born in 1909, only to die eight months later. Elliott was born the following year. Two more sons, another boy named Franklin Jr., and John, came in 1914 and 1916, respectively. Reticent about her sexual relationship with Franklin, she counseled Anna on the eve of her first marriage that sex for women was an ordeal to be borne.[49]

Uncertain in dealing with her domestic responsibilities, Eleanor, said by her children to be inconsistent and unpredictable in her mothering, depended on Franklin's mother, Sara, for assistance, which Sara gloried in providing. Although Eleanor had inherited an income of $8,000 a year (equivalent to some $160,000 today), Franklin earned little as a lawyer and depended on his mother for funds to support the family's expensive lifestyle. Sara paid the bills for Franklin and Eleanor, building and furnishing a New York townhouse for them that was a twin of her own. The homes had connecting doors so she easily could drop in unannounced, with Eleanor lamenting years later, "You were never quite sure when she would appear, day or night."[50] Sara hired nursemaids and disciplined the children, leading Eleanor to later admit, "FDR's children were more my mother-in-law's children than they were mine."[51]

As the dowager of Springwood, the imposing Roosevelt home known as the "Big House" at Hyde Park, Sara donated to charity. She supported sewing clubs for village women and contributed to a settlement house in New York's Greenwich Village, but she insisted her daughter-in-law keep personally aloof from the needy. Eleanor wrote in her autobiography that early in her marriage she "had lost a good deal of my crusading spirit where the poor were concerned, because I had been told I had no right to go into the slums or into the hospitals, for fear of bringing diseases home to my children."[52]

Newly wed, Franklin and Eleanor share a moment with Franklin's mother, Sara Delano Roosevelt, at her childhood home in Newburgh, New York, on 7 May 1905. Mother and son gaze tenderly at each other while Eleanor looks down. Courtesy of the Franklin D. Roosevelt Library, Hyde Park, New York.

The wealthy and well-traveled Sara exuded the self-confidence that Eleanor lacked, making her initially grateful for Sara's help but soon weary of her mother-in-law's interference.

When Franklin launched his political career with his surprising election to the New York state senate from a Republican district in 1910, Eleanor happily moved with him to Albany, glad to be away from Sara. She soaked up some political atmosphere by entertaining her husband's associates and watching debates in the legislature, but she did not support woman suffrage until Franklin came out for it in 1911. She wrote later that she "took it for granted that men were superior creatures."[53] She did not actively work for or against the suffrage amendment that was added to the U.S. Constitution in 1920.

Eleanor continued to act the part of the submissive spouse after the Roosevelts moved to Washington, D.C., in 1913. To his delight Franklin was appointed assistant secretary of the navy by President Woodrow Wilson, following in the footsteps of Uncle Ted even to the point of renting Bamie's home at 1733 N Street NW, where Eleanor had visited before her marriage. His position required Eleanor to spend hours calling on the wives of other officials, then a necessary, if empty, social ritual. To assist with her burdensome responsibilities she hired a social secretary, Lucy Page Mercer, a beautiful and charming young woman with an impeccable background, even though her family had lost its money. Eleanor had no way of knowing that this chance act was to change the course of her own life.

In 1918 Eleanor's world of conventional duties crumbled, inflicting a blow that struck her to the core. Franklin was stricken with pneumonia while returning from an inspection trip of military fortifications in Europe toward the end of World War I. As Eleanor unpacked his luggage, she discovered a packet of love letters from Lucy. She now had indisputable proof of what she must have surmised but had not wanted to face—her husband was in love with another woman, one who was younger, more chic, livelier, and more attractive than she. "The bottom dropped out of my own particular world, and I faced myself, my surroundings, my world, honestly for the first time. I really grew up that year," she told Joseph P. Lash.[54]

When or even if Franklin and Lucy engaged in a physical relationship remains a matter of conjecture, but there is ample evidence that the handsome couple were romantically involved for two years. The affair probably started in the summer of 1916 after Eleanor took the children to the Roosevelt summer home on Campobello Island in New Brunswick, off the coast of Maine. According to two of the Roosevelt children, Anna and Elliott, Eleanor refused to have sex with Franklin following the birth of John in March 1916, possibly inadvertently contributing to his affair with Lucy. John's birth had fulfilled Franklin's wish to have as many children as Uncle Ted.[55] In that period when birth control was illegal and forbidden by the Episcopal Church, couples commonly practiced sexual abstinence to avoid having more children.[56]

While discreet in their behavior, Franklin and Lucy were seen together in Washington society when Eleanor traveled to Hyde Park and Campobello, keeping her youngsters away from what was considered Washington's unhealthy climate. The irrepressible Alice Roosevelt Longworth, her own marriage marked by infidelity, invited Lucy and Franklin to dine at her home without Eleanor and may even have tried to warn her cousin about the relationship, but Eleanor closed her ears to any hint of scandalous conduct.[57] Quite willing to sanction Franklin's romance, Alice believed that the intense Eleanor "always seemed to manage to hold Franklin back from having a good time."[58]

In addition to her social and domestic responsibilities, Eleanor threw herself into volunteer efforts stemming from U.S. entry into World War I in 1917. While she stayed away from the suffrage campaign, the war gave her a patriotic rationale for social service akin to her Rivington Street experience. She donned a Red Cross uniform and tirelessly served meals in sweltering temperatures to soldiers passing through Washington's Union Station, discovering a latent skill at organization that would serve her well in the future. She took charge of a Navy Department effort to have women knit socks and scarves for servicemen. The Red Cross wanted to send her to England to set up a canteen there, but she declined to go because of her family.[59] War work made her feel competent and needed. "I loved it," she recalled later; "I ate it up."[60]

Eleanor's zeal to support the war led to her first bruising experience with the press, adding to the strain in her marriage. Subscribing enthusiastically to the federal government's efforts to persuade housewives to conserve food, Eleanor naïvely allowed herself to be interviewed by a woman reporter for the *New York Times.* Calling attention to the family's "ten servants," the resulting article said that Mrs. Roosevelt had profited from the conservation campaign since she did "the buying, the cooks see that there is no food wasted, the laundress is sparing in her use of soap; each servant has a watchful eye for evidences of shortcomings in others, and all are encouraged to make suggestions in the use of 'left overs.' "[61]

Acutely aware that the interview made the family into a laughingstock, Franklin sarcastically wrote his wife, who had gone reluctantly to Campobello in the summer of 1917, "All I can say is that your latest newspaper campaign is a corker and I am proud to be the husband of the Originator, Discoverer and Inventor of the New Household Economy for Millionaires."[62] Eleanor replied, "I never will be caught again that's sure and I would like to crawl away from shame."[63] In her later career she kept her promise to be more careful in her press dealings as she developed close friendships with women reporters who helped perfect her public image.

The discovery of the love letters gave irrefutable proof of what Eleanor probably had suspected for some time: Franklin had betrayed her with a woman whom she had befriended. Profoundly hurt, she offered him a divorce. Franklin, who found in the adoring Lucy qualities of femininity that the high-minded Eleanor lacked, was sorely tempted, but practical considerations held him back. Sara, concerned about the effect of a divorce on the grandchildren and the family name, was appalled at the idea and threatened to cut off her financial support.[64] Louis Howe, the disheveled gnome-like newspaperman who acted as Franklin's political mentor and later as Eleanor's, adamantly told Franklin that a divorce would ruin his political career. Finally, to the relief of the insecure Eleanor in an era when divorce equated to scandal, Franklin decided to stay married, at least in terms of appearances, for the sake of his political career and their children.

Eleanor set two stipulations—he was not to see Lucy again and the Roosevelts would have no sexual relationship. Franklin agreed, although long-concealed evidence has recently been uncovered that shows Franklin continued to keep in contact with Lucy, who married a wealthy widower, Winthrop Rutherford, in 1920.[65] The second stipulation apparently was never violated, although Franklin and Eleanor developed a remarkable political partnership that made its impact on history. If political ambition had been a factor in Franklin's marriage, it served as a glue to cement the couple for three eventful decades to come. Eventually Eleanor would arrive at the point where she recognized the potential for leadership that politics would give her personally both with and without her husband.

CHAPTER 2

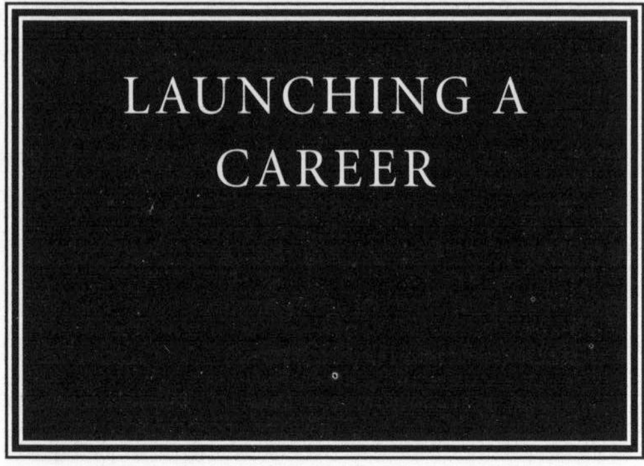

LAUNCHING A CAREER

"With some outstanding exceptions, women who have gone into politics are refused serious consideration by the men leaders. Generally they are treated most courteously, to be sure, but what they want, what they have to say, is regarded as of little consequence."

Eleanor Roosevelt in 1928 from her article "Women Must Learn to Play the Game as Men Do," in *The Red Book Magazine*

In the midst of her own marital stress Eleanor drew on her position as the wife of an important official in an effort to benefit others, a step that she would take repeatedly in the future. Shocked by the poor conditions she encountered on visits to veterans at St. Elizabeth's Hospital, a federal mental institution, she worked behind the scenes politically to improve the situation. Since St. Elizabeth's came under the domain of Secretary of the Interior Franklin Lane, Eleanor turned to her friendship with Lane and his wife, Anne, to press for action. She easily got the secretary's ear because the Lanes were members of an informal Sunday evening supper club that frequently met at the Roosevelt home and to which Eleanor served scrambled eggs, one of the few dishes she knew how to prepare.[1]

As the result of her entreaties to look into the situation, Lane appointed a committee to investigate the ill-funded hospital, where lack of attendants meant patients were kept locked on cage-like porches. The committee report resulted in increased appropriations for the hospital, leading Eleanor to conclude that the hospital had been transformed into "a model of its kind."[2] As part of the transformation she used her influence with the Red Cross and a women's patriotic organization, the Colonial Dames, to set up recreation and occupational therapy programs for shell-shocked patients.[3] The success of her efforts offered a satisfying taste of what could be accomplished through backstage political contacts and commitment to public service.[4]

Keeping busy prevented Eleanor from dwelling on her circumstances, made more difficult by the fact that Franklin and all of their children were stricken with influenza shortly after she had discovered Franklin's affair. Eleanor managed to care for them as well as continue her Red Cross work. She commented stoically in her autobiography, "I was learning that what one has to do usually can be done."[5] Although she gave no hint of Franklin's infidelity, she wrote that the World War I period taught her "more about the human heart."[6]

Fluent in French as a result of her days at Allenswood, she took part as a translator at the 1919 International Congress of Working Women in Washington, where she became acquainted with members of the Women's Trade Union League, an organization she joined three years later. It channeled the charitable interests of upper-class women into political and social support for trade unions. When Franklin returned to Europe in the winter of 1919, following the armistice the previous November, he took Eleanor along on the trip, intended to oversee the liquidation of naval installations there. She toured what had been the front, a depressing experience that gave her the impression of walking alongside ghosts.[7]

Eleanor paid an emotional and physical price for carrying on in the midst of personal travail, confiding in her diary at the end of 1919 that her self-confidence was gone.[8] In Europe she came down with pleurisy. A doctor told her to be examined for tuberculosis when she reached home, but she thought she had recovered and discounted this advice, apparently mistakenly, since the reactivation of an old and undiagnosed case of tuberculosis figured in the cause of her death forty-three years later.[9]

Pictures of Eleanor at the close of World War I show an extremely thin woman, the victim of an eating disorder who could not keep down food and who was unwilling to look directly at a camera.[10] In a letter to Franklin in 1919, she wrote that she had had dinner with Mama, "but I might as well not have eaten it for I promptly parted with it all."[11] As is common with sufferers from such disorders, her teeth and gums loosened; she also endured headaches and extreme fatigue. Years later she told Lorena Hickok of making many trips alone during this period to Washington's Rock Creek cemetery to find comfort in Saint-Gaudens's statue of a hooded figure, popularly called "Grief."[12] It had been erected by the author Henry Adams, a friend of Eleanor's, in memory of his wife who had committed suicide, purportedly after learning of her husband's unfaithfulness.

When Franklin was selected as the Democratic candidate for vice president in 1920, he wanted her to ride with him on his campaign train to garner support from women voting for the first time in a presidential race. She was pressed to provide photographs and to talk to reporters, neither of which she was prepared to do. She granted only a single interview in which she said she was a Democrat in spite of her relationship to Theodore Roosevelt and that she favored the League of Nations, bitterly opposed by the Republicans, as a way to prevent war.[13] "I take such bad photographs," she told one of Franklin's staff members.[14]

The only woman on the campaign train, Eleanor was surrounded by card-playing newspapermen and politicos, who watched her standing dutifully by Franklin's side during whistle-stop appearances and listening raptly as he gave the same speech repeatedly. Shy and ignored by the men who bantered with her husband, she benefited from the attention of Louis Howe, who recognized her quick mind and organizational ability as he coached her in the art of politics. By now a convert to suffrage, she responded to Howe's efforts to pull her into the campaign, as he brought her drafts of speeches to critique and persuaded her to unwind more with the traveling newspapermen. She and Howe formed a relationship that eventually mirrored that of family members and would be vital in her own political development.

The election, as foreseen, turned into a disastrous defeat for Franklin and his presidential running mate, James M. Cox, who inherited voter discontent with the Democratic administration of Woodrow Wilson. His high-handed efforts to support the League of Nations, along with his crippling stroke that resulted in an apparent lack of effective government for months prior to the election, propelled the return of the Republican Party to power.[15] Nevertheless, the campaign whetted Eleanor's interest in politics as she cast her first vote, at Hyde Park, for the Democratic ticket.

When the Roosevelts returned to New York after the election, she joined the New York State League of Women Voters, a nonpartisan organization to encourage voter education that grew out of the National American Woman Suffrage Association. It was one of several steps, including cooking and typing lessons, that she took to fashion a life for herself apart from her previous round of social and family obligations. During the winter and spring of 1921, Eleanor attended both the state and national conventions of the league. She met women like Carrie Chapman Catt, key organizer of the league, who were committed to pacifism and progressive political action, particularly the Sheppard-Towner Act to give federal grants for maternal and child-care clinics.

League membership put Eleanor squarely in the midst of social feminists who had formed the Women's Joint Congressional Committee in 1919 to lobby for education, mother and child health care, a constitutional amendment outlawing child labor, and increased funds for the federal Children's Bureau and Women's Bureau along with U.S. participation in the World Court. The league, like most other women's organizations, opposed the Equal Rights Amendment, advocated by Alice Paul's National Woman's Party to eliminate discriminatory laws against women, taking the position that working women needed protective legislation.[16]

As chair of the league's state legislative committee, Eleanor became a close friend of Elizabeth Read, a lawyer, and her life partner, Esther Lape, a journalist and activist. Finding herself for the first time in her life in the company of professional women, Eleanor enjoyed dinners in their Greenwich Village apartment, where the three read French poetry aloud and plotted political strategies both within the league itself and on the broader political field. With Read's help, Eleanor studied the *Congressional Record* and wrote reports on pending legislation for league members.

Eleanor soon rose to the position of state vice chair with special interests in the promotion of world peace, women's right to jury service, and equal prosecution of men and women in prostitution cases.[17] She first ventured into the world of political journalism in August 1921, presenting readers of the state league's *Weekly News* with a "comprehensive digest" of proposed changes in New York's primary election law. Having learned to gather facts systematically, she subsequently wrote other articles for the bulletin, using her new skill of typing.[18]

The same month Eleanor's first article appeared, the Roosevelt family received a blow that changed their lives and perhaps the course of American history. Handsome, muscular Franklin developed infantile paralysis while at Campobello. He would never walk again, although he struggled for years to regain movement in his legs and mastered the art of giving the illusion in public that he had done so. According to biographers, polio changed Franklin by giving him insight into both physical suffering and rural poverty. His firsthand experience with poor farm families living near Warm Springs, Georgia, where he went in search of treatment, led him to champion government aid for the poverty-stricken in his later political career.[19]

With Eleanor as his round-the-clock nurse during the most acute phase of his illness, Franklin bonded with her in an enforced intimacy that may have ameliorated to some extent what one son called the "armed truce" between his parents that existed after Eleanor's discovery of the Mercer affair.[20] Summoning Howe to help her move Franklin back to New York from Campobello, Eleanor found the weeks and months to follow in 1921 and 1922 "the most trying winter of my entire life."[21] There were not enough bedrooms in the Roosevelts' overcrowded townhouse for all members of the household, which now included Howe, so Eleanor "slept in one of the little boys' rooms."[22] Anna, resentful that she had a small room while Howe had a big one, created scenes at the dinner table. Finally, Eleanor went on an uncontrollable crying jag, "the one and only time I remember in my entire life having gone to pieces in this particular manner."[23] All her life, however, especially in the early years of her marriage, she suffered from spells of depression, which she referred to as "Griselda moods," after a character in Chaucer, in

Eleanor and four of her five children prepare to stargaze at Campobello, the Canadian island off the coast of Maine where the Roosevelt summer home was located, in 1920, the year before Franklin contracted polio there and the family's life changed forever. From left to right, Elliott, John, Franklin D. Jr. with "Chief," the family dog, and Anna. Courtesy of the Franklin D. Roosevelt Library, Hyde Park, New York.

which she shut herself "up like a clam, not telling anyone what is the matter."[24]

Sara had different ideas than Eleanor on Franklin's future. She wanted him to retire to Hyde Park and be content with a wealthy squire's existence, much like his father's, setting off acrimonious family arguments. Franklin himself, backed by his doctor, had the last word. He struggled to use crutches and made every effort to recuperate and regain a normal life. In the contest between Eleanor and Sara over Franklin's future, Eleanor—and politics—won out. No doubt a desire to maintain Franklin's morale motivated Eleanor, but surely she harbored at least a subconscious desire to look after her own well-being. She would not have welcomed a life under Sara's thumb at Hyde Park.

Joining with Howe in determination to keep Franklin from succumbing to invalidism, Eleanor brought visitors to see him and emerged as a political surrogate. By December 1921 she had resumed her duties with the state League of Women Voters. According to legend, Eleanor, prodded by Howe, became politically active to keep the Roosevelt name viable in the Democratic Party while Franklin recuperated. Her league activity, however, shows that she moved toward the political realm before Franklin's illness. With political advice from Franklin himself before he was stricken, Eleanor and her two friends, Read and Lape, successfully maneuvered the reelection of a mutual friend, Narcissa Vanderlip, a liberal Republican, as the league's state chair.

In two years the three women unexpectedly found themselves on a national stage. Asked by Edward Bok, who had attained fame as the editor of the *Ladies' Home Journal*, to direct a contest offering a $100,000 prize to the American citizen who proposed the best plan to preserve world peace, Lape agreed to do so with the proviso that Eleanor and Vanderlip be invited to work with her. The well-publicized competition called for the winner to receive half the prize on selection of his or her plan and the remainder after the U.S. Senate either ratified the winning proposal or it was approved in a referendum. The contest resulted in more than 22,000 entries and gave Eleanor the chance to publish her first article in a national magazine. As the wife of a former vice presidential candidate, she announced details of the competition in the *Ladies' Home Journal* in October 1923, noting its novel attempt to solicit public opinion through the medium of mass communications.[25] Franklin himself prepared one of the entries, although he apparently did not submit it due to Eleanor's role in the contest.[26]

The winning plan, by a retired college president, called for cooperation with the League of Nations, but not actual membership. It produced a storm of criticism from Senate isolationists, who claimed that the contest's "democratic diplomacy" undermined congressional authority. A Senate committee launched an investigation, but Bok and Lape defended themselves successfully in testimony before it. The investigation halted, although the peace plan was scrapped.[27]

While Eleanor accompanied Lape to the hearing, she did not testify, but the experience illustrated her commitment to the peace movement during the 1920s and introduced her to the kind of political hostility that she would encounter in future years. It also produced the first item (simply the fact that she had ordered a telephone for the award committee to use) in what eventually became her voluminous Federal Bureau of Investigation file.[28] It was kept by J. Edgar Hoover, who viewed with suspicion peace advocates and reformers on grounds they might be linked to Communists, whom he detested as anti-American.

As a prominent antiwar advocate during the 1920s, Eleanor was allied with other women pacifists on whom Hoover kept a close eye. Eleanor applauded two of them in particular: Jane Addams, first president of the Women's International League for Peace and Freedom and founder of Chicago's Hull House, the nation's best-known settlement house, and Carrie Chapman Catt, who had led the successful women's suffrage campaign and subsequent organization of the League of Women Voters. Eleanor was present in Washington in 1925 for Catt's first national conference on the Cause and Cure of War, made up of a coalition of women's groups.

In 1922 Eleanor met two women who became her closest companions during the years ahead. They were Marion Dickerman, the first woman to run for the legislature in New York State, and her partner, Nancy Cook, the dynamic executive secretary of the women's division of the New York State Democratic Committee. Cook had managed Dickerman's surprisingly strong showing in the election even though she did not win. At Cook's request a trembling Eleanor, afraid that her voice could not be heard, nervously undertook to give a fund-raising speech at a division luncheon without, she wrote later, "the faintest idea of what I was going to say or what work the organization was really doing."[29] To overcome her fear of an audience, she followed advice from Howe, who sat in the back of the room and critiqued her performance, insisting she stop giggling in embarrassment. He told her: "Have something you want to say, say it, and sit down."[30]

The eloquent Dickerman, who had been a dean at a New Jersey state normal school, impressed Eleanor, who became inseparable from her and Cook. Franklin liked both the witty Cook and dignified Dickerman. He valued them as political allies and referred to them jovially as "our gang."[31] Nevertheless, he and Howe made snide comments about their lesbian relationship, calling Eleanor's friends "she-males," while Alice Longworth dubbed her cousin's new friends "female impersonators."[32]

In 1925 Franklin urged the three women to build a stone cottage, called Val-Kill after a nearby stream, on the Roosevelt estate at Hyde Park, possibly because he thought Eleanor would be happier with a retreat away from Sara.[33] He also might have been influenced by feelings of guilt because he was spending more and more time away from New York seeking to regain the use of his legs in a warmer climate, first on a houseboat in the South and later at Warm Springs. In the absence of Eleanor, who did not enjoy boating trips and disliked the racial segregation practiced at Warm Springs and elsewhere in the South, his attractive personal secretary, Marguerite LeHand, called Missy, accompanied him. She acted as his hostess and, possibly, substitute wife.[34] Busy with her women friends and newfound political interests, Eleanor appeared relieved that Missy, who devoted herself totally to Franklin, could serve as his companion.

Franklin donated the land for the Val-Kill cottage and oversaw the architecture.[35] Dickerman and Cook made it their home and Eleanor frequently joined them there instead of staying at Big House under her mother-in-law's eye. So tightly knit in the 1920s that they had linen for Val-Kill embroidered with the initials EMN (Eleanor, Marion, Nancy), the three women worked and played together, even to the point of engaging in nocturnal pillow fights.[36] In a building behind the cottage the trio, with Franklin's blessing, established Val-Kill Industries under Cook's management to make replicas of early American furniture with the intent of providing jobs for unemployed workmen in the Hudson Valley.

In 1927 Eleanor, Cook, and Dickerman also purchased Todhunter School, an elite girls' school in New York City, installing Dickerman as the principal. Eleanor, whose didactic manner was said to resemble a schoolteacher's, scored as a successful and popular teacher, instructing students in drama, current events, and American history. Although Eleanor's friendship with Dickerman and Cook cooled while she was in the White House and they argued over use of their joint property, for years her relationship with the two women spurred her political and career interests.

A threesome whose motto might well have echoed that of Dumas's Three Musketeers—"all for one and one for all"—Nancy, Marion,

Eleanor works with three of her close friends at the Democratic State Committee Headquarters in New York City in 1929: Nancy Cook (seated), Caroline O'Day, and Marion Dickerman, right. Courtesy of the Franklin D. Roosevelt Library, Hyde Park, New York.

and Eleanor carried on political warfare against reactionary forces to push progressive causes advocated by newly enfranchised women voters.[37] They saw the Democratic Party as the logical conduit for their efforts, which included campaigns for minimum wages and maximum hours, an end to child labor, and the right of workers to organize. In an article titled "Why I Am a Democrat," written for the Junior League *Bulletin* in 1923, Eleanor contended, "On the whole the Democratic Party seems to have been more concerned with the welfare and interests of the people at large, and less with the growth of big business interests [than the Republican Party]."[38]

Through Cook and Dickerman, Eleanor acquired another intimate friend, Caroline O'Day. A wealthy and artistic widow, she helped promote Val-Kill Industries. O'Day became chair of the women's division of the state Democratic Party in 1923 and later was New York's congresswoman at large (a position no longer in existence).

Eleanor did not confine her teaching, which she loved, to the wealthy at Todhunter. She gave weekly readings to women workers in evening classes organized by the Women's Trade Union League (WTUL), headed by the fiery Rose Schneiderman, an immigrant from Russian Poland, and her associate, Maud Swartz. It brought together upper-class and working women, some of whom were militant Socialists.[39] Joining the league in 1922, Eleanor assisted in fundraising for its headquarters in Manhattan. She widened her circle of friends as she ended her readings by serving cookies and hot chocolate to women who represented different social strata than her cultivated, well-educated friends like Lape, Reed, Dickerman, and Cook.[40] As the WTUL changed its focus from organizing to lobbying for protective legislation setting minimum wages and maximum hours for women, Eleanor endorsed this approach, favored by the league's leadership of working-class women.

While polite on the surface and seemingly tolerant, Sara disliked the lifestyle of Eleanor's close friends. She objected to Eleanor staying at Val-Kill with Cook and Dickerman and criticized independent women like them who smoked and on occasion wore trousers and neckties.[41] She expressed even stronger disapproval of Eleanor's labor union associates who spoke in the unpolished language of New York's Lower East Side. As a result Eleanor hesitated to invite Schneiderman to Hyde Park since Sara looked down on her politics, Jewish background, and personal manner.[42]

Yet Sara, perhaps in determination not to be overlooked by Eleanor, involved herself in her daughter-in-law's activities. She gave a tea for members of the Women's Trade Union League at her New York home and expressed disappointment when only thirty members attended, although 600 invitations had been extended.[43] In 1927 she hosted a luncheon for members of the National Council of Women at which Eleanor was the guest of honor. At this event Eleanor met Mary McLeod Bethune, president of the National Association of Colored Women, who later became one of her closest African American political allies.

If not always in tune with Franklin's and Eleanor's ambitions, Sara did not want to be excluded from their pursuits while she continued to be a dominant force in their children's lives. In 1924 she insisted that Anna, in spite of her vigorous objections, make a debut at the age of eighteen. She sent her to Newport to stay with cousin Susie Parrish for a traditional week of debutante parties. Refusing to side with her daughter and veto a debut, Eleanor forced Anna to conform to standard upper-class behavior for young women. But she herself did not go to Newport to be with Anna. By 1924 Eleanor's own life had broadened much beyond the world in which she had been born. She had decided to work in partisan politics, resigning her office in the League of Women Voters in favor of political action as a Democrat.

In her attitude toward Anna and in other actions related to public appearances, on the surface Eleanor clung to the conventional even though she considered herself a progressive reformer. For example, her 1925 radio debut on behalf of the Women's City Club of New York, which she called a "clearing house for civic ideas," contained a relatively conservative message. Her broadcast called attention to the club's investigation of dance halls as dangerous influences on young women, although she open-mindedly noted that club members had found a surprisingly "low percentage of disaster . . . in spite of unwholesome surroundings."[44]

Eleanor had joined the club, initially founded by suffragists to persuade women to vote and influence the political process, two years before and had been elected vice president, gaining contacts with veterans of the suffrage movement who had moved into party politics. Among them was Belle Moskowitz, a labor reformer and close adviser of Alfred E. Smith, the four-time governor of New York and Democratic presidential hopeful. First becoming acquainted with Smith during Franklin's years in Albany, Eleanor emerged, like Franklin, as one of Smith's strong backers in his unsuccessful 1924 bid for the Democratic presidential nomination. Franklin staged his preliminary political comeback when he gave a rousing nominating speech for Smith at the Democratic national convention that year.

Managing to propel himself to the podium using crutches and accompanied by his son, James, Franklin gave the illusion that he could walk again while the convention crowd roared its approval.

Along with Dickerman and Cook, Eleanor watched intently from the gallery. After working with other women to organize support for Smith throughout upstate New York, where the Democratic Party was weak, she had succeeded in persuading Smith that women delegates to the national convention should be named by the women's division rather than by male party bosses. By now more accustomed to being interviewed, she told a reporter, "We go into the campaign feeling that our party has recognized us as an independent part of the organization and are encouraged accordingly."[45]

She was far less encouraged when the male politicos at the national convention rejected a proposal from a subcommittee of women she chaired to submit social-welfare planks for the party platform. The group, particularly interested in a resolution calling for states to ratify a constitutional amendment against child labor, had worked for three months to put together recommendations for legislation endorsed by national women's organizations. In addition to their stand on the child-labor amendment, the subcommittee backed the League of Nations and called for a federal department of education, equal pay for women, a forty-eight-hour workweek, living wages, and employment bureaus.[46] Their efforts were to no avail. The women were kept waiting all night outside a locked-door meeting of the Resolutions Committee that refused to hear their appeal.[47] Eleanor had learned a hard political lesson—that men did not surrender power easily. As she wrote later, "I was to see for the first time where the women stood when it came to a national convention. They stood outside the door of all important meetings and waited."[48]

At the state Democratic convention it was Eleanor's turn to speak, seconding Smith's renomination as governor, and in the process exacerbating the rift between the Hyde Park and the Oyster Bay Roosevelts. The previous day New York Republicans had picked their gubernatorial candidate, Eleanor's cousin, Theodore Roosevelt Jr., to run against Smith. Prodded by Howe, Eleanor and her women coworkers campaigned against Teddy Jr. by attempting to tie the candidate to the Teapot Dome scandal of the Harding administration. Although he was innocent of personal wrongdoing, he had previously served as assistant secretary of the navy under Harding, following in the footsteps of both his father and Franklin. To promote Smith, Eleanor shadowed Teddy Jr. during campaign appearances around the state in a car with an enormous teapot on top spouting steam. In her autobiography she apologized at least to some degree by saying, "I do think this was a rough stunt."[49] Cousin Alice never forgave her for it.[50]

Along with O'Day, Cook, and Dickerman, Eleanor had emerged as a leader of the women's division. A fifth woman, Elinor Morgenthau, also joined their circle. Unlike the other members she was a happily married wife and mother. Her husband, Henry Morgenthau, a well-to-do gentleman farmer, was a neighbor of the Roosevelts in the Hudson Valley and Franklin's political crony. The Roosevelts frequently invited the Morgenthau family to picnics at Hyde Park, making them "the only Jewish family the Roosevelts were intimate with socially," according to the Morgenthaus' son.[51] For six years in the 1920s the five women drove through every one of the 114 counties in New York State advocating causes sought by women reformers in the Democratic Party. These included improved education, sanitation, and housing; child health care; parks and playgrounds; protective legislation for women workers; and the right of women to serve on juries. They called their effort "Trooping for Democracy."[52]

With considerable help from Howe as well as O'Day, Dickerman, Cook, and Morgenthau, in 1925 Eleanor undertook to edit a monthly magazine, the *Women's Democratic News*, published by the women's division of the New York State Democratic Committee to promote Smith's political fortunes. Under Howe's guidance Eleanor, an antiwar activist, wrote editorials on the need for women to work for world peace, as she mastered page layout, proofreading, and other journalistic skills. Echoing social feminist ideals of the period, the magazine did not see women as either victims or candidates for the Equal Rights Amendment being pushed by Alice Paul. Instead, it pictured political activity within the Democratic Party as an enhanced opportunity for women to serve society without relinquishing their customary family roles.

Giving interviews, writing articles, and raising money for the state Democratic Party, Eleanor presented herself as a traditional wife helping her husband's career in the 1920s, although she became more outspoken as she gained experience. She witnessed the sordid side of politics firsthand as well as the idealism that drove some into public life. Driving voters to the polls and working with local Democratic committees, Eleanor wrote later, she witnessed "how people took money or its equivalent . . . for their votes and how much of the party machinery was geared to crooked business."[53] But this did not deter her because she also saw examples of unselfish service. She readily recognized that the suffragists' dream of women voting as a bloc to purify politics had evaporated and that women needed education, organization, and encouragement to make use of the ballot at all.

Disheartened when she realized that Democratic men were not willing to share actual power with women within the party, even though they had granted them equal representation in district committees, she published an article bylined "Mrs. Franklin D. Roosevelt" in *The Red Book Magazine*, a popular monthly, in April 1928. Titled "Women Must Learn to Play the Game as Men Do," it called for "women bosses" who could compete with men, although she explained that her idea of a boss was a "high-minded leader."[54] An editor's note introduced Eleanor as a woman "whose life has been spent in a political atmosphere," calling attention to her family background as the niece of Theodore Roosevelt and a descendant of New York chancellor Robert R. Livingstone, who had administered the oath of office to George Washington.[55]

After detailing Franklin's political career, the editor recited Eleanor's own involvement in the Democratic Party and the Women's City Club along with her service on the boards of the Foreign Policy Association and the City Housing Corporation. The introduction ended, however, with a stereotypical reassurance of Eleanor's femininity: "Active as she is politically, Mrs. Roosevelt is devoted to her home, is the mother of five children, and is one of the most popular and charming hostesses in the best circles of society."[56]

But the contents of the article conveyed a feminist message: "The fact is that generally women are not taken seriously," she wrote. "With certain exceptions, men still as a class dismiss their consequence and value in politics, cherishing the old-fashioned concept that their place is in the home."[57] Even so, she said women should learn to work with and like men in politics, not form their own political party—a direct slap at the National Woman's Party. Although her son James told her he would not write for such a magazine as *The Red Book*, known at the time for light fiction, she wrote Franklin, "I am glad of the chance."[58]

By this time she was earning money as a writer and eager to have the opportunity to do so. Her first-person style of writing was addressed to other women attempting to merge traditional and modern roles, but it fell far from being inflammatory and seemed a bit puritanical if not preachy. The previous year she had written an article titled "What I Want out of Life: A Prominent Society Woman Reveals Her Purpose," for *Success Magazine* and disclosed that she sought "the privilege of being useful, for in no other way, I am convinced, can true happiness be obtained."[59] She emphasized politics as a way for "empty nesters," women over forty like herself whose children were grown or away at school, "to guard against the emptiness and loneliness that enter some women's lives after their children are grown."[60]

By 1927 she had seen her own children more or less removed from the family circle. Anna had married a stockbroker, Curtis Dall, in 1926 in part "to get out" of the conflicts between her mother and grandmother, she said later.[61] Eleanor's eldest son, James, was at Harvard University and the younger boys were either in or headed for Groton, the upper-class boarding school attended by Franklin.

Was Eleanor herself willing to be a political boss? An article on her by S. J. Woolf in the *New York Times Magazine* certainly did not give this impression. It described her as a wife, mother, and teacher who refused to allow her public life to "interfere with her devotion to her home, nor has she sacrificed her private life in any respect to her public activities."[62] In public Eleanor operated within the constraints of her position as an upper-class married woman of her era.[63] Her gentility, marked by graciousness in social interactions, may have given the impression that she was politically naïve. She continually reassured Franklin that she was only his stand-in, as when she wrote her husband, "I'm only being active till you can be again."[64] Her actions, on the other hand, belied her words and surface appearances, illustrating the complexities of social roles that she carefully finessed.

In 1928 both Franklin and Eleanor represented pinnacles of power in the Democratic Party. Franklin reemerged from Warm Springs and again gave a resounding nominating speech for Al Smith at the Democratic convention in Houston, leading to Smith's nomination for president on the first ballot. Eleanor, having shown herself as a gifted political strategist, headed the Bureau of Women's Activities of the Democratic National Committee. She worked with Belle Moskowitz to organize Smith's preconvention campaign for the nomination. Yet, Eleanor was assigned no role at the convention and chose to remain behind at Hyde Park while Franklin delivered his stirring address.[65] Perhaps she did not go because she assumed Franklin's return to politics meant the end of her own participation.[66]

Nevertheless, she agreed to cochair women's activities in the Smith campaign, chiefly by organizing his headquarters, since she still found speaking "something of an ordeal."[67] More importantly, she made no effort to interfere with a party draft to nominate Franklin for governor of New York. In fact, she made a crucial call on the phone to Franklin at Warm Springs and turned the receiver over to Smith, who persuaded Franklin to make the run.[68] Apparently she remained ambiguous about his candidacy, noting in her autobiography that she considered it one of the aspects of her life to which she had to adjust: "I sometimes wonder whether I really wanted Franklin to run."[69]

While Eleanor did not campaign for her husband, she continued her vigorous efforts in support of Smith, directing the organization of national campaign committees, including those aimed at new voters—middle-class businesswomen and their working-class sisters. She told voters that Smith's Roman Catholic religion should be no barrier to his election. A well-known supporter of Prohibition herself, she attempted to divert attention from the fact that Smith opposed Prohibition, then required by the Eighteenth Amendment to the U.S. Constitution. She did so by claiming that women advocates of Prohibition within the Democratic Party were more interested in the Eighteenth Amendment than in constitutional amendments giving the vote to African Americans and considered Prohibition enforcement "more important than truth or fair play."[70] The *New York Times* praised her by saying, "Mrs. Roosevelt has replied with all the heat which many men have felt but do not venture to express."[71] Yet she herself did not speak up for racial justice, assuring an Alabama Democrat that Smith "would never try to do violence to the feelings of Southern people."[72]

Smith met an overwhelming defeat but Roosevelt squeezed by with a narrow margin of victory, although his defeat had been expected. Eleanor found herself in the role of governor's wife and made a tactless and uncharacteristically ungracious comment to reporters, "No, I am not excited about my husband's election. I don't care. What difference can it make to me?"[73] She feared that it would curb her own pursuits. With her strong organizational skills, she soon worked out a plan for it to interfere as little as possible with her interests.

As the governor's wife, Eleanor decided to devote half of the week to ceremonial duties in Albany. The other half she spent at Todhunter, where she was associate principal as well as a teacher of history, literature, and public affairs. When she was not at the governor's mansion, Missy served in her stead as hostess. By this time it was obvious that the Roosevelts had divided into two camps, each assembling a group of intimates who did not always see eye to eye with each other.[74] But the marriage endured, based on family loyalty, personal ambition, and a desire to attain political objectives, all of which required the maintenance of appropriate public appearances.

In an effort to conform to expectations that the governor's wife not play an openly partisan role, Eleanor resigned as editor of the *Women's Democratic News*, although she continued her work behind the scenes.[75] While Franklin had Missy, Eleanor now had her own equally devoted secretary, Malvina Thompson, known as Tommy, a tart-tongued young woman who had worked for Eleanor during the Smith campaign and continued to assist her part-time. Over the years she became indispensable to Eleanor as a confidante, gatekeeper, critic, and friend, the person who, Eleanor said, "makes life possible for me."[76]

Eleanor remained in close touch with her key political contacts, including Mary W. (Molly) Dewson, the no-nonsense civic secretary of the Women's City Club, president of the New York Consumers League, and leading member of the Joint Legislative Conference, a coalition of labor and women's organizations seeking social legislation in New York State. The conference, chaired by Eleanor in the early 1920s, pushed for unemployment compensation, minimum wages, and pensions, objectives adopted by Franklin in response to the influences of progressive reformers. Eleanor gave up her office in the Women's City Club after Franklin's election, but she and Dewson continued to be closely allied in Democratic Party politics. They worked together on Franklin's reelection campaign for governor in 1930. When he ran for president in 1932, they had back-to-back desks at the headquarters of the women's division of the Democratic Party, but Eleanor's name was kept off the division's masthead.[77]

Eleanor's correspondence showed she had no hesitancy in advising Franklin about appointments. She warned him not to make Belle Moskowitz an advisor on grounds she was too attached to Smith to serve Franklin's interests.[78] "I hope you will consider making Frances Perkins Labor Commissioner," she wrote Franklin, even though she denied for the rest of her life that she had played a part in Perkins's selection.[79] Lash contended that Eleanor minimized her influence on Franklin because she knew her success depended on "how well she buried her tracks."[80]

On the other hand, perhaps, Eleanor may not have been duplicitous. She knew Franklin listened to her views, but she also knew that he did what he wanted to do. According to Perkins, Franklin did not consult with Eleanor, but "liked her as a reporter," believing her "when she came back and said, 'Now I saw this, and this and this'... [but] when most men would have asked their wives what they thought, he didn't."[81]

As the governor's wife, Eleanor acted as her husband's legs as well as his ears. She represented him on inspection tours of state institutions, following Franklin's instructions to check the contents of cooking pots to make sure they corresponded with the menus presented by those in charge.[82] Earl Miller, a New York State highway patrolman assigned to be her bodyguard, assisted her on these trips, which enabled the couple to know each other well.

A former acrobat and boxing champion, the muscular Miller, twelve years younger than Eleanor and known as a ladies' man, ignored class barriers by considering himself her social equal. To bol-

Franklin and Eleanor enjoy a summer day at the Val-Kill swimming pool in Hyde Park with Missy LeHand and Earl Miller (about 1930). Courtesy of the Franklin D. Roosevelt Library, Hyde Park, New York.

ster her self-confidence he encouraged her to ride the horses he gave her and coached her in diving, offering Eleanor the personal attention and appreciation her own family did not provide. He urged Eleanor, whom he called "The Lady," to smile for press photographers and cooperate with journalists.

Their intimacy sparked rumors of romance, although no definite evidence of a love affair has been found. According to one scenario, Miller can be compared to a fun-loving nephew who endears himself to a staid aunt.[83] For example, home movies revealed the normally earnest Eleanor being gagged by Miller, who was costumed as a pirate, in a homespun drama.[84]

Franklin's governorship, while it may have curtailed Eleanor's most overt political activity, boosted her career as a magazine journalist. From 1928 to 1932 she published more than twenty articles in mass periodicals, mainly women's magazines. Loosely geared to social feminism, they included her personal views on relatively noncontroversial topics such as marriage, careers, education, and the wives of famous men. Although not overtly political, they drew on her personal experience and served to position the Roosevelts as a model couple. Without mentioning any of the strains in her own marriage, she published an article in 1931 titled "Ten Rules for Success in Marriage," in which she described a good marriage as one of adjustment from romance to companionship.[85] The test of companionship, she explained, lay in a wife's contribution to her husband's success in his chosen pursuit. She gave the impression she was referring to her own marital partnership, and perhaps she was. In her autobiography she wrote of Franklin, "I was one of those who served his purposes."[86] She could have added that he also served her purpose—to build a fulfilling career.

CHAPTER 3

MERGING THE PERSONAL AND THE POLITICAL

"The basis of all useful political activity is an interest in human beings and social conditions, and a knowledge of human nature."
Eleanor Roosevelt in her 1933 book, *It's Up to the Women*

When Franklin ran for President in 1932, Eleanor curtailed her political involvement on the surface. "I did not work directly in the campaign, because I felt that that was something better done by others," she explained later, adding, "I went on many of the trips and always did anything that Franklin felt would be helpful."[1] In 1932 it was not considered seemly for a candidate's wife to be too visible.[2] Her assigned office was not in New York City's Biltmore Hotel, the official campaign headquarters, where Molly Dewson busily recruited women workers, but across the street where Howe's office was located.[3] Since Eleanor acted as a conduit to keep communication open between Howe and James A. Farley, chairman of the Democratic National Committee, who did not always see eye to eye, New Yorkers repeatedly saw Eleanor and Howe hurry across Madison Avenue to straighten out campaign differences.[4] Eleanor also conferred with Dewson, who oversaw the printing of millions of "Rainbow Fliers," political messages on colored paper designed to appeal to women voters. Working in the background through trusted lieutenants,

Eleanor continued a political style that she had developed as the governor's wife and would perfect in the White House.[5]

Eleanor's limited campaign participation in public corresponded with her views on women in politics expressed in articles she sold to mass-circulation magazines, with Howe acting as her agent. Picturing political participation against a backdrop of women's traditional family responsibilities, she advocated moderation that approached tokenism in terms of women holding office. She did not deal specifically with the role of candidates' wives, probably because she did not see a definite place for them in politics.

Nine months before Roosevelt's landslide election, *Home* magazine published an article by Eleanor titled "What Do Ten Million Women Want?"[6] She contended that women did not want a woman president, but she argued that the "time had come for a woman to fill a place in the Cabinet," perhaps floating a trial balloon to assess sentiment on the possible appointment of Frances Perkins to the position of secretary of labor.[7] In the article Eleanor defined areas she considered important to women voters: education, Prohibition, uniform marriage and divorce laws, and a crackdown on crime. Like other writers for women's magazines of the day, she glorified the role of housewives, urging women to be active in politics to improve community life for their children.

Adopting a less feminist tone than in her article two years earlier urging women to "play the game as men do," Eleanor mirrored the political situation of women at the start of the 1930s. By gaining suffrage in 1920, women had lost a specific objective for political power. Initially, male politicians had feared that women would emerge as a voting bloc, but elections during the 1920s dispelled this possibility. Women, when they voted at all, separated themselves by class and ideology much as their husbands did. No longer committed to the common goal of suffrage, women's groups splintered among themselves. Given no more than surface courtesy and representation within party circles, women were "exactly where men political leaders wanted them: bound, gagged, divided and delivered to the Republican and Democratic parties," one suffragist, Anne Martin, observed cynically.[8]

In presenting a tepid argument for women in politics, Eleanor portrayed herself as a middle-of-the-road mother concerned mainly with her home and children. Certainly, Franklin gave the impression that she had modest talents for public life. Interviewed by *Good Housekeeping* in 1930, both Eleanor and Franklin commented on her role as a governor's wife. While Eleanor pointed to a decline in the time required for the occupation of motherhood because of expanded schooling and reliance on professional experts, she stressed that women still needed to put their families first. Using her own example of teaching at Todhunter School, she wrote that "until all my children were away at school, I stayed at home," a scenario that skipped her volunteer activity in women's reform networks and the Democratic Party in the 1920s.[9]

Pressed by the interviewer to say what accounted for his wife's "success as a wife and mother," Franklin first answered, "Great Scott," before crediting her with "something which every member of the Roosevelt family seems always to have had, a deep and abiding interest in everything and everybody."[10] Asked further if she had "special abilities of any kind," he replied, "None!" although he conceded in response to more prodding that she had become "a good executive because she is interested in people and in doing things."[11] He did not say that he considered her a political partner, nor did she voice a desire to be one. In the climate of the times, it probably would not have been wise to express their relationship in terms of any kind of equality, even if that had been the case. But, in the period when Franklin eyed the White House, it was not. Eleanor seemed cast as a subordinate and not a chief one at that.

Eleanor and Franklin did not always agree politically. As governor he was not willing to sponsor child-labor legislation, which she had backed, and he abandoned support for Prohibition over her objections. Furthermore, in 1932 he had withdrawn his advocacy of the United States' joining the League of Nations and the World Court, two causes in which she strongly believed. She knew that he and his confidants could not be counted on to accept her views. The "Brains Trust," as Franklin's key advisors were called, considered her too idealistic, too assertive, and a thorn in their flesh. Rexford G. Tugwell, one of the members, was startled when he heard comments from other advisors that one of their first jobs was "to get the pants off Eleanor and onto Frank."[12]

In spite of her high-pitched voice, Eleanor by this time had become a sought-after public speaker herself, setting herself on a parallel track with her husband. While she insisted in her autobiography, "I played no role at all" in Franklin's speeches, she admitted he sometimes used material from letters or articles that she had given him.[13] "But I never expected him to pay any attention to my ideas—he was much too good a speaker to need advice from me," she continued.[14] She might also have added that he had a team of accomplished speechwriters.

Not surprisingly, Eleanor longed for status of her own and wanted to be seen as an individual in her own right. In an article titled "Ten Rules for Success in Marriage," which she wrote the year after the *Good Housekeeping* interview, she described marriage as a process of adjustment from romance to companionship but said neither husband nor wife should be "the dominating person in the household."[15] She urged women to "have a plan, some central idea, as definite a pattern for your life as possible, and a clearly understood object for the joint project."[16]

While it was becoming quite clear at this point what Franklin's object was, Eleanor's own contribution to the couple's "joint project" remained undefined. Her 1932 income tax return listed her occupation as "teacher, writer and editor."[17] It reported she made $25,000 from these sources. She also earned money from giving paid speeches and a series of broadcasts on child rearing and family relations for a cold cream manufacturer. Combined with proceeds from a family trust, this gave her a total taxable income of $33,000. From it she donated $5,000 to charity.[18]

During Franklin's 1932 campaign for the presidency, Eleanor preferred gathering political intelligence on her own and reporting to Franklin rather than standing by his side on smoke-filled campaign trains.[19] In mid-October she left his train to go back to her students at Todhunter School in New York, which offered progressive education. She justified her departure by explaining, "Why, I have to teach school tomorrow."[20]

When Franklin won in a landslide, Eleanor feared that the White House would stifle her, limiting her opportunities to gain income that allowed her a feeling of independence and self-worth. Since Franklin had to depend on his mother, Sara, to pay many of the family's bills, Eleanor's desire to earn her own income represented a breaking away from Sara over her objections. "When I began to earn money it was a real grief to her," Eleanor wrote.[21] She had no intention of giving up all her paid activities to live in the White House, and she did not, but she realized that she had to move carefully.

In an unprecedented move after the election, Eleanor continued to earn money. She delivered a series of twelve network radio commentaries in the preinaugural period, chiefly on children and families. Pond's, the cold cream manufacturer, paid her $1,800 per broadcast.[22] In the face of newspaper criticism that she was exploiting her position "for commercial purposes," she announced she would not accept additional radio contracts, although by 1934 she changed her mind.[23]

Regardless of the election, Eleanor planned to fulfill her contract with Bernarr Macfadden, a physical culture faddist and publisher of pulp magazines, to edit a new monthly parenting magazine, *Babies—Just Babies*, for middle-class families.[24] *Time* magazine claimed Macfadden's motivation for hiring her may have been to ingratiate himself with Franklin in hopes of getting a top political appointment.[25] If so, his strategy did not succeed. Eleanor took the job, which paid her $500 a month, partly to provide income for her daughter, Anna Roosevelt Dall, who was named associate editor.[26] In the process of divorcing her husband, Curtis Dall, a stockbroker, Anna needed employment.

Both Eleanor and her daughter contributed to the first issue of the baby magazine in October 1932, with humorous accounts of their trials as young mothers with crying infants.[27] As editor, Eleanor avoided controversial topics, penciling in "no" on a memo suggesting an article on birth control.[28] The publication featured slick-paper photographs of smiling infants and consumer advice, along with fiction and lullabies, but it did not do well financially.

After six months Eleanor withdrew from the magazine, in reaction to ridicule and disagreements with Macfadden. Lacking the prestige of her name, *Babies—Just Babies* ceased publication. When members of the Women's National Press Club, a leading organization of Washington women journalists, spoofed her efforts at their annual party by singing, "We are new to the business of running the show. We are babies, just babies, just babies," the first lady had had enough.[29] She wrote to Lorena Hickok that Macfadden pressured her to rewrite the editorial announcing her resignation because the first one "said I was giving up the magazine too emphatically."[30] She continued writing for other publications.

Having rejected a life as a society matron, Eleanor had no desire to be first lady and face endless rounds of teas, receptions, and dinners. She recognized that the demands of entertaining and other duties would make it impossible for her to continue teaching at Todhunter. Before moving into the White House in 1933, she reluctantly resigned from the school, even though the previous year she had told a reporter that she liked teaching better than "anything else I do."[31] She wrote later, "I had watched Mrs. Theodore Roosevelt and had seen what it meant to be the wife of the President, and I cannot say that I was pleased at the prospect."[32]

Without the opportunity to express herself through teaching, Eleanor found writing her main career outlet. Before Franklin's inauguration on 4 March 1933 she began a column, "Passing Thoughts of Mrs. Franklin D. Roosevelt," for the *Women's Democratic News.* Mainly chronicling her ceremonial activities as first lady, it ran from February 1933 until December 1935 when the *News* merged with the *Democratic Digest.* In an article titled "What I Hope to Leave Behind!" published in *Pictorial Review*, a popular magazine, a month after the inauguration, she supported careers for women if they made "a woman more of a person so that her charm, her intelligence and her experience will be of great value to the other lives around her."[33] It voiced her own determination to pursue a career in a new, demanding, and somewhat uncomfortable situation.

In addition to obligating her to spend time at official functions, the move to Washington separated her from close friends like Dickerman and Cook, as well as Earl Miller, whom Franklin had elevated from state police sergeant to personnel director for the New York State Department of Corrections. The new job kept him in Albany and out of Washington. Years later Dickerman revealed that Eleanor had written a letter to Cook rebelling against "the prospect of being a prisoner of the White House" and threatening to divorce Franklin and run away with Miller.[34] Dickerman said Howe, to whom she and Cook showed the letter, had shredded it and ordered them "not to breathe a word of this to anyone."[35] If Eleanor had contemplated such a possibility, it would have been a reflection of emotional stress at the thought of being first lady. Elopement with Miller, at the time already planning the second of his three failed marriages, would have seemed totally out of character for Eleanor with her strong sense of duty and family loyalty.

Regardless of the veracity of Dickerman's recollection, Miller and Eleanor remained close friends. She entertained Miller at Val-Kill and visited him during vacations while she lived in the White House. Miller taught her to shoot a pistol when she insisted on refusing Secret Service protection. He gave her guard dogs and played billiards and other games with her, providing companionable relaxation that was otherwise absent from her life.[36] Her son Elliott wrote that Miller instilled "self-assuredness" and "courage" in her. In return, according to Elliott, she gave him "doting" affection.[37] Another son, James, thought that his mother and Miller may have had a full-blown affair.[38]

Dickerman and Cook were not the only close friends to whom Eleanor confided her fears that she "would have nothing to do except stand in line and receive visitors and preside over official dinners."[39] She made similar statements to Frances Perkins, whom Franklin named secretary of labor, telling Perkins that she respected Lou Henry Hoover for continuing her active engagement in the White House with the Girl Scouts, since presidential wives "were expected to show no interest in public affairs."[40] Anticipating leisure hours, Perkins said, Eleanor "sent a couple of horses to Washington, planning to ride every day . . . thought she might study a language, Spanish perhaps [and] was going to catch up on her reading."[41]

One measure of the tension between the Roosevelts was the fact that Eleanor never shared her reservations about life at 1600 Pennsylvania Avenue with Franklin. "From the personal standpoint, I did not want my husband to be President," she wrote later; "I realized, however, that it was impossible to keep a man out of public service when that was what he wanted. . . . It was pure selfishness on my part, and I never mentioned my feelings on the subject to him."[42] In not doing so she violated two of the ten rules she had laid down in her magazine article on success in marriage: "Be honest" and "talk things over . . . meet every situation in the open."[43] Like many others, Eleanor found it easier to give advice than to practice it. Open communication did not mark the Roosevelt marriage. Franklin did not tell her when he decided to run for president in 1932, although she was well aware through Howe that Franklin was getting ready to challenge Smith for the Democratic nomination.[44]

Eleanor had known several of her predecessors as first lady, but none of them presented a viable role model. She definitely did not want to confine herself mainly to being a hostess like her aunt Edith. Having lived in Washington during the Wilson administration, she had known both of the wives of Woodrow Wilson. Eleanor had not taken part in Ellen Wilson's campaign, criticized by the press, to demolish substandard alley dwellings occupied mainly by African Americans. She undoubtedly was aware that Congress had passed legislation, later ruled unconstitutional, against back-alley slums, only when the president's wife lay on her deathbed and made it her final request.[45] She also knew that Wilson's second wife, Edith, had been accused of trying to run the government when she controlled access to her husband after he suffered a major stroke.

Eleanor's immediate predecessor, Lou Henry Hoover, a graduate of Stanford University, had taken some steps to update the role of the first lady, although the depression that hit in 1929 made her, like her husband, President Herbert Hoover, exceedingly unpopular with both the public and the press. Between 1929 and 1933, Lou Henry Hoover addressed the public on several occasions via the radio.[46] Her radio talks, the first ever given by a first lady, celebrated the work of voluntary organizations in attempting to ameliorate Depression conditions. They were in keeping with her husband's philosophy against direct government assistance. Serving as honorary president of the Girl Scouts, an organization to which she had been deeply committed for years, Hoover spoke twice on efforts by Girl Scouts to assist with Depression relief activities. She also broadcast a feminist message to members of 4-H Clubs in 1929, challenging gender roles by urging boys as well as girls to learn homemaking skills.

In addition, Hoover was the first president's wife to entertain an African American in the White House. In response to inviting Jessie DePriest, the wife of African American congressman Oscar DePriest, to tea along with the wives of other congressmen, she encountered a storm of criticism from southern whites.[47] Herbert Hoover, however, did not want his wife or family members to be seen as public figures. Living primarily in his shadow, Lou Henry exercised little political influence and eschewed contacts with journalists.[48] When meeting with reporters, which she did only to discuss her favorite organizations, she requested that women correspondents sit cross-legged on the floor like members of a Girl Scout troop.[49] This arrangement did little to improve her public image of being cold and distant.

One enterprising reporter, Bess Furman of the Associated Press (AP), desperate for a feature story on the president's family, dressed up like a Girl Scout to enter the family living quarters as part of a group of Christmas carolers.[50] Not surprisingly, Furman was overjoyed when Eleanor became first lady because she did not shy away from publicity. Howe, the architect of Franklin's political success, continued to encourage Eleanor's own political interests as a way of drawing more women into the Democratic Party.

Franklin did not insist that Eleanor remain in the background, although he had no particular role for her in his administration. When, as Eleanor put it in her autobiography, she tentatively told Franklin that being a hostess at official functions would not take all her time and that "he might like me to do a real job and take over some of his mail," he rejected her offer. She wrote that he replied, "Missy [LeHand], who had been handling his mail for a long time, would feel I was interfering."[51]

When Franklin was occupied with plans for his presidency prior to the inauguration, Eleanor kept busy by working on two nonfiction books published the following year. In addition, she wrote a children's textbook on U.S. government, *When You Grow Up to Vote.*[52] The first of the adult books, a tribute to her beloved father, was an edited version of letters to his family describing hunting expeditions before his marriage. Titled *Hunting Big Game in the Eighties: The Letters of Elliott Roosevelt*, the book won praise from reviewers as cultural history offering insight into the personalities making up the Roosevelt family.[53]

The second volume, *It's Up to the Women*, called on women to help pull their families through the grim economic conditions facing the nation while righting social wrongs. Based on Eleanor's speeches and articles, the slender volume interwove recipes, model budgets, and child-rearing tips with an appeal to women to initiate progressive change as they reared healthy children.[54] The most controversial chapter embraced the right of women to work outside the home, although Eleanor emphasized home responsibilities above all: "If a woman falls in love and marries, of course her first interest and her first duty is to her home, but her duty to her home does not of necessity preclude her having another occupation."[55]

Urging women to become more active politically, Eleanor pictured the results of woman suffrage as disappointing: "The vast majority of women . . . remain as indifferent to the vote and how they use it as are the vast majority of men."[56] In fact, she wrote that it would be a long time until women worked their way up the political ladder. Eventually a woman would be elected president, she predicted, but this would be far into the future: "I do not advise any woman to try to be President, or in fact to hold any important office until she has gained experience in minor offices first. . . . every woman in public office will be watched far more carefully than a man holding a similar position."[57]

The book met a favorable response, although reviewers noted its middle-class orientation. It touched on Eleanor's wide-ranging moral interests as an advocate for peace, education, abolition of poverty, women's and minority rights, and other worthy causes.[58] While it lacked a clear-cut plan of action, its ideas fit within Franklin's New Deal policies and were loosely drawn from those of liberal women reformers, the social feminists with whom Eleanor had allied herself in the 1920s. Suzanne La Follette pointed out in the *Saturday Review of Literature* that the book would not be helpful to the "wives of miners or steel workers" but said "its platitudes are inspired by good liberal principles and benevolent intentions."[59]

In another review historian Mary R. Beard contended, "Mrs. Roosevelt still sees social arrangements in the bright autumn of a bourgeois culture. . . . Her world of minds and manners is largely bounded by the middle class, but within it there is noblesse oblige—a type of her own making."[60] Marked by sometimes hazy and convoluted language, the work expressed Eleanor's attitude toward women's roles as she entered the White House. She wanted to maintain her own career, encourage others to follow her example, and inspire women to take part in building a better world. The book contained nothing about the position of first lady that Eleanor feared would constrain her activities.

Initially Eleanor barely concealed her hostility toward being first lady, giving a stony-faced stare to a woman reporter who gushed during the celebration at Hyde Park after Franklin won the presidential nomination, "Mrs. Roosevelt, aren't you thrilled at the idea of being in the White House?"[61] A more astute journalist, Lorena Hickok, a top political reporter for the AP, observed Eleanor's look and sought to find out why the prospect had little appeal. The opportunity arose when Hickok, whose friends called her Hick, was assigned to cover Eleanor during the final month of the 1932 presidential campaign. On lengthy cross-country train trips, the two women exchanged life stories and shared confidences, even though their backgrounds could hardly have been more dissimilar. Neither had experienced a happy childhood, although Hickok, unlike Eleanor, had suffered from economic as well as emotional deprivation.

Brutalized by her father, a butter maker in South Dakota, Hickok started work as a hired girl at the age of fourteen after the death of her mother.[62] Taken in by a cousin in Battle Creek, Michigan, she finished high school there and began her journalism career writing items about visitors to Battle Creek for the local newspaper. Dropping out of Lawrence College in Appleton, Wisconsin, she concentrated on journalism, advancing to the *Milwaukee Sentinel* and, after an unsuccessful fling in New York, moving to Minneapolis. She enrolled in the University of Minnesota but soon gave up college to become a star reporter at the *Minneapolis Tribune* where she covered murder trials and University of Minnesota football, a beat that made her one of the first women sports reporters. In 1927 she returned to New York and joined the AP, where she won coveted political assignments in spite of prevailing prejudice against women journalists.[63]

A large woman who struggled with her weight, Hickok, sexually oriented to other women, developed a passionate attachment to Eleanor. Yet, when she first had seen her in New York in 1928 at the Democratic national headquarters, Hickok considered Eleanor, who was nearly six feet tall, "very plain," with prominent front teeth and unbecoming clothes, and thought she looked "rather awkward and ungainly" when she stood still. On the positive side she watched Eleanor, said to dance beautifully in evening gowns, move "with the grace of a fine athlete."[64] As their relationship flowered in 1932,

Hickok gave Eleanor her most treasured possession, a sapphire and diamond ring that she had received from a famous singer, Ernestine Schumann-Heink. Eleanor wore the ring until her death.[65] While the exact nature of the intimacy between Eleanor and Hickok remains unclear, the journalist undoubtedly offered stimulating and supportive affection at a time when Eleanor was separated physically from Earl Miller and growing more distant from Cook and Dickerman.

For years Eleanor and Hickok exchanged daily letters, some of which contained erotic references. Scholars are split on the question of whether they had a lesbian relationship in terms of physical contact, although there is no dispute on their emotional closeness. Hickok burned some of the correspondence after Eleanor's death and retyped other letters to provide edited versions. She placed these in the Franklin D. Roosevelt Library with the stipulation they not be opened until ten years after her death, which occurred in 1968.[66]

What is clear is that Hickok played a significant role in introducing Eleanor to the public in her new role and in advancing her journalistic career. Hickok advised Eleanor on press relations, helping her establish White House press conferences for women reporters only shortly after the inauguration, although Hickok herself, since she was based in New York, never covered them. She gave Eleanor tips on writing for magazines, paved her way for successful interaction with other women journalists, and suggested she keep copies of her daily letters, an idea that eventually became the basis for Eleanor's successful syndicated newspaper column, "My Day."[67]

Of even more initial importance, Hickok wrote glowing AP news stories on the first-lady-to-be, showing her as an independent-minded modern woman who still personified traditional feminine virtues of caring deeply for her family as well as society at large. Following Franklin's landslide election as president, Hickok wrote a three-part series, announcing that Eleanor would give up her position at Todhunter School but would remain as editor of *Babies—Just Babies* so she could earn money to give "to people who need help."[68] The series also pointed out that Eleanor refused Secret Service escorts, wore $10 dresses, and drove her own car.

Hickok's glowing portrayal of Eleanor as a new kind of first lady turned her into a public relations appendage of the Roosevelt administration, with Hick clearing stories in advance with either Eleanor herself or Howe in violation of AP rules. After suppressing a comment Eleanor had made on her paid radio series during the campaign—that the girl of today "faces the probability of learning, very young, how much she can drink of such things as whisky and gin"—Hickok had been disciplined by the AP. It cut her pay after a newspaper printed the remark that outraged supporters of Prohibition, a hot election issue.[69] The night before Franklin gave his inaugural address on 4 March 1933, Eleanor read the speech to Hickok, whose passionate loyalty to the Roosevelts suppressed any desire to scoop her competitors by calling in the story to her employers. "That night," she wrote later, "Lorena Hickok ceased to be a newspaper reporter."[70] She left the AP in June to go to work for the Roosevelt administration as a confidential investigator of relief programs for the Federal Emergency Relief Administration.

On inauguration day itself Hickok returned to her reportorial role before going back to New York, conducting an exclusive interview with Eleanor copyrighted by the AP. It stood out as the first interview ever given by a president's wife in the White House and took place in a bathroom, the only place where the two could find privacy.[71] The previous day Eleanor had taken Hickok to see the cemetery statue of *Grief*, which had brought her solace after discovering Franklin's affair with Lucy Mercer. Apparently Eleanor wanted Hickok to join her in seeking inner peace before the inauguration.

The interview gave Eleanor's impression of public reaction to Franklin's inaugural address that asserted his "firm belief that all we have to fear is fear itself" and promised a New Deal to a Depression-stricken nation.[72] Before going to inaugural balls in her gown of an unflattering shade called "Eleanor blue," Eleanor had watched huge crowds listen to Franklin. She told Hickok, "You felt that they would do anything—if only someone would tell them what to do."[73] In the interview she promised to simplify White House social life, reduce expenses, and serve as her husband's "eyes and ears," reporting to him on the concerns of the American people.[74]

As she carried out those intentions, Eleanor greatly expanded the concept of what a first lady could or should do, adding her own sense of mission and personal preferences to the tasks before her. In her autobiography she stated that Franklin "never told me I was a

Eleanor smiles at the side of Franklin during his first inauguration as president of the United States on 4 March 1933. Sen. Joseph T. Robinson accompanies them. Courtesy of the Franklin D. Roosevelt Library, Hyde Park, New York.

good reporter, nor, in the early days, were any of my trips made at his request," but because he listened to what she said, she "decided this was the only way I could help him, outside of running the house which was soon organized and running itself under Mrs. Nesbitt."[75] This reference was to Henrietta Nesbitt, whom Eleanor installed as a budget-minded head housekeeper and put in charge of domestic details to free herself for more congenial pursuits.

To Hickok's dismay her interview did not get much attention, but another AP story did. Written by Bess Furman, the star woman reporter in the AP Washington bureau, it emphasized that Eleanor had startled Washington by breaking several social precedents on her first day as first lady. When three thousand guests arrived for tea, instead of the one thousand expected, Eleanor expanded tea-pouring from the State Dining Room to the East Room for the first time and invited in members of the press. After finishing her interview with Hickok, she entertained seventy-five persons for dinner, in-

Eleanor meets the press after flying to Los Angeles on 6 June 1933, making her first transcontinental flight, which served to publicize aviation as well as the Roosevelt administration and the role of the first lady. Courtesy of the Franklin D. Roosevelt Library, Hyde Park, New York.

cluding her spiteful Republican cousin, Alice Longworth, who delighted in making fun of her. The new first lady met her guests personally at the door, instead of waiting for them to assemble and then ceremoniously descending to greet them. Furman ended her account with a bated-breath summary: "Washington had never seen the like—a social transformation had taken place with the New Deal."[76]

The transformation involved social action as well as social activity and carved out a new role in White House political communication. Previously, wives had not been pressed into service as conscious symbols of an administration's attitude toward the public. Eleanor, on the other hand, acted as a personal representative of her husband, even in tense situations, thereby elevating the role of the first lady.

Shortly after the inauguration, Howe took Eleanor on a surprise visit to a group of "bonus marchers," unemployed World War I veterans who had come to Washington to demand payment of promised bonuses for military service. Some 20,000 had marched on the capital in 1932 and been evicted from their encampment in July by Gen. Douglas MacArthur, army chief of staff under President Hoover. Using tanks and troops, MacArthur burned down the veterans' camp, injuring scores of persons, a move that cast blame on Hoover for callousness toward former servicemen.

To avoid a similar disaster, an ailing Howe took charge of dealing with a second contingent of 3,000 marchers, who arrived in Washington in May 1933. The administration housed the veterans in an abandoned camp near the White House and gave them food from relief supplies. Without advance notice to the marchers, Howe insisted that an unaccompanied Eleanor, as she put it, "walk around among the veterans and see just how things were."[77] He remained in her car while she introduced herself, toured the camp, spoke to the men and joined them in singing old war songs. In view of her determination to avoid Secret Service escorts, Eleanor made light of security concerns: "Several people inquired what protection we had had, and seemed a little horrified when I answered, 'None,'" she wrote.[78] She did not add that the Secret Service responded to the incident by giving Howe two pistols, one for her, which she uneasily carried with her, and one for himself. [79]

Although the marchers did not get the checks they wanted, Eleanor's visit demonstrated presidential concern for their welfare. A left-wing veteran, disappointed when the marchers did not follow the Communist line and protest more vehemently, commented wryly, "Hoover sent the Army, Roosevelt sent his wife."[80] The "bonus marchers" disbanded several days after Eleanor's visit, with most of the men joining the Civilian Conservation Corps (CCC), one of the key New Deal programs established during the administration's first 100 days of legislative activity to cope with the Great Depression. It placed unemployed young men in camps to work on conservation projects and learn job skills. During the years to come, Eleanor visited numerous CCC camps and other relief facilities to publicize New Deal programs.

Her most immediate task as first lady was presiding over the White House, official residence of the president and his family since 1800, when Abigail Adams had hung her laundry in the East Room, which she called "the great unfinished audience Room."[81] Familiar with the historic mansion where she had visited Uncle Ted and Aunt Edith as a young woman, Eleanor understood established protocol, commenting, "I think it is a beautiful house with lovely proportions, great dignity, and I do not think any one looking at it from the outside or living in it can fail to feel the spell of the past."[82] Nevertheless, she put a personal stamp on the mansion, operating the cage-like elevator herself and treating the staff with greater informality than the Hoovers had allowed.

Eleanor oversaw the rearrangement of family living quarters on the second and third floors to provide space for FDR's two key staff members, Howe and Missy LeHand, as well as Sara, who often visited. Rooms were assigned to the five photogenic Roosevelt children, Anna, James, Elliott, Franklin D. Jr., and John—ranging in age from twenty-six to sixteen. Two still were students, Franklin Jr. at Harvard and John at Groton, the boarding school Roosevelt sons traditionally attended. Anna, preparing for a divorce, needed space for both herself and her two children, six-year-old Sisty (Anna Eleanor) Dall and three-year-old Buzz (Curtis) Dall, who were frequently photographed with Eleanor. She insisted that a swing for them be hung from a tree on the White House lawn in spite of regulations forbidding it.[83]

Since White House beds were too short for the tall Roosevelts, Eleanor replaced them with furniture made at the Val-Kill factory. She used family possessions, including Franklin's naval prints and her collection of photographs of friends and relatives, to ornament the second-floor family living quarters. One of her Val-Kill partners, Nancy Cook, assisted with the redecoration, which emphasized a homey feel. According to Robert Sherwood, a speechwriter for Franklin, "the progressivism of Franklin and Eleanor Roosevelt certainly did not extend to interior decoration."[84]

Sherwood said their White House rooms were "as nearly as possible duplications of the rooms at Hyde Park," with upstairs bedrooms containing furnishings "which might have come out of an old and ultra-respectable summer resort hotel."[85] He described most of the rooms as "dingy with the darkness of southern mansions from which the sunlight is excluded by surrounding colonnades and big trees," but he loved the Roosevelts' warm hospitality.[86] Even though the White House was spruced up when the British monarchs, King George VI and Queen Elizabeth, visited in 1939, Eleanor paid scant attention to interior decorating in the face of the Depression and World War II.[87]

For herself Eleanor chose the two-room Lincoln bedroom suite, using the larger room as her office/sitting room. She closed off the west sitting hall outside her suite with screens and brightened the furniture with chintz slipcovers, making the area a cheery place to meet her staff and serve tea and coffee to family, staff, and guests.[88] A small bedroom and study across a corridor from her suite was set aside for Hickok, who moved into the White House after she left the AP. When the house was full, Hickok, like other close friends, occupied a daybed in Eleanor's sitting room.[89] Described by one White House aide as a "heavy-set, mannish woman," Hickok initially dined with the family, but later kept to herself and did not participate in social events, perhaps because Franklin feared that there might be gossip about her and Eleanor.[90]

Eleanor's Lincoln suite adjoined Franklin's study, known as the Oval Room. A portrait of Eleanor that Franklin particularly liked hung over the door facing his desk and a portrait of his mother behind the desk. His small bedroom next to the study contained two bed tables, on one of which Eleanor left material for him with the notation "F-read."[91] Franklin eventually blocked the sliding doors between his suite and Eleanor's with a large highboy, barring free access between the two areas.[92] It served as a tangible reminder of the emotional distance between the couple, who saw relatively little of each other in the White House. Eleanor entered Franklin's bedroom briefly each day to say good morning while he ate breakfast. She stopped by again before he went to sleep, taking advantage of the opportunity to perch on his bed and talk about personal and political matters that concerned her.[93] During the day Franklin was occupied with official business and they rarely met.

In her daily letters to Hickok, Eleanor poured out frustrations but said that she did not feel sorry for herself: "I'm only unhappy [in] spots & heaven knows, most people are."[94] Servants noted a lack of intimacy between the two, whereas they witnessed numerous incidents of warmth between Franklin and his attractive secretary, who enjoyed each other's company outside of office hours. Lillian Parks, a maid, noticed, "FDR was spending his evenings with Missy LeHand. Eleanor Roosevelt was spending her evenings with Lorena Hickok."[95] While the staff members deferred to Eleanor, whom they respected for her kindness and crusading instincts, they grew to love the vivacious, lighthearted LeHand, respond to her requests, and appreciate her importance to the president.[96] Parks concluded, "We really had two mistresses in the White House."[97]

Observing LeHand's entry into Franklin's suite at odd hours in her bathrobe, the servants surmised, like the Roosevelts' daughter, Anna, that LeHand was "the office wife" who also lived in the White House.[98] Both Eleanor and LeHand maintained a show of friendship, although Eleanor avoided Franklin's daily cocktail ritual for his intimate circle where LeHand held sway. Dinners that followed included numerous guests; Franklin and Eleanor almost never dined by themselves.

While Eleanor's interests chiefly lay outside domestic matters, she realized the need to exercise oversight of the White House, noting that "a house that is always on exhibition should look its best at all times."[99] Although some visitors complained about shortcomings in housekeeping and interior decoration, particularly during World War II, Eleanor dutifully tried to make improvements in the mansion. In 1934–1935 she conferred with an architect friend, Eric Gugler, on refurbishing the Red Room, helping select fabrics and colors for upholstery and wall coverings, and two years later sought his advice on the Blue Room.[100] In 1935 she proudly led reporters on a tour of the new White House kitchen featuring the latest electrical appliances that had been installed at her suggestion, making the first changes in the cooking area since the Taft administration of 1908–1912.[101]

To decorate family quarters and offices Eleanor selected paintings and other works by artists who were on the public payroll as part of New Deal relief efforts. Recognizing that she could not act solely on her own, she consulted with the Commission of Fine Arts on objects to be displayed in the White House. In 1941 she set up a permanent Subcommittee on Furnishings and Gifts for State Rooms of the White House, thereby establishing it as a national museum.[102] This group remained in place until Jacqueline Kennedy launched a major restoration effort in the early 1960s.

As she took charge of the White House, Eleanor's most notable action was hiring her Hyde Park neighbor, Henrietta Nesbitt, to be the official housekeeper. Nesbitt, whose prior experience was limited to running a home bakery, was employed in spite of the recommendation of Chief Usher Ike Hoover that a professional manager be selected instead.[103] Nesbitt first came to Eleanor's attention when she baked whole-wheat bread that Eleanor liked for an event sponsored by the League of Women Voters in Hyde Park.

Hoover, who had worked at the White House for more than forty years and had vivid memories of Eleanor's uncle Ted and aunt Edith, described Eleanor as extremely well organized at the time of Franklin's first inauguration. "Mrs. Roosevelt knew just what she wanted," he wrote in a memoir published following his death six months after the Roosevelt administration began.[104] He was succeeded by Howell G. Crim, a proper individual easily shocked at apparent breaches of manners. Crim took notice when Eleanor did not change her dress or comb her hair between appointments.[105]

Eleanor employed Nesbitt, who remained in the job during the entire Roosevelt administration, because, according to Lash, "she would do Eleanor's bidding."[106] Nesbitt needed work, could keep accounts, was frugal and unpretentious, and worshipped Eleanor as a friend. After her customary morning horseback ride in Rock Creek Park, Eleanor began her working day by meeting with Nesbitt. The housekeeper brought menus for her to approve and the two women discussed the number of guests expected and arrangements for them. Eleanor also hired Nesbitt's husband, Henry, an unemployed salesman, as White House custodian.

As head housekeeper the economy-minded Nesbitt supervised the purchase and preparation of food and directed some thirty African American servants, some of whom had worked for the Roosevelt family for years.[107] One of Eleanor's first acts was to discharge white servants and replace them with black staff. The move appeared to be in part a money-saving mechanism, since she had been told to cut White House expenses by 25 percent and black servants received less pay.[108] When a former white servant complained, Eleanor answered, "I have had my own servants for a great many years [and] they happen to be colored." She noted that "government expenses had to be curtailed," but added disingenuously, being "white or colored has nothing whatever to do with dismissal."[109]

Others disputed this version. Margaret Truman pointed out that the stature Eleanor achieved after leaving the White House "interferes with an accurate assessment of her years as first lady." According to Truman, Eleanor did away with segregated dining facilities at the White House for white and black staff by simply firing white servants, except for the housekeeper, and hiring only black servants. If these servants accompanied the first family to Hyde Park, they had to eat in the kitchen because they were not allowed in the white servants' dining room.[110] Truman emphasized that White House staff integration did not occur until the administration of her father, President Harry S Truman, who succeeded Franklin.[111]

Eleanor brought with her a personal maid, Mary Foster, who died within the year. She was replaced with Mabel Haley Webster, who had worked for the Roosevelts in Washington at the time of Franklin's affair with Lucy Mercer and "knew all the Roosevelt secrets," according to Parks.[112] Staff members had good reason to be discreet and develop camaraderie. Eleanor fired servants who could not get along with each other.[113] When Webster's son died, Eleanor went to the funeral, endearing her to the servants, since it was almost unheard of in 1930s Washington for a white woman to attend an all-black gathering.[114]

Eleanor gave Nesbitt $2,000 a month from Franklin's salary to cover the cost of family food at the White House, since government funds covered only state functions.[115] Out of this amount Eleanor also laid aside money for Christmas expenses. In keeping with the hard economic times, Eleanor encouraged Nesbitt to serve seven-

and-one-half-cent-per-person meals originated by home economists at Cornell University.[116] The first lady distributed menus for the meals, which she had published in *It's Up to the Women*, at her press conferences but assured reporters they were not given to guests. A typical low-cost lunch, for example, included hot stuffed eggs, tomato sauce, mashed potatoes, prune pudding, and coffee.[117]

Unfortunately, Nesbitt did not plan varied and appealing fare, a fact that Eleanor ignored, apparently considering conversation at meals and economy more important than cuisine.[118] Nesbitt repeatedly served food to Franklin that he disliked, claiming, "One of the hardest jobs Mrs. Roosevelt and I shared was trying to coax vegetables down the President."[119] Defending herself against newspaper stories that said the president was displeased with boiled calf liver and green beans three days in a row, Nesbitt wrote years later, "Well, he was supposed to have them."[120] Curiously, the newspaper stories were inspired by Eleanor herself, who jested about Franklin's dismay over his meals in her daily newspaper column, "My Day," which began at the end of 1935. This led to headlines that the president was in a "tizzy-wizzy" over spinach.[121] Alonzo Fields, the chief butler, described the food under Nesbitt's regime as "good and wholesome," but added, "its presentation was poorly done, with no desire to please or excite the appetite."[122]

Overlooking the cuisine, Fields said, "The Roosevelts were not hard to please . . . and had the old White House rocking with their gaiety and laughter."[123] Eleanor delighted in entertaining personal guests on the spur of the moment. An usher, J. B. West, recalled Eleanor racing through the White House, "skirts flapping around her legs." On her way to numerous appointments, West remembered, she would "jump into her waiting car, and call out to the driver: 'Where am I going?' . . . and on her way back, she gathered up people to bring home to lunch."[124] He said she sometimes invited so many "she forgot who they were."[125] Nesbitt, who was heartily disliked by the staff for her imperious manner, reacted to complaints about White House food by blaming the Roosevelts for being too hospitable. "How can the food taste good when I have to keep watering it down?" she exclaimed bitterly.[126] Bess Truman, Eleanor's successor as first lady, eventually fired Nesbitt for insubordination.

Blanche Cook, Eleanor's recent biographer, treated Eleanor's insistence on retaining Nesbitt in the face of widespread criticism as symptomatic of Eleanor's "passive-aggressive behavior" in a complex marriage.[127] Since Franklin was physically incapacitated, food was particularly important to him as a source of pleasure. Eleanor's unwillingness to replace Nesbitt with a more accomplished household manager, Cook argued, was her way of rivaling Franklin's power in the White House by setting up her own court of aides.

With the exception of Howe, who fit in both camps, the White House was divided, even in terms of guests, between what West called "the President's people" and "Mrs. Roosevelt's people."[128] LeHand reigned over Franklin's court, which included Stephen T. Early, press secretary, whom Franklin called "Steve the Earl"; Marvin McIntyre, appointments secretary; Gus Gennerich, the president's bodyguard; and Missy's assistant, Grace Tully. Among the black staff Franklin's valet, Irvin McDuffie, and his wife, Lizzie, long-term Roosevelt servants, were particularly close to Franklin. He was completely dependent on his valets to lift him in and out of bed and chairs and to take care of his personal needs. From her office, painted pink unlike other offices painted green, LeHand arranged entertainments for Franklin and brought in convivial friends to amuse him.[129]

By contrast Eleanor's guests, who sometimes met Franklin through her, often worked on governmental or social justice projects and tended to be a more serious-minded lot.[130] Her demanding schedule, compounded by piles of correspondence, kept her occupied far into the night.[131] By the time of Franklin's third-term election in 1940, the five Roosevelt children, whose numerous divorces and remarriages made tabloid headlines, all had homes and families of their own. When they visited the White House with their spouses and children, Eleanor "saw them briefly by appointment or at breakfast, treating them like other guests," according to West.[132]

Anna and her children left the White House in 1935 when she married John Boettiger, a newspaper correspondent. The couple moved to Seattle where Boettiger took the job of publisher of the *Seattle Post-Intelligencer.* The newspaper was owned by press magnate William Randolph Hearst, who had turned against Franklin after having been instrumental in securing his nomination in 1932, but presumably wanted to keep personal contact with the administration. In 1943 when Boettiger was on military duty, Anna returned to the White House as her father's confidential assistant and ally, a position that strained relations with Eleanor.

According to Lash, both Eleanor and Franklin "demanded a fierce and absolute loyalty from friends and associates."[133] Aides and family members changed sides only at their peril, as Harry L. Hopkins, Franklin's chief relief administrator, learned. Drawn together by mutual interest in welfare programs, Eleanor and Hopkins worked closely on relief issues during the early years of the New Deal, with Hopkins amenable to Eleanor's advocacy of more relief jobs for women.[134] Eleanor advanced Hopkins's career by introducing him to Franklin's inner circle. After Hopkins's first wife died in 1937, he moved into the White House with his five-year-old daughter, Diana, whom Eleanor attempted to mother.

The close association between Hopkins and Eleanor ended when Franklin made Hopkins secretary of commerce in 1938 and he seemingly lost interest in social programs, upsetting Eleanor greatly.[135] A young woman friend of Eleanor's to whom Franklin showed some attention received a warning from Hopkins that she had better be careful or Eleanor would "freeze" her out as she had him.[136] Eleanor's secretary, Tommy, saw it differently. She was sure Hopkins simply had dropped Eleanor after using her as a conduit to Franklin.[137]

The Roosevelts' son James also ran afoul of the divided White House. Acting as his father's aide, first as an assistant and then as his personal secretary, James and his wife, Betsey, moved into the White House in 1937. Tensions developed when Franklin made a favorite of the attractive Betsey, while Eleanor was miffed because she thought Betsey was trying to usurp her role of first lady.[138] James left the post in 1938 after confronting stress-related illness and a failed marriage with Betsey.

In some cases Franklin's advisors found it hard to deal with Eleanor, widening the gap between the two camps. Harold L. Ickes, secretary of the interior, to whom Eleanor addressed many inquiries from correspondents regarding federal facilities under his department, feared that she might be part of a group plotting against him in the mid-1930s.[139] Displeased with efforts by Eleanor and Howe to personally manage Arthurdale, a resettlement community for unemployed miners near Reedsville, West Virginia, Ickes found little comfort in talking to Franklin. The president brushed aside Ickes's objections to what he considered wasteful spending, saying, "My Missus, unlike most women, hasn't any sense about money at all."[140] Unlike Hopkins, who was committed to putting money into the hands of the unemployed as soon as possible, Ickes wanted to spend funds given to his Public Works Administration cautiously and economically.[141]

When Eleanor criticized some Interior Department officials, Ickes, a nervous, irascible individual, complained that she interfered in his domain.[142] Keeping his cabinet post throughout the Roosevelt years in spite of their differences, Ickes worked with Eleanor on issues of civil rights, to which they were both committed, and assistance to Native Americans, since the Interior Department included Indian reservations. Eleanor publicized exhibitions and marketing of Indian handiwork promoted by the Indian Arts and Crafts Board created in 1935 as part of the so-called Indian New Deal. Attacked by critics for pushing a "back-to-the blanket" approach to Native Americans, the effort was designed to preserve traditional culture.[143]

Eleanor's executive staff, including Nesbitt, enabled her to carry out a crowded schedule of official duties, political activity behind the scenes, and personal pursuits. Key figures were her confidential secretary, Tommy, and her experienced social secretary, Edith Benham Helm. They assisted at countless ceremonial functions and helped handle the huge deluge of mail that arrived daily for the first lady. Helm, like Nesbitt and White House ushers, met with Eleanor each morning to go over endless details pertaining to her position. Helm brought lists of invitations and advised Eleanor on official protocol.

Though pathbreaking in many respects, Eleanor carefully adhered to the conventional schedule of events on the White House social calendar long set by tradition. Her first year, for example, she observed a social season from 16 November 1933 to 8 February 1934, alternating dinners for Supreme Court justices, the vice president, cabinet members, Speaker of the House, and senior diplomats with receptions for members of Congress, the diplomatic corps, government officials, and top military brass.[144] Among Eleanor's first acts as official hostess was to lift the ban on women smoking, even though she did not smoke herself.[145] Initially she asked for cigarettes to be passed around and would pretend to smoke, although after she had established the custom of women smoking she stopped doing so.[146] After Prohibition officially ended, she served domestic wines with dinner. Ickes, generally hard to please, faulted Eleanor for offering "undrinkable" champagne along with "ordinary roast mutton" and carrots at the annual official dinner for the cabinet in 1934.[147]

With her usual whirlwind of activity, Eleanor did not stop with established events. She introduced "many large-scale teas, receptions, and garden parties where guests sometimes numbered in the thousands," remembered Mollie Somerville, a secretarial aide.[148] Fields said she "invented the double-header tea," scheduling one group of 400 to 500 at 4 p.m. and a similar group at 5 p.m., while keeping costs down.[149] He added, "During those days most anyone was invited to the White House. . . . Mrs. Roosevelt didn't refuse any group admittance, and nothing delighted her more than to give them a sip of tea, coffee or lemonade and cookies."[150]

At these events Helm served coffee while Tommy poured tea. Eleanor initially thought the teas were "useless burdens" but later realized they "had real meaning and value."[151] As she put it, "to many people the White House, in itself, symbolizes the government, and though standing and shaking hands for an hour or so, two to three times a week, is not exactly an inspiring occupation, still I think it is well worth while."[152] Learning to greet hundreds at receptions, she wrote that in spite of pains in her arms, shoulders, and back, "I was lucky in having a supple hand which never ached."[153] Teas were among the multitude of social events that fell into the domain of Helm, who recognized the political implications of White House entertaining.

Helm worked with Henry Junge of Steinway & Sons in New York, a firm specializing in grand pianos, to locate musicians to perform at White House dinners. Ickes found these East Room events "tiresome," with guests being forced to sit in extremely uncomfortable chairs.[154] Others applauded Eleanor for seeking music that crossed racial and ethnic boundaries. Elise Kirk, a music historian, concluded, "Thus, the White House resounded with the rich, moving voices of black singers and choirs from all over America in a way that was never heard before in the mansion."[155] For example, the Sedalia Quartet, an African American group from South Carolina, sang on 17 May 1933.[156]

Known for her formality and impressive demeanor, Helm was well versed in the ways of Washington society dominated by local elites known as "cave dwellers."[157] Having been social secretary for the second Mrs. Woodrow Wilson and Lou Hoover, Helm volunteered to help Eleanor "for a few days" after Franklin's first inauguration.[158] The daughter of an admiral and the widow of another one, Helm had become acquainted with Eleanor on shipboard when the two women were returning home from peace conferences following World War I. Eleanor soon convinced her to accept the social secretary job permanently, a position she kept throughout the Roosevelt and Truman administrations.

Curiously, in 1941 a routine FBI investigation of the social secretary, considered a model of propriety, led to long-standing animosity between Eleanor and J. Edgar Hoover. Eleanor became incensed when she discovered that the FBI was checking on Helm due to her appointment to the Advisory Commission to the Council of National Defense. She rebuked Hoover in a letter complaining of "Gestapo methods," and, while he apologized, he neither forgot nor forgave the attack.[159]

In Eleanor's personal hierarchy Helm was subordinate to Tommy, whom Eleanor called "the person who makes life possible for me."[160] Her tribute appeared in a feature story on Tommy in the *New York Herald Tribune* written by Emma Bugbee, who covered Eleanor's women-only press conferences. Although previous first ladies had secretaries, Tommy elevated the role to that of chief assistant, occasional critic, and intimate friend. After the *Saturday Evening Post*, a major magazine, ran an article on the importance of LeHand in White House operations, Eleanor sought equal publicity for Tommy. Betraying some jealousy, Eleanor told her press conference that she wished "somebody would write a piece equally interesting about my secretary, Malvina Thompson, who is equally important to me."[161] Bugbee obliged with a long story quoting Tommy as saying, "Everything I do is conditioned by her [Eleanor's] needs."[162]

The daughter of a locomotive engineer, Tommy grew up in the Bronx and, after finishing high school, taught herself typing to pursue secretarial employment. Obtaining a job with the New York State Democratic Committee in 1922, she first worked for Eleanor part-time when she organized women's campaign activities. Tommy became so devoted to Eleanor that she chose to leave her husband, Frank Scheider, a New York schoolteacher, to accompany Eleanor to Washington. She and Scheider were divorced in 1938. Tommy had a long-standing relationship with Henry Osthagen, an engineer, but they did not marry due to the demands of her job. Eleanor's personal efforts to find a job for Osthagen in the Interior Department further fueled Ickes's resentment of her, although he agreed to her request.[163]

Known as a feisty, down-to-earth individual, Tommy routinely worked eighteen-hour days, juggled Eleanor's schedule, accompanied her on travels, took notes on her speeches to record what portions went over well, and served as her gatekeeper.[164] Parks said Tommy "had a look that said 'no' before you asked."[165] She decided who Eleanor should see and prevented her from being taken in by "unscrupulous people," according to Franklin's cousin, Margaret Suckley.[166] When Hickok first sought access to Eleanor, she developed a friendship with Tommy, who paved the way for her to gain Eleanor's confidence.[167]

Tommy sorted Eleanor's personal correspondence, picking out about fifty letters per day to bring to her attention and drafting letters for her signature. Eleanor worked on her correspondence early in the morning and late at night, leaving a basket of letters with instructions for Tommy to answer them when she came to work each morning.[168] When Tommy got behind in typing replies dictated by Eleanor, she would redictate Eleanor's responses to other secretarial aides. Tommy did not know conventional shorthand and could not pass on her notes.[169]

The bulk of the letters went to the correspondence unit in the White House, where staff members divided them into two categories. Helm took charge of those dealing strictly with social matters, while Ralph Magee, the unit head, aided by Tommy, supervised some two dozen persons who answered the remainder.[170] Eleanor drew far more mail than her predecessors, receiving some 300,000 pieces in 1933 alone, most of which asked for help during the Depression. The avalanche of letters, from children as well as adults, was triggered to some extent by people who wanted her to give messages to the president.[171] When one person, for example, wrote, "I know you can buttonhole him at breakfast and make him listen,"

Eleanor replied humorously, "He would be at breakfast all day and far into the night if he even scanned my mail!"[172]

Letters in the 1930s portrayed the desperation of individuals hit by foreclosures, unemployment, lack of medical care, and other distressing circumstances.[173] Discovering that the correspondence unit was using form letter responses that dated back to the days of the Cleveland administration, Eleanor and Tommy set up new guidelines for replies, referring requests for assistance to government agencies when appropriate.[174] Although the initial flood of letters abated somewhat, by Eleanor's own count she received 90,000 in 1937 and about 150,000 in 1940.[175]

Eleanor saw mail as a valuable means of keeping in touch with the American people and making the role of first lady one of advocacy for the people. She also used it for her journalistic career. In August 1933 she began writing a page for the *Woman's Home Companion*, a widely circulated monthly women's magazine, for which she received $1,000 per page.[176] Readers of the feature titled "I Want You to Write Me" were urged to consider Eleanor a friend to whom they could confide their problems: "It is hard to find just the friend we would like to talk to. Often it is easier to write to someone whom we do not expect ever to see."[177] Eleanor directed readers to send their letters to the magazine. It paid Anna $350 a month to handle mail for the page, which was set up in a question-and-answer format.[178] Although Eleanor did not answer individual letters sent to the magazine, her general willingness to correspond with individuals doubtless added to her White House mail.

Obviously unable to attend to all her mail personally, Eleanor read some fifty letters each day, leaving her staff to deal with the remainder.[179] A sampling of staff response to her correspondence from young people showed that she personally helped about 1 percent of the needy youth who wrote her, with another 5 percent of the letter writers directed to New Deal agencies, 3 percent to charities, and an additional 3 percent to educational institutions.[180] The vast majority, 88 percent, were turned down with form letters, as inappropriate in some cases as those that Eleanor had replaced. For example, an impoverished farm boy who asked for a mule received a reply that the first lady could not help him "because of the similar number of requests she receives."[181]

Yet, the letters gave Eleanor a clear picture of the needs of young people and propelled her into becoming the administration's staunchest advocate of programs to aid them. She lobbied Franklin on behalf of the National Youth Administration, established in 1935, to provide job training and work-study programs to keep young people in school, leading him to refer to it as "the Missus organization."[182] Her correspondence from youths and adults alike gave Eleanor insight into the lives of ordinary Americans during a period of tremendous stress and served as a source of material for her own career as a writer, lecturer, and commentator.

In the White House Eleanor moved indirectly as a political leader, pushing the cause of women appointees behind the scenes. Holding a press conference, previously unheard of for a first lady, on 6 March 1933, just two days after Franklin's inauguration and two before the first of his own, a nervous Eleanor stated that she did not wish to send a special message to American women because her husband had delivered his inaugural address to all Americans, including women.[183] She did not wish to "trespass on my husband's prerogatives," as she expressed it, but she thought "there were many things, even connected with my own activities, which might be useful and interesting if well written up."[184] Her hesitant manner revealed her uncertainty about what activities to publicize.

Eleanor's disinclination to speak on the record about her political involvement led to erroneous reports that she was responsible for the appointment of the first woman cabinet member, Frances Perkins, as secretary of labor. In reality the credit belonged to Molly Dewson, who headed the women's division of the Democratic Party in 1932 and was determined that women receive high offices to demonstrate their competence and commitment to public life.[185] In seeking appointments for women, Dewson worked closely with Eleanor. In mid-April 1933 Eleanor and Dewson met with two other leading Democratic women, Nellie Tayloe Ross and Sue Shelton White, to set priorities for women's patronage.[186]

As she pressed James A. Farley, the head of the Democratic National Committee, to reward outstanding women campaigners, Dewson kept Eleanor informed of her efforts, a necessity since Farley had pledged himself to check all women's appointments with Eleanor.[187] The women labored hard to get their share of political jobs. Although Dewson took Farley a list of 100 qualified women in April, by June only seven had been appointed, and in July Dewson wrote Eleanor, "Heavens but the nicest of men are slippery as eels."[188]

In August a disgusted Dewson wanted to know if Franklin was "really opposed to women who are well-equipped" to serve as diplomats in small Latin American countries.[189] Eleanor replied that "they would be quite useless as representatives because of the different attitude toward women in those countries. Therefore, Franklin did not feel that he could appoint any women, and he says he could have told us this two months ago if we had asked him."[190] As this exchange showed, Eleanor tried to ameliorate the lack of communication between Dewson and male Democrats.

Social feminists saw Eleanor as their representative in the White House who stood up for what they believed—that women could bring a more humanitarian approach to politics than men—and also supported their practical quest for employment. Yet, her position was somewhat marginal. Franklin respected the abilities of professional women, many of whom he had met through Eleanor, going back to the days when she had formed a threesome with Cook and Dickerman.[191] Still, neither Dewson nor Eleanor was admitted to his inner circle of advisors.[192]

As first lady Eleanor could and did use her position to spotlight the hardships faced by women during the Great Depression. She consulted frequently with Ellen S. Woodward, head of women's relief operations, and Florence Kerr, who worked under her, and supported their battles for funds for their programs to help unemployed women.[193] She saw the White House as a staging area to call attention to hardships facing American women, planning a White House Conference on the Emergency Needs of Women for November 1933, to which she invited female members of Congress and other prominent women.[194]

From the opening days of the Roosevelt administration to its close twelve years later, Eleanor's public appearances, which included giving paid and unpaid speeches throughout the nation as well as visiting countless sites of innumerable federally funded relief projects, had political overtones expressed in a nonpolitical way. Her commercial lecture topics, chiefly youth, civic responsibility, peace, and White House life, lent themselves to nonpartisan gener-

Eleanor pays an inspection visit to Camp Tera for unemployed women on Bear Mountain, New York, on 7 August 1933. It was known as a "she-she-she" camp to distinguish it from the CCC (Civilian Conservation Corps) camps for young men. Courtesy of the Franklin D. Roosevelt Library, Hyde Park, New York.

alities expressed before large, primarily female audiences. Press photographers took picture after picture of Eleanor surrounded by women and often children. Sometimes she was shown with African Americans and other minorities, symbolizing her willingness to reach out to Americans of all backgrounds. As one communications scholar wrote, Eleanor's "personal investment in the success of the individual drove her rhetoric, which was neither as polished nor as smooth as her husband's."[195] It spoke to ordinary people as part of a political program that aspired to aid the downtrodden segments of society even if it did not always do so.

Eleanor's interests and activities put a compassionate public face on a political coalition that often ignored the liberal approach she personified. For example, Franklin did not favor a bonus for veterans. He did not press for civil rights laws that would antagonize southern conservatives in Congress on whom he was dependent for passage of New Deal legislation. Eleanor's efforts served to reassure different constituencies that the administration cared for all Americans, even if it did not take action to benefit them. She soon became the first presidential family member to be taken seriously as a political operative in Washington.[196]

If Eleanor's involvement seemed episodic and lacking in direction, part of this could be attributed to the experimental nature of the New Deal itself. As Perkins pointed out, "The notion that the New Deal had a preconceived theoretical position is ridiculous. The pattern it was to assume was not clear or specific in Roosevelt's mind."[197] As Franklin met with his "Brain Trust" to develop political strategies, he had little time or inclination to consult Eleanor or other women, with the exception of Perkins, who considered herself a member of the president's inner circle.

Eleanor spoke up for women who were discriminated against in various New Deal programs. She protested the wage differentials between men and women approved in many of the National Recovery Administration codes that were hallmarks of administration policies, opposed the dismissal of wives on grounds of making more jobs available to men in both the public and private sectors, and insisted that more women be included in relief efforts such as the government's chief welfare program, the Works Progress Administration (WPA). Her efforts fell short as she, like other social feminists of the day, placed reform and relief efforts ahead of women's equality.[198] On grounds that women workers needed special protective legislation, Eleanor opposed the proposed Equal Rights Amendment during most of her life.

Yet, through her ceaseless public contact she promoted what Perkins called the "intellectual and spiritual climate . . . that the people mattered."[199] Perkins said that Franklin was "enormously proud of [Eleanor's] ability, although he rarely talked about it except to someone in whose sympathy he felt complete confidence."[200] In cabinet meetings he called attention to Eleanor's visits to distressed areas, according to Perkins, with comments such as "You know my Missus gets around a lot," or "my Missus says that they have typhoid fever in that district," or "my Missus says the people are leaving the dust bowl in droves because they haven't any chance there."[201] In Perkins's view Franklin took action based on what Eleanor had seen and valued her political partnership.

In her constant traveling to observe conditions facing ordinary Americans battling extreme poverty, in her speeches and writings,

Eleanor and Franklin show themselves comfortably at home in the White House on their 1934 Christmas card. Courtesy of the Franklin D. Roosevelt Library, Hyde Park, New York.

and in her involvement with government programs that attempted to aid the unfortunate, she emerged as the conscience of the administration, even if her efforts, like those directed at Arthurdale, did not always meet with public approval.[202] She showed that she cared, and the vast majority of Americans responded positively. Through a process of trial and error she transformed her personal need to be active and useful into a potent political force within an administration in which she had feared there would be little place for her at all.

CHAPTER 4

CLAIMING THE PUBLIC STAGE

"No woman can really reach a place of recognition unless she has actually earned that place."

Eleanor Roosevelt speaking on the role of women in public life during a sponsored radio broadcast in 1934*

When Eleanor met about thirty-five "newspaper girls," as she called them, for her first press conference on 6 March 1933 on the first floor of the White House, she passed around a box of candied grapefruit peel to mask her nervousness. She wrote in her autobiography, "Most of the women facing me were total strangers. . . . I only hope they did not know how terrified I was in entering this untried field."[1] With the exception of Howe, who encouraged her to make friends with the press and continually sharpen her public communication skills for political purposes, she knew that "many people around my husband were doubtful whether I could handle press conferences without getting myself and him into trouble."[2] She sensed displeasure from the White House ushers as she entered the Red Room to meet women reporters "with fear and trembling."[3]

---

* ERP, Speech and Article File, script for Simmons radio broadcast, 18 September 1934, FDRL.

Eleanor holds one of her first press conferences for women reporters only in the Monroe Room of the White House in the spring of 1933. Courtesy of the Franklin D. Roosevelt Library, Hyde Park, New York.

Offering reassurances that she would not attempt to compete in her husband's domain, she stressed that the press conferences would be limited to women journalists and directed at women readers, offering news of special interest to them. She told her listeners that their job was an important one: "tell the women throughout the country what you think they should know. . . . You are the interpreters to the women of the country as to what goes on politically in the legislative national life, and also what the social and personal life is at the White House."[4] There were practical reasons for the gatherings, too. She wanted to save time by seeing women reporters in a group rather than making herself available for individual interviews.

Although the White House usher's office provided press releases about social functions, Eleanor knew journalists wanted more details to spice up their stories, most of which appeared in women's and society sections. Filled with advertisements for department stores, patterns for home sewing, and household products, these sections were mainstays of early twentieth-century newspapers. Eleanor hoped that regular press conferences would stop journalistic snooping, which had included bribery of White House servants, to get information on social events during previous administrations. She therefore "decided that everything that was legitimate news should be given out by me."[5] Apparently she saw the press conferences as one way to take charge of the news spotlight now beamed in her direction. She may have been uncertain how to do it but she intended to try.

The conferences were only part of the public communication activities that Eleanor undertook during her White House years in spite of her conflicting feelings over being first lady. She was the first presidential spouse, and to date the only one, to earn sizable sums on a sustained basis while first lady. In April 1933, a month after her first conference, she signed a contract for a monthly syndicated newspaper column on general subjects pertaining to White House life such as the president's daily schedule. In 1935 she launched a much more popular daily column, "My Day," a diary-like account of her personal activities and observations, somewhat akin to a blog today. At the same time she wrote magazine articles and performed on the lecture circuit.

Her tireless traveling gave her fresh material for her writing and speeches and allowed her to report to her physically incapacitated husband and to appear on his behalf. During the first eight years of the Roosevelt administration, Eleanor traveled about 300,000 miles on fact-finding trips and trips to symbolize New Deal concerns, stopping in every state except South Dakota. She traveled for both personal and official reasons, visiting her own children who were widely scattered and inspecting projects of every description. During World War II she flew across the Atlantic and the Pacific, making notable trips to England, the South Pacific, and Latin America under difficult conditions. Eleanor enjoyed the stimulation of traveling and meeting new people. She also was able to translate her traveling into dollars and cents because she shared what she saw and learned with readers, listeners, and paying audiences.[6]

Eleanor's tax returns for 1933–1935 showed net earnings averaging about $26,750 annually, investment income from inherited funds of about $8,700 annually, and annual charitable contributions ranging from $2,000 to $6,100.[7] Her taxable income increased markedly while she was first lady, averaging about $70,000 a year, $62,000 after expenses, from 1937 to 1939, with some 27 percent going for taxes and 5 percent for charity.[8] These figures included $75,000 (the same amount as her husband's annual salary as president), which she received in 1937 from the *Ladies' Home Journal* for rights to serialize her autobiography, *This Is My Story*, an account of her childhood and married life up to 1924.[9] Praised for charming simplicity that told the tale of her ugly duckling childhood, the book, which contained no hint of Franklin's affair with Lucy Mercer, sold well.

During World War II her taxable income remained relatively high, due in part to numerous articles she wrote for the *Ladies' Home Journal*, as well as her monthly question-and-answer column, "If You Ask Me," which she began in 1941. Her average annual earnings from 1941 to 1944 increased to $76,000, but taxes took almost half (49 percent) of her taxable income, and she donated 17 percent to charity, mainly to the American Friends Service Committee, the American Red Cross, and the International Students Service.[10]

Eleanor also earned respectable sums from sponsored radio broadcasts giving her views on education, White House activities, and other relatively noncontroversial topics. Her broadcasts brought in $36,000 in 1934, $29,832 in 1935, and $32,535 in 1937. Her diverse sponsors paid her $500 a minute, the same amount given the highest-paid radio stars. Sponsors included a roofing concern, the Simmons mattress company, the American typewriter industry, a shoe manufacturer, and Pond's Cold Cream. She authorized her payments to go directly into a special fund of the American Friends Service Committee, a Quaker social service organization, to benefit the Arthurdale resettlement project for unemployed West Virginia miners, one of her main interests among New Deal programs. This arrangement ended in 1937 after critics in Congress contended she was improperly avoiding income taxes.[11] Subsequently, she paid taxes on her radio income before turning it over to the committee.

Nevertheless, Eleanor chose not to tell the public exactly how much she gave to the Quaker organization or to account for all her earnings from books, magazine articles, and newspaper columns while first lady. United Press (UP) news articles estimated that two total payments, one of $66,000 and one of $75,000, went to the American Friends Service Committee, during an eighteen-month period in 1934–1935.[12] Eleanor confirmed neither figure. While some questions arose at her press conferences about the money she made, it was not subject to the intense scrutiny that a first lady's earnings would be today. Possibly her husband's advisors took lightly complaints that she was commercializing her position because they thought it good politics for her to reach directly to an audience of women. Although a mattress manufacturer complained that it was unfair for her to broadcast for Simmons, his rival, since the prestige of the Roosevelt name would unduly influence customers, she simply replied ingeniously that broadcasting for one sponsor was no more unfair than writing for one magazine instead of another or buying a dress from a particular designer.[13]

Unsure of herself and ambivalent about the value of her own efforts, Eleanor drew on a reservoir of determination to make the most of opportunities that presented themselves. When a listener complained that she was not worth payment of $3,000 for a six-minute broadcast, she replied in a letter that her position as the president's wife was responsible for what she received.[14] But in her broadcast she took a different tack, claiming that no woman was awarded recognition unless she was able to "deliver the goods."[15] And deliver Eleanor did for her sponsors.

While intellectuals smirked at what they considered trite comments, both spoken and written, her observations appealed to average citizens. For Simmons, for example, Eleanor discussed such subjects as parents' attempts to sanitize movies attended by children, her own visit to an all-star baseball game, and the humorous side of New Deal programs and personalities. She explained how hard it was for Franklin to change vacation plans, since "the ship upon which he is to sail is kept in a constant tizzy-dizzy of shining buttons and brass."[16]

In addition, she used the radio to refute charges that she neglected her husband. She read a letter asking, "Why do you take so many trips; think of your poor husband sitting at home alone in the evening with no one to keep him company by the fireside?" Eleanor's answer: Her critic lacked "the remotest idea" of White House life and besides Franklin was too busy to miss her.[17]

Her programs served as public relations vehicles for the White House as well as reflections of her own personality. In March 1935, for example, she broadcast a staged press conference at which she was interviewed by five women journalists who attended her conferences. One questioner asked her if she ever used a ghostwriter, allowing Eleanor to deny rumors to this effect. She stated, "I dictate, or sometimes write in long hand, every word of every article or speech which I make."[18]

When another questioner asked her about a new outfit for Easter, she minimized interest in it, replying, "I have ordered a blue suit . . . but it is so long since I ordered it, I have forgotten what it is really like."[19] It was a politic answer for the Depression era when millions lacked money for new clothes and a president's wife who flaunted her wardrobe would have drawn opprobrium. A third reporter asked her what the New Deal had done for women, and Eleanor quickly responded with a list of sex-stereotyped relief jobs: sewing, canning and preserving, serving school lunches, working as aides in nurseries, schools, and libraries and on playgrounds, doing clerical work for local government, and acting as census takers.[20] No questions were asked about the pay scales for women, which were lower than those for men.

At the time Japan attacked Pearl Harbor on 7 December 1941, drawing the United States into World War II, Eleanor had a contract to give a series of news commentaries for the Pan-American Coffee Bureau, a trade association of Latin American coffee growers. She presented a scheduled commentary only hours after the attack, urging listeners to rally for the war effort and speaking to the nation before Franklin did. After completing the series, she gave up sponsored radio programs during World War II, but her income remained considerable.

A significant part came from the *Ladies' Home Journal.* Out of the total, Eleanor paid Thompson for performing secretarial work not connected with the official duties of being first lady and George Bye, who took over as her literary agent when Howe became incapacitated prior to his death in 1936.

Since so much of what she made went for taxes, charity, and expenses, Eleanor contended that she left the White House with less capital than she had at the beginning of her tenure as first lady. Not everyone saw her earnings in this light. Even as close a political ally as Frances Perkins saw Eleanor as a self-promoter, commenting later that "the striking fact about Eleanor Roosevelt to those of us who knew her for many years was how much she did for herself."[21] While critics accused Eleanor of being greedy, many Americans approved of her activities on grounds her income went mainly to help others, a point that she stressed to the women reporters who covered her. In 1934, for example, she told her press conference group off the record that she expected to resume commercial broadcasting to "get the money for a good cause and take the gaff."[22]

Pursuing opportunities in writing, broadcasting, and on the lecture circuit, Eleanor was determined to have a paid career while in the White House. Family members attributed it to her psychological need for reaffirmation of her own self-worth. According to her son Elliott, his mother sought "power and influence, provided it was in her own right and her own name."[23] Her women-only press conferences offered an opportunity for Eleanor to establish herself as an individual in her own right and make the amorphous position of first lady into one of actual importance in public life.

At the same time they helped mask her emotional state as she undertook her new role. She confided her unhappiness to Hickok in May 1933, after leading a group of women reporters on a tour of two historic shrines in Virginia: Stratford, ancestral home of Robert E. Lee, and Monticello, Thomas Jefferson's home. Eleanor wrote, "Monticello was lovely, and everyone is kind, but my zest in life is rather gone for the time being. . . . my mind goes round and round like a squirrel in a cage. I want to run and I can't, and I despise myself."[24] Involving herself in never-ending pursuits enabled her to ward off attacks of depression to which she was subject throughout her life.

By holding the conferences, Eleanor gained unprecedented opportunities to influence portrayal of the role of first lady, drawing on the concept of the press conference as a "pseudo-event," calculated to call attention to a specific person or idea.[25] The inspiration for the conferences apparently came from Hickok, but Howe warmly welcomed the idea. Hickok told Eleanor that newspapers were cutting staff due to economic pressures, and women journalists, who routinely were paid less than men, would keep only a toehold on employment "unless they could find something new to write about."[26] One journalist who covered the conferences, Mary Hornaday of the *Christian Science Monitor*, was sure that Hickok "persuaded Mrs. Roosevelt that everything she did was news."[27]

The assumption that what she did would, and perhaps should, interest others lay behind Eleanor's decision to continue paid pursuits while she was first lady. In the 1920s she had started writing magazine articles, drawing on her personal experiences of learning how to take part in politics after suffrage was won. They also were a way for her to dramatize her own life experience with the goal of making it helpful to others. Her press conferences, which focused on her White House life, constituted a logical extension of publicizing her activities as a force for good. Why then was she fearful of the press conferences? No doubt because of the novelty of a president's wife subjecting herself to a format that allowed journalists to ask potentially embarrassing and impertinent questions.

Years later she referred to every press conference as "a battle of wits," and revealed that the conferences were not easy for her or the reporters.[28] In particular, she remembered that the press women asked her "all sorts of trick questions" when they were trying to find out if Franklin would run for an unprecedented third term in 1940, but she said she avoided giving direct answers.[29] Her apprehensions about her White House press conferences appeared to be unfounded. Most of the women reporters wrote favorable stories that reached millions of readers via major wire services of the era, particularly the AP and UP, as well as individual newspapers. The 1935 broadcast version of a simulated press conference, which featured reporters who asked only questions that she wanted to answer, mirrored what usually transpired.

As a group, the women who covered the conferences, underpaid and downtrodden as they were in male-dominated newsrooms, viewed Eleanor as a valuable news source and welcomed the opportunity to frequent the White House. Ann Cottrell Free, who began covering the conferences in 1941, remembered decades later how women reporters rushed up the White House stairs in an unseemly dash for front-row seats in the second-floor Monroe Room.[30] When they were seated, Eleanor entered, followed by Thompson and Helm. Following a pleasant "Good morning, ladies," she shook each reporter's hand before announcing her schedule and taking questions.[31] Although they complained privately that the conferences did not always produce interesting news, the women as a group supported Eleanor. Some actively helped her avoid awkward situations by coming to her defense if questions seemed hostile. They saw her as naïve and in need of their protection.

The conferences enlarged the scope of the first lady's position by publicizing it in an open forum at a time when women were beginning to break through barriers limiting their roles in public life. By the 1930s it was acceptable for women to write magazine articles and books or even speak on politics before large audiences. In June 1920 Theodore Roosevelt's sister and Eleanor's paternal aunt, Corinne Roosevelt Robinson, a published poet, writer, and professional lecturer, had become the first woman to give a nominating speech at the national convention of a major political party when she spoke before 14,000 Republicans in the Coliseum in Chicago.[32]

Displaying the tension between the Oyster Bay and Hyde Park Roosevelts, Robinson nominated an old friend and military hero, Gen. Leonard Wood, to run for president on the GOP ticket, although her cousin Franklin now was high in Democratic circles. After Wood was passed over for a ticket composed of Warren G. Harding for president and Calvin Coolidge for vice president, Franklin became the Democratic nominee for vice president. This had prompted Eleanor, still better known as Theodore's niece than as Franklin's wife, to move haltingly into political activity to further her husband's chances.[33]

As the actions of the two Roosevelt women showed, both Democratic and Republican parties recognized the potential for votes in newly enfranchised women able to cast ballots for the first time in 1920 in a presidential election. Yet, woman suffrage did not immediately emancipate women from sex-role stereotyping. Twelve years later when Franklin was elected president, women in politics still ran the risk of being considered unfeminine and overstepping their bounds.

Eleanor's decision to hold press conferences startled Washington, countering the traditional idea, held by many women as well as men, that presidential wives, like genteel women in general, should remain in the background of their husbands' lives. Traditionally, first ladies had remained relatively aloof from the press. Illustrating the split in the Roosevelt family itself over public activity by women, Eleanor's beloved aunt, Anna "Bamie" Roosevelt Cowles, unlike her sister Corinne, determinedly kept herself in the private sphere, even though she was a shrewd political observer.

During the years that Eleanor was starting her career, Bamie spoke approvingly of Grace Dodge, a philanthropist who helped found Teachers College at Columbia University and the YWCA, noting, "She certainly accomplished a lot without ever having her name come before the public."[34] Yet, Bamie was proud of her sister's accomplishments and supportive of Eleanor's career, although she died before her niece became first lady. As Eleanor charted her own course in the White House, she had her aunts before her as examples of strong, independent women, but neither provided clear guidance for her career.

When Eleanor, spurred by Hickok and Howe, first showed interest in holding press conferences, a committee of women journalists helped Howe organize them. Members included Bess Furman of the AP; Ruby A. Black of the UP; Katharine Dayton of the Consolidated Press; Ruth Finney, a correspondent for Scripps-Howard newspapers; and Ruth E. Jones, society editor of the *Washington Herald*.[35] Jones compiled a list of Washington newspaper women eager to attend. She submitted it to Stephen Early, Franklin's press secretary, with a recommendation that only one woman from each of the main Washington newspapers, which then numbered five, be admitted. In response Early certified forty representatives of Washington newspapers, press associations, and Washington bureaus of major daily newspapers.[36]

Even before the conferences officially started, women journalists began to form a protective shield around Eleanor to make sure that she would not embarrass herself unwittingly. In 1981 Dorothy Roe Lewis, who had covered Eleanor for Universal Service, a night wire service for Hearst newspapers, reported in the *New York Times* that Eleanor had rushed up to her and three other reporters, Hickok, Black, and Dorothy Ducas, Lewis's counterpart at International News Service, Hearst's day wire service, to leak a scoop before Franklin's inauguration in 1933. Lewis recalled that Eleanor told them her husband had refused to join with President Hoover in ordering bank closures to ensure the safety of deposits, but the reporters were afraid this news would start a financial panic and declined to print the story.[37] Years later Ducas commented, "The women always covered up for Mrs. Roosevelt. All kinds of things were said [by her] that shouldn't be said in print."[38]

The formal organization of the conferences turned out to be less important than the informal manner in which they operated. An inner circle of confidantes proposed topics, planted questions, and received invitations from the Roosevelts for visits to the White House as well as Hyde Park. One key figure was Furman, a hardworking former schoolteacher from Nebraska, whose career at the AP depended mainly on the stories she wrote about the first lady. Another was Black, a slight, spunky feminist who had established her own Washington news bureau after running afoul of male editors who refused to employ women. The UP hired her as its first permanent woman staff writer, even though she was only part-time, because Eleanor would not admit men to her press conferences. Well aware that she owed her highly prized job to the first lady, Black idealized Eleanor. Martha Strayer, a prim former secretary, whose career at the *Washington Daily News* was her life for forty-three years, took shorthand notes on the conferences.[39] She assured Eleanor that she was "a very grand person" and the conferences "a very grand idea."[40]

Others in the circle included Genevieve Forbes Herrick, known as "Geno," who was a top "front-page girl" for the *Chicago Tribune;* Elizabeth May Craig, who represented Guy Gannett newspapers in Maine; and Emma Bugbee, the chief woman reporter for a leading New York newspaper, the *Herald Tribune.*[41] Bugbee's postinauguration request to see the family quarters in the White House resulted in a luncheon and tour there for several women reporters. This so impressed Bugbee's New York editors that they told her to remain in Washington for four months to cover the first lady and sent Bugbee back from time to time.

Hickok, who received frequent reports from Eleanor on the press conferences, disparaged the group's professionalism. She considered Herrick, known for interviews with Al Capone and other gangsters, the only journalist at the press conferences whose credentials matched her own. "God damn it, professionally I ranked so far above the rest of that mob, except Geno," Hickok wrote late in life to Malvina Thompson.[42] Anne O'Hare McCormick, a *New York Times* columnist and the first woman journalist to win a Pulitzer Prize, did not bother to attend Eleanor's press conferences. Instead, Eleanor told Hickok she arranged for McCormick to interview Franklin.[43]

Hickok's explosion to Thompson came after Eleanor wrote in a draft of her autobiography that she had learned, following Hickok's exclusive inauguration day interview with her, not to play favorites among reporters. The comment presumably made light of Hickok's professional standing, which in Hickok's view entitled her to the interview, and failed to acknowledge Eleanor's friendship with her inner circle of reporters. After Hickok's objection Eleanor omitted it from the published version of the autobiography.[44]

Hickok left the AP in June 1933 and went to work directly for the Roosevelt administration as the chief investigator of relief programs for the Federal Emergency Relief Administration, headed by Harry Hopkins. In this capacity she wrote reportorial accounts of Depression conditions throughout the country and sent them directly to Hopkins with copies to Eleanor, who passed them on to Franklin. Hopkins, who did not trust bureaucratic or press accounts of the Depression, told her, "Tell me what you see and hear. All of it. Don't ever pull your punches."[45] And Hickok did not, sending back firsthand reports of crushing poverty, including accounts of appalling conditions among unemployed minors in West Virginia. They intensified Eleanor's interest in the controversial Arthurdale project to aid the miners along with other efforts to ameliorate Depression conditions that Eleanor raised at her press conferences.

Before beginning her new job, Hickok, accompanied by Eleanor, took a monthlong vacation. The two women drove by themselves in Eleanor's gray roadster through New England and the Gaspé Peninsula of Canada. During the summer of 1934 they also vacationed together, camping in Yosemite National Park. Eleanor's press conference group agreed to keep the trips off the record and made no attempt to cover them, testimony to Eleanor's hold over her personal press corps. Local journalists were not so obliging. They followed the two women around in San Francisco on their return from Yosemite, eager to take flash photographs, which in those days required the explosion of black powder near their subjects.[46] After reporters pursued the two in Portland, where the women had booked an inexpensive hotel, Eleanor told Hickok that she realized it was hopeless to try to be inconspicuous and that "from now on I shall travel as I'm supposed to travel, as the President's wife and try to do what is expected of me."[47]

Hickok saw this as a premonition of Eleanor building a wall

within herself to separate her public and private roles. Eleanor reflected later, "It was almost as though I had erected someone a little outside myself who was the President's wife. I was lost somewhere deep down inside myself. That is the way I lived and worked until I left the White House."[48] Perhaps this was one of Eleanor's contributions to developing the institution of the first lady—recognition of the fact that the modern president's wife needed for political purposes to construct a public image for herself that might veer sharply from her private reality.

In March 1934, Eleanor decided to go with Hickok on an inspection trip of social conditions in Puerto Rico and the Virgin Islands. Representatives of her press conference group were permitted to go along, as well as a male photographer, Sammy Shulman, chosen from the White House photo pool. The trip was prompted in part by Black, who spoke Spanish fluently and was a correspondent for a Puerto Rican newspaper, *La Democracia*. In addition to Black, three other women journalists close to Eleanor made the trip: Furman, Ducas (representing Hearst newspapers), and Bugbee, whose staunchly Republican newspaper, the *Herald Tribune*, nevertheless saw Eleanor as a prime subject of lively feature stories.

Bugbee's editors were not disappointed. The trip generated colorful news articles as the first lady, followed by her press entourage, strolled down the worst streets in San Juan. Surrounded by clamoring adults, nearly naked children, barking dogs, and stray pigs, she peered into garbage dumps while Shulman, who had been drafted into the Secret Service to protect Eleanor on the tour, busily clicked his camera.[49] The women journalists downplayed the presence of Hickok, presumably out of loyalty to Eleanor. A skeptical *Time* magazine, on the other hand, depicted the trip, which took place while Hickok celebrated her fortieth birthday, as a boondoggle for Eleanor's friend. It described Hickok as a "rotund lady with a husky voice, a preemptory manner, [and] baggy-clothes" who has "gone around a lot with the first lady."[50]

The first presidential-level fact-finding tour undertaken by a first lady, the trip called attention to the miserable conditions under which many residents of Puerto Rico and the Virgin Islands lived, even though Eleanor did not visit areas of actual unrest and labor strikes.[51] Her tour alerted Franklin and administration officials to the

Devoted members of Eleanor's press conference group gather around her on 5 March 1934 during her trip to Puerto Rico and the Virgin Islands. From left, Emma Bugbee, New York Herald Tribune; *Dorothy Ducas, International News Service; Ruby Black, United Press; and Bess Furman, Associated Press. Courtesy of the Franklin D. Roosevelt Library, Hyde Park, New York.*

need for more action to address poverty in these areas. It prompted the president to pay his own visit to Puerto Rico four months later and led to the implementation of limited relief projects there, including low-cost housing named for Eleanor and plans for resettlement communities.[52] On balance, however, the New Deal had a mixed record on treatment of Caribbean dependencies as part of its overall Latin American policy that supported dictatorships.

For the most part the women journalists liked the sex-segregated conferences, with the exception of May Craig, an outspoken extro-

Eleanor and Lorena Hickok walk down a squalid street in San Juan, Puerto Rico, accompanied by officials and a crowd of small children to inspect conditions there in March 1934. Courtesy of the Franklin D. Roosevelt Library, Hyde Park, New York.

vert and one of the few women accredited to the president's press conferences, as well as to the first lady's. Craig opposed the omission of men on grounds it was unfair to bar men when women journalists knew how disheartening it was to face sex discrimination themselves. Eleanor, on the other hand, argued that she did not wish to "encroach on my husband's side of the news," indicating a desire to shape news along gender-specific lines.[53] While presidential press conferences did not exclude women in principle, in practice they were rarely there because editors considered political coverage beyond the abilities of most women journalists.

By limiting the conferences to women Eleanor gained immense gratitude from some who covered her, particularly Furman and Black. Furman, who was forced to leave the AP before the birth of her twins in 1936 because of a policy against employment of pregnant women, later covered the first lady for the *New York Times*, after running her own feature service. While she maintained that she remained objective, Furman wrote laudatory stories about the first lady and considered Eleanor the "star to which my journalistic wagon was suddenly hitched."[54]

Although a fervent member of the National Woman's Party, which pushed for the Equal Rights Amendment, Black did not want men admitted to the press conferences because that would have meant the end of her UP job. Her devotion to Eleanor led a male journalist to write that "even" other women journalists were "amazed at the extremes of Ruby's [Black's] idolatrous attitude toward the first lady."[55] Black wrote the first biography of Eleanor, an admiring work that appeared in 1940, picturing her as a happily married political partner.[56]

Both Furman and Black, like some of the other reporters, enhanced their personal lives through contact with the first lady. Black told readers of the *Matrix*, a magazine published by Theta Sigma Phi, a journalism sorority, that Cornelia Jane, her baby daughter, was invited to the White House for her first party and first movie as a guest at "'Sistie' Dall's (Eleanor's grandchild's) birthday party."[57] Eleanor dined at Furman's home, knitted blankets for Furman's twins, and was godmother to one. Women journalists received invitations for their children to play with the Roosevelt grandchildren, flowers from the White House greenhouse when they were ill, and White House Christmas cards for themselves and their families.[58]

Until World War II broke out, press conference admission was controlled by Early, who delegated routine accreditation matters to Tommy. By 1941 the number of women accredited had risen to more than 100. Many were part-time social columnists for newspapers outside of Washington, although a few radio correspondents and government publicity writers also were admitted.[59] Wartime security concerns led the women journalists themselves to form Mrs. Roosevelt's Press Conference Association and take responsibility for accreditation, setting up a committee that limited attendance to full-time representatives of daily newspapers, weekly newsmagazines, wire services, and broadcasting companies. The number of accredited reporters dropped sharply to thirty-three in 1942 but increased to fifty-six by 1945. Reporters had special admission cards along with Secret Service cards with their photographs and fingerprints.[60]

When Gordon Cole, a male reporter for *PM*, a liberal daily newspaper in New York, sought admission in 1942, the association rejected his application after Eleanor said she might refuse to hold press conferences if men attended.[61] Eleanor's response came after she had received blistering criticism in the press for alleged administrative failings as assistant director of the Office of Civil Defense, a six-month unpaid job in 1941–1942 that ended with her resignation. Obviously, she much preferred the warm atmosphere of her women-only group to adversarial encounters.

The next year, however, she dropped the women-only requirements to allow men to attend her press conference after she returned from an exhausting trip to South Pacific war zones.[62] Twenty did, but only one asked a question. Resulting feature stories highlighted a war-between-the-sexes angle instead of more substantive reports on her trip. One male reporter wrote, "I felt like I had blundered into the powder room of an art gallery."[63]

The association went out of existence after the death of Franklin on 12 April 1945, but the friendly relationship between Eleanor and some of the women who covered her lasted throughout her lifetime and helped advance her later career at the United Nations.

Male journalists scoffed at the prospect of Eleanor holding press conferences, although they could not ignore them totally. When Furman told her boss, Byron Price, AP bureau chief, about plans for them, he predicted that the conferences would last less than six months—"the only poor prediction I ever heard him make," Furman recalled.[64] According to Hornaday, "Mostly the men preferred to ignore Mrs. Roosevelt and her views."[65] This attitude apparently influenced the editing of news articles based on the press conferences.[66] The *Washington Post*, for example, paid no attention to Eleanor's advocacy of legislation to provide "old age pensions, a permanent ban on child labor, better unemployment insurance, better health care for the country as a whole, [and] better care for mothers and children generally" at her press conference on 27 February 1935.[67] The next day's story on the first lady was titled "Mrs. Roosevelt Entertains at Luncheon and Musicale."[68]

Male ridicule of the press gatherings increased after publication of a photograph taken at the second conference, on 13 March 1933 on the second floor of the White House. It showed women journalists clustered around Eleanor, who was seated in a chair, while some of the reporters sat on the floor around her. Men journalists promptly labeled the women "the incense burners."[69] The press conferences soon were "furnished with straight-backed chairs," one newsmagazine noted.[70] Putting an end to the "girls at Mrs. Roosevelt's feet" crack of columnists, Eleanor insisted that all attending be seated.[71]

The conferences endured for the twelve years that Eleanor remained as first lady. They totaled 348 conferences in all, or about a third of the 998 that her husband held during his presidency. Franklin used his conferences to announce policies and programs as he bantered with reporters and cultivated their friendship.[72] By contrast Eleanor's press conferences, which she began by announcing her weekly schedule, seemed to have little purpose except to showcase her and other Democratic women as role models. Franklin's conferences were relatively brief—less than a half-hour, while Eleanor's rambled on two or three times longer.

Furman captured the difference between Franklin's and Eleanor's conferences in an AP story: "At the President's press conference, all the world's a stage. At Mrs. Roosevelt's, all the world's a school. . . . Give Mrs. Roosevelt a roomful of newspaper women, and she conducts classes on scores of subjects, always seeing beyond her immediate hearers to the 'women of the country.'"[73] Reverting to her days as a teacher at Todhunter, Eleanor sometimes used the conferences to lecture on women's duties as citizens. If Furman had extended her analysis of the press conferences to political aspects, she could have noted how they served as vehicles to allow both the president and his wife to counterbalance the pro-Republican slant of a majority of the nation's newspapers in their editorial policies.

Without doubt, many of the nation's newspapers opposed Roosevelt, although the total may not have been as high as the 85 percent he customarily cited, but this opposition came from owners, not working journalists.[74] Enmity toward Franklin, originally centered in the *Chicago Tribune*, *New York Daily News*, and *Washington Times-Herald*, publications associated with the McCormick/Patterson families, later spread to Hearst newspapers and eventually to the Scripps-Howard chain. It reached a crescendo over domestic reforms like Social Security and pre–World War II debates between isolationists and interventionists.[75]

In spite of editorial page criticism, Franklin charmed an overwhelming majority of the Washington press corps from the day of his first press conference onward, White House reporters said.[76] Support lessened during the second term, prompting Eleanor to write Hickok she was worried over Franklin's attitude toward the press corps: "The old attitude of friendliness is gone & instead of indifference which I could understand is this resentful feeling which I regret."[77] Nonetheless, Franklin generally captivated the working press with jaunty self-confidence as well as a sense for news that enabled him to feed reporters information they could readily use in their news articles.[78]

Eleanor appealed to the women who covered her far differently. Appearing insecure and sometimes uncertain as to what to do or say, she brought out women reporters' feelings of superiority to her along with their sympathy. While Franklin gained recognition from columnists as the "best newspaperman who has ever been President of the United States," Eleanor was seen by her press corps as an innocent idealist trying to do the best she could.[79]

Journalists at her press conferences wished for more exciting news than they often got, but regarded the first lady compassionately. Ducas, whose International News Service switched from supporting to opposing Franklin in 1935 at the bidding of its owner, William Randolph Hearst, found Eleanor gullible—"easily led by people she felt were her friends." Ducas saw her as a woman seeking love and affection while attempting to "do good" under a somewhat "prissy" exterior.[80]

Male journalists continued to attack the professional credibility of Eleanor's press conferences. A syndicated 1938 "Washington Merry-Go-Round" column by Drew Pearson criticized the "loving protectiveness" of her press corps. The column claimed that her devotees cautioned her against frank remarks, reminding her to change words like "ridiculous" to "regrettable," which she would do while "beaming gratefully."[81] Clearly, most reporters assigned to Eleanor did not consider themselves her adversaries. Lacking a set rationale for the conferences, except to meet the "news girls," Eleanor answered questions on everything from her clothes and family to her opinions on war and peace.

As she moved from topic to topic, Eleanor maintained that she could not comment on political issues, even though she often did. In particular, she used the conferences to defuse criticism directed at her role in the Arthurdale resettlement project in West Virginia. It was led by Sen. Tom Schall, a Republican from Minnesota, who claimed she wanted to spend government money to set up an Arthurdale furniture factory, which would be similar to her Val-Kill enterprise and compete with private enterprise. In response, on 23 April 1934 Eleanor assured the press conference group that she and her partners had never received "one cent of interest" from Val-Kill Industries and had no plans to start a similar business in West Virginia, but she expressed support for a government factory at Arthurdale to make post office boxes.[82]

The subject of Arthurdale came up again a week later at a typical press conference that began with Eleanor listing her heavy schedule of forthcoming engagements. These included a broadcast for Child Health Day; a picnic lunch for senators' wives at the White House; two speeches to organizations in Philadelphia—one to the Young Women's Christian Association and the other to Hadassah, a Jewish women's group—a visit to the federal prison for women at Alderson, West Virginia; attendance at a conference on Negro education at the Department of Commerce; a ceremonial trip with her husband to Jamestown, Virginia, to commemorate the landing of English settlers there in 1607; a day in Westchester County, New York, with Rep. Caroline O'Day; and a speech before the League for Political Education at the Theodore Roosevelt House in New York City.

After she finished announcing her engagements, she briefly answered a few questions related to Sen. Schall's attack, saying he had not come to see her at the White House as she had expected, before moving on to sweeping generalities on economic planning: "To me it seems as if our intelligence would force us to believe that planning would have to be done on a large scale, just as we plan our own home, through the country and through the world."[83] Such statements, given without specifics, left reporters yawning. Days elapsed before they figured out the real news from that particular conference hidden in her routine announcements. She was going to New York to campaign openly for the reelection of O'Day to Congress, the first time a first lady had taken an active part in a congressional race.

Like Franklin at his press conferences, Eleanor carefully limited the use of direct quotations. This contributed to bland statements, such as the only one that she allowed to be quoted from her first press conference, "The time is one that requires courage and common sense on everybody's part."[84] Some reporters grumbled that Eleanor spoke in platitudes, but the women rarely drew out Eleanor's views on substantive political and social questions. Instead, they were expected to glean human-interest tidbits. Most of the journalists wrote feature stories for women's and society sections in newspapers, which in effect spelled out the parameters of acceptable conduct for women in an era when about three-fourths of American women did not hold jobs outside the home.[85] The conferences provided hundreds of stories geared to these sections, such as accounts of ceremonial activities like the annual Easter eggroll on the White House lawn.

By contrast, when Eleanor responded to a request from Black and spoke out at a press conference in April 1933 against a Hoover administration act to discharge married government workers whose spouses also were on the federal payroll, her statement received relatively little news play.[86] Reporters displayed less interest in her feminist stand than in her fall from a horse during her daily ride.[87] The legislation, called the Economy Act, stayed on the books until 1937.

The bad behavior of Eleanor's two beloved dogs, Major and Meggie, also made headlines. Major, a police dog given her by Earl Miller, had been present at Eleanor's first press conference, although he had created a disturbance and had to be led away.[88] When he bit Sen. Hattie Caraway at Eleanor's party for Frances Perkins on 29 April 1933, an assertive Furman persuaded a reluctant Eleanor to let her write the story, which appeared on the AP wire from coast to coast.[89] Eleanor would much rather have had the focus on the party itself, which foreshadowed her annual White House festivity for women reporters and officials not allowed to attend the exclusive all-male Gridiron Club dinners. On these gala occasions top male journalists satirized the president, who was the guest of honor along with key administration officials. Eleanor tried to counter by offering the excluded women an entertaining evening. She invited celebrities such as Fannie Hurst, a best-selling author, and encouraged humorous skits.[90] Hurst, a celebrity of the day who pushed the New Deal, stayed in the Lincoln bedroom and other White House guest quarters.

Several months after Major's fall from grace, Furman herself was bitten on the lip by Meggie, Eleanor's Scottie, when Eleanor gave Furman a ride home on 27 December following a post-Christmas visit to hospitalized veterans that Furman covered. Eleanor took Furman to a hospital emergency room and even called the AP, offering to write the story for Furman in an effort to apologize.[91] An astonished deskman turned her down, although the AP ran a feature on the incident after the *Washington Post* found out about it. It drew more attention than the Caraway story, with newspapers writing quips such as "if the President's wife's dog bites a reporter—that's news."[92] To Eleanor's sorrow her dogs had to be banished from the White House.[93] A realist, she understood that her pets had become press liabilities in her role as first lady. The press conferences made Eleanor more aware of both the positive and negative effects of press coverage.

Society reporters welcomed Eleanor's willingness to provide accounts of official entertaining, which had been difficult for them to get during the Hoover administration. On the same day that Eleanor held her first press conference, she and her daughter, Anna, had attended a tea given for them by the Newspaper Women's Club. Unlike the Women's National Press Club, a rival group that competed more directly with men journalists, the Newspaper Women's Club was composed of both society writers and the prominent women they wrote about. Eleanor readily accepted honorary membership in the Newspaper Women's Club, but relations between her and society journalists remained lukewarm, perhaps because Eleanor's dutiful view of purely social activities did not fit the society reporters' ideal of social leadership.

Her closest friends among the press women, like Furman and Black, were members of the Women's National Press Club, which Eleanor herself eventually joined as an active member. She faithfully attended the Women's National Press Club stunt parties, which mimicked the Gridiron dinners and poked fun at her as first lady. Members of both clubs, however, received invitations to the annual Gridiron Widows parties at the White House. At the first Gridiron Widows party of 8 December 1934, members of the American Newspaper Women's Club, for instance, dressed like characters from *Alice in Wonderland* to perform a skit.[94]

Hope Ridings Miller, society editor of the *Washington Post*, be-

Eleanor joins in a gala party staged by the Newspaper Women's Club in Washington on 17 March 1936 following Franklin's second inauguration as president. Annette B. Harris (left) and Margaret Hart, two members of the group—which was made up mainly of society page reporters—welcome her. Courtesy of the Franklin D. Roosevelt Library, Hyde Park, New York.

lieved that Eleanor felt little affinity for fashion and society, even to the point of preferring to socialize with those who had little interest in these directions. "Mrs. Roosevelt's closest friends were very homely girls and Lorena Hickok was one of them," Miller recalled years later.[95] "Mrs. Roosevelt was homely herself and felt comfortable with them. She felt she could do something for them—build up their ego." But Miller said society writers refrained from being hostile toward the first lady: "She gave us plenty to write about; usually when press people write mean things they don't have anything else to write."[96]

Asked repeatedly about her own wardrobe at the press conferences, Eleanor displayed defensiveness in regard to spending money on new outfits when millions of Depression-stricken Americans had no money for clothes at all. When reporters told her she had been chosen to head the list of the best-dressed American women of

1934, she simply answered, "Was I? I didn't know it."[97] Her apparent lack of interest in clothing did not endear her to society reporters used to writing detailed descriptions of the dresses of prominent women, copy that pleased editors because it pleased advertisers. In fact, Eleanor probably was not as uninterested in fashion as she appeared to be. In her "My Day" column two decades later (3 December 1954), she referred to "that title" of best-dressed woman as one of the "grandest" things in her life.[98] She apparently realized that a first lady traditionally had been expected to promote the American fashion industry.

As a presidential candidate's wife, Eleanor had presented an unfashionable appearance that shocked at least one woman reporter. Kathleen McLaughlin of the *Chicago Tribune*, who later wrote about Eleanor for the *New York Times*, felt compassion for Eleanor at the 1932 Democratic national convention. "She was so long and so tall and she was wearing black cotton stockings and a very simple, unchic, straight-line dress, black, with red floral sprigs; and a very large hat, rather flat-crowned; black gloves and a pedestrian handbag," McLaughlin recalled.[99]

Once in the White House Eleanor made an attempt to improve her wardrobe, in keeping with her desire to perform her role properly. She bought fashionable clothes at reduced prices from Arnold Constable, a New York store, in return for allowing the store to publicize photographs of her wearing the new finery. According to Anne Wassell Arnall, the photographer who took the pictures, Eleanor had no interest in being a model and made no effort to attend to her makeup or hair before the photographs were made.[100] Perhaps this was because she was inured to comments about her unflattering photographs. When Hickok remarked that it was a shame that they did not capture her warmth, Eleanor shrugged and said, "My dear, if you haven't any chin and your teeth stick out, it's going to show on a camera plate."[101]

For years she had hated to be photographed because she was convinced she was ugly, playing an unnerving game with Howe to see which one could find the ugliest picture of himself or herself.[102] Yet she realized that press photographers had a job to do and she cooperated with them. Max Desfor, a retired AP photographer, remembered some seven decades later how a little boy had looked up at her when she toured a poor area of Washington. At Desfor's request she "knelt down in the mud and brackish water and spoke to the little boy and it made a lovely picture," he recalled. Desfor found her "very modest, simple, plain-spoken, very gracious to the photographers, knew what to do when she was asked and she did it. . . . stayed pretty much in the background when the President was around.[103]

Eleanor's arrangement with Arnold Constable would raise ethical questions today, but in the 1930s reporters were not as interested in investigating the private dealings of presidential spouses as they became later in the twentieth century. At 5 feet 11 inches tall and weighing 160 pounds while she was first lady, Eleanor presented a striking appearance in a long ball gown.[104] A study of her bills and correspondence shows that she liked fine fabrics and patronized well-known New York stores in addition to Arnold Constable. Unfortunately, most styles of the day did not flatter older women, and Eleanor did not appear to advantage in the matronly daytime outfits considered suitable for women of her age. The press conferences provided an opportunity for her to generate a more positive public image than her customary photographs showed.

From their beginnings the conferences had obvious political overtones even though this aspect was played down. The meetings served to publicize administration concerns, as when Eleanor told the press women on 16 May 1933 of her peaceful visit to the camp occupied by the "bonus marchers." The following week Eleanor used the conferences to float a trial balloon for establishing forest work camps for unemployed women. After widespread complaints that these camps would take women from their homes, Eleanor and Secretary of Labor Perkins announced the first camp would be for single women only.[105]

Throughout their existence the conferences presented Eleanor as the most visible member of a woman's network in politics and government that sought to advance feminist goals if not feminism itself.[106] She used the conferences to introduce prominent women in the New Deal, including Secretary of Labor Perkins; Nellie Tayloe Ross, director of the mint; Hilda Smith, in charge of women's camps for the unemployed; Ellen S. Woodward, director of women's relief work in the Federal Emergency Relief Administration; Dr. Louise Stanley, chief of the Bureau of Home Economics; and Mary Anderson, head of the Women's Bureau. Their presence, however, did not necessarily mean women were not discriminated against, since women on relief earned less than men. Similarly, it did not mean that the journalists thought it newsworthy to write about these guests, and they usually did not, except possibly to mention their names.

The press women also met notable visitors not connected with the administration. These included Rose Schneiderman, president of the National Women's Trade Union League, and the aviator Amelia Earhart, a frequent guest. In April 1933 Earhart took Eleanor on a night flight to Baltimore with both women wearing evening dresses as a stunt to promote the glamour of flying in the early days of commercial aviation. At Eleanor's invitation Furman went along in return for the fact that she had kept quiet about plans to make Eleanor an honorary member of the Daughters of the American Revolution (DAR) after having been blacklisted for active membership, apparently due to her liberal activities.[107] Since the DAR was a prominent conservative organization of the era, that story would have been a bigger one than the night flight, but Furman did not want to offend Eleanor.

Other visitors were connected with foreign policy. Among them were Ishbel MacDonald, daughter of the British prime minister, and Dame Rachel Crowdy of the League of Nations. The most memorable were King George VI and Queen Elizabeth of England, who made a historic trip to Washington in 1939 to seek U.S. support at the start of World War II in Europe. During the war the women were introduced to Madame Chiang Kai-shek of China and Queen Wilhelmina of Holland.

From time to time the Roosevelt administration made sure that Eleanor's press conferences furnished front-page stories and turned them into vehicles of overt political communication. Male journalists had more respect for them as news sources after Franklin referred reporters at his press conference to Eleanor in response to questions about the end of Prohibition and the return of alcoholic beverages to the White House. Consequently, on 3 April 1933 Eleanor announced at her press conference that beer would be served as a first step in the repeal of Prohibition. On 29 January 1934 she announced that wine would soon be on White House tables.

Because Eleanor was known to be a teetotaler, male reporters assumed that Early, the president's press secretary, and Howe, his political strategist, decided it made political sense for the first lady to act as a spokesperson on White House use of alcoholic beverages.[108] Eleanor could, and did, refer to her personal abstinence as a partial appeasement of the Prohibitionists, still an active political force.[109] For example, when she announced the return of beer to the White House, she expressed the hope that "a great many people who have used stronger things will be content with legal beer so that the cause of temperance will be really served," adding, "I myself do not drink anything with alcoholic content but that is purely an individual thing."[110]

Eleanor received help in preparing her statement, but it did not come from Early or Howe, but from Martha Strayer of the *Washington Daily News*, who, assisted by a few other women reporters, served as Eleanor's unofficial press advisor. Unlike the president's press conferences, which dealt with public policy and matters of state, Eleanor's conferences depended on the goodwill and organizational skill of the reporters themselves. This meant that those closest to her were accused of compromising their professional objectivity in the process.

Eleanor initially tried to help her special friends among the press corps by offering them government jobs. She proposed that both Strayer and the canny Furman, who initially sought personal ties with Eleanor by mentioning her admiration for Hickok, be hired part-time to do publicity work for the National Recovery Administration. This New Deal agency had launched a "Buy Now" campaign to persuade consumers to spend money to aid the economy, and Eleanor wanted the veteran reporters to help publicize it. Although both women needed extra money for family responsibilities, they tactfully declined, explaining that it would compromise ethical standards for them to be on the payroll of agencies that they covered.[111] Nevertheless, Strayer continued to advise Eleanor on her press conferences, suggesting planted questions on the "buy now" campaign.

With the exception of a Filipino reporter, all of the women accredited to Eleanor's press conferences were white. Eleanor would have accepted African American reporters, but Early, a Virginian who subscribed to the segregation of the era, enforced the policy of the white-only White House Correspondents Association that banned black journalists from presidential news conferences. Following the policy, Early ruled that presidential press conferences were open only to representatives of daily newspapers and wire services. Because the African American press was mainly weekly, this requirement effectively excluded its journalists.[112] Early insisted the same policy be applied to the first lady's conferences.

In February 1941, Early told Eleanor that he had turned down an accreditation request from Mrs. Bedford Lawson, who "represents colored weekly newspapers printed in Pittsburgh."[113] He contended that if she were accepted, other correspondents for weekly newspapers, both black and white, would seek admission, increasing attendance by hundreds of persons. Early also viewed Lawson's request suspiciously as a subterfuge by "certain colored leaders" attempting to "force their admission to the President's conferences."[114] Nine months later, when Thompson asked Early if a reporter for the *Washington Afro-American*, also a weekly, could attend, Thompson received the same negative response.

Since some of the women who were accepted sold freelance articles to weekly newspapers, even if they were not actually employed by them, Early's opposition appeared to reflect his own bias against racial equality. It also was attuned to the political reality that Franklin needed the votes of southern congressmen to push through New Deal legislation. As African American voters became a more powerful force in 1944, Early, however, went around the press corps to admit the first African American reporter to the president's news conference. None attended Eleanor's, however.[115] In terms of development of the first lady's role it was significant that Early saw Eleanor's conferences as roughly parallel to those of her husband.

No doubt Early lacked sympathy for Eleanor's activities pertaining to race in the city of Washington, where African Americans were barred from restaurants, theaters, hotels, libraries, and even taxis used by the white population. In 1936, for example, after Eleanor visited the National Training School for Girls, a reformatory for young women, she told her press conference about deplorable conditions there. She also announced that she would hold a garden party at the White House for the offenders, many of whom were African American.[116] Early became furious, but did not express his views directly to Eleanor herself, presumably because he did not want to jeopardize their working relationship.[117]

The party took place as scheduled, although the African American inmates were served in a separate tent, and the press could watch the event only through the bars of the iron fence surrounding the White House grounds. Eleanor's concern for the training school shamed Congress into appropriating $100,000 to improve the facility, but outraged Southerners who complained she had entertained "'nigger whores'" and circulated a crude drawing of the first lady dancing with an African American labeled "Nigger-Lover Eleanor."[118]

Her advocacy of more justice for African Americans, as well as her other controversial activities, prompted some of Franklin's advisors to urge her to stay in the background during the election campaign of 1936. In fact, Eleanor reduced her press conferences from a high of thirty-eight in 1934 to twenty-four in 1936. Furman recorded in her diary that three subjects were off limits at the press conferences prior to the election: birth control, a *McCall's* magazine article attacking Eleanor for her role in Arthurdale, and statements by the historian Mary Beard that men had robbed women of their history.[119]

Behind the scenes, Eleanor continued to coordinate the efforts of volunteers, who handed out "rainbow fliers" giving the Democratic Party's position on election issues and championed the right of women to claim equal representation on the Democratic Platform Committee for the first time.[120] Beneath her gracious patrician manner lay a sharp-minded political operative. In a detailed memo sent in July to Franklin (whom she called "The President"), Farley, Early, Dewson, and two Democratic National Committee officials, Charles Michelson and Stanley High, she mapped out a coordinated publicity campaign for the November election, covering radio, speeches, movies, pamphlets, fliers, and news releases, along with a research department. Its task would be to check on all "inconsistencies" in the record of Franklin's Republican opponent, Gov. Alf Landon of Kansas. "My feeling is that we have to get going and going quickly," she emphasized.[121]

By contrast, on the campaign trail she only smiled and waved, leaving Furman to report that Mrs. Roosevelt "seemed to me remarkably retiring."[122] To the surprise of Franklin's campaign staff, crowds clamored to see Eleanor, a first lady who had become the public face of the New Deal, connecting with ordinary Americans during a time of economic collapse.[123] Confined to a minor role in public, she started writing the first volume of her popular autobiography, *This Is My Story.*[124]

No plaster saint on racial issues, Eleanor occasionally showed insensitivity in language, using terms from time to time like "pickaninny" and "darky" in her writings.[125] The 1930s were, as one author put it, hardly "an equalitarian wonderland," with New Deal job programs often discriminating against women and African Americans and segregating employees by race.[126] Race per se, however, rarely came up in the press conferences, except when it seemed to be an accidental slip, as when Eleanor remarked on 15 June 1933 that Arizona copper miners were unemployed due to unfair competition from "South African savage labor."[127] On the other hand, she sometimes used the conferences to speak up for greater civil rights. After the United States entered World War II, she told the women reporters that there should be no discrimination in the legislation establishing the Women's Auxiliary Army Corps.[128]

Although the press women included her visits to African American churches, schools, and segregated military facilities when they reported her schedule of activities, racial issues remained mainly in the background. Sharing the general prejudices of the day, the women did not necessarily endorse Roosevelt's interest in better treatment for African Americans. In her diary Furman recorded a "blue Monday" in 1934 when the press conferences yielded only one story—"about a Negro to sing at the White House"—instead of feature material more generally acceptable to all southern, as well as northern, AP clients.[129] Eleanor's support of the 1935 appointment of an African American educator, Mary McLeod Bethune, to the national advisory committee of the National Youth Administration (and later to the post of director of the agency's Negro affairs) was not the kind of news that many of the women reporters sought.

When the chief topic at press conferences focused on plans to entertain the visiting King and Queen of England in June 1939, Furman, then covering the conferences for her own feature service, wrote in her diary that Eleanor was asked "with malice" by a reporter if the monarchs would "meet the artists" who performed for them at the

White House.[130] Since Marian Anderson, a celebrated African American singer, was expected to be one of the performers, Eleanor's reply that artists "are always presented to the people for whom the dinner or party is given" represented a major statement of her continued opposition to segregation.[131] As Eleanor's protector, Furman seemed more interested in the first lady avoiding criticism from Southerners than in news articles promoting her views on racial justice. She apparently thought that the reporters should avoid this controversial topic.

Eleanor's celebrity status, enhanced by her visible public role, increased following the election of 1936. In the spring of that year she had gone on a paid lecture trip, offering to speak on topics such as "The Mail of a President's Wife" and "A Typical Day at the White House." In 1937, to her surprise, she filled an auditorium with an audience of 16,000.[132]

By this time the press conferences were actually competing for public attention with Eleanor's own newspaper column, "My Day," which she had started at the end of 1935. The first "My Day" column was hastily distributed for publication on 30 December 1935 to vie with another unusual Washington offering, a column by Eleanor's acid-tongued Republican cousin, Alice Roosevelt Longworth. Distributed by United Features, a syndicated service that had signed Eleanor to a five-year contract, "My Day" was sent daily by telegraph wire to subscribing newspapers. It contained accounts of her "daily doings," similar to those she had been sending Hickok in letters, which the two had discussed as the basis for a future book.[133]

At this point Eleanor's intense friendship with Hickok was waning. Perhaps Eleanor thought it would be better to capitalize on her activities now than to wait. Her cousin's famed wit regarding politics failed to transfer well to the printed page and her column soon died, while Eleanor's survived. "My Day" enabled the first lady to speak for herself, although in a muted voice, rather than have her views transmitted to the public via her press conferences. It continued for nearly three decades until her death in 1962, growing increasingly political and outspoken after Eleanor left the White House.

Ridiculed by intellectuals as shallow and trivial, the initial "My Day" described domestic details of White House life and paraded before its readers the names of well-known women in the New Deal with whom Eleanor had dealings. In her first column she wrote that "the house was full of young people, my husband had a cold and was in bed having milk-toast," so she retired to her room and read reports on problems of youth.[134] When the U.S. Supreme Court outlawed the Agricultural Adjustment Administration, one of her husband's key New Deal agencies, she portrayed Franklin as reacting nonchalantly, taking his usual swim in the White House pool.[135]

Undertaken with Franklin's approval, "My Day," with its picture of good-humored family life, turned into an effective political weapon during the campaign of 1936. It helped counteract unfavorable publicity stemming from Eleanor's own ceaseless activities and her children's divorces. In "My Day" she appeared self-effacing by calling attention to others at her press conferences. For instance, in referring to an appearance by Hallie Flanagan, director of the Federal Theatre Project, she wrote, "When I have a guest at these conferences, . . . I can sit back and listen with the knowledge that the [press] girls will take something with them of real interest."[136]

Newspapers immediately bought the column, sometimes pairing it with the Longworth column in advance of the 1936 elections. They paid for the column based on the size of their circulation. United Features predicted she would make about $1,000 a month from "My Day," but she kept the amount quiet.[137] When her press conference group asked what she would earn, she evaded an answer, saying, "I have the same contract they make with anyone else. So I have no idea what I will get."[138] She added that she would give some of the money to charity and keep some for herself. The women did not press further out of loyalty to her and a sense of her vulnerability. As Hope Ridings Miller of the *Washington Post* put it, "She did the best she could for the country and herself with the gifts she had."[139]

While the column presented Eleanor as a devoted wife and mother who carried her domestic concerns into the broader world around her, it carried feminist overtones. Remarks such as this one poked at men: "There are practical little things in housekeeping which no man really understands."[140] Criticizing an assertion that there were no great women playwrights, she wrote in 1937 that women, far from being intellectually inferior to men, "know not only what men know, but much that men will never know. For, how many men really know the heart and soul of a woman?"[141]

Professional journalists laughed at "My Day," which lacked the accurate detail considered a vital part of the newspaper craft. The journalists who attended her press conferences thought it an amateurish affair based only on Eleanor's position, although they changed their minds when Eleanor used it to break actual news stories. "Mrs. Roosevelt was always looking for ways to earn money," Hornaday recalled; "we resented that when she wrote her column competing with us."[142] Her husband downplayed "My Day" by distinguishing it from a "worthwhile column" and reminding his own press conference that Eleanor "simply writes a daily diary."[143]

Editors who purchased her column took it seriously, trying to correct her grammatical and reportorial mistakes. Writing Eleanor in 1937, George Carlin, her syndicate head, enclosed a memorandum from one client who commented: "I note with sorrow that the First Lady has turned cannibal. Her lead sentence . . . is 'We had a lunch of some 50-odd ladies yesterday' . . . and a little further down she goes on with this fearful orgy . . . 'We returned in time for lunch and had a very distinguished group of doctors. . . .' I have carefully changed these two sentences lest we lose our vegetarian readers."[144] Eleanor accepted the reprimand in good grace, but not humbly: "I am afraid that my desire to eat them all crept into print."[145]

Her desire to have a life separate from her official duties sometimes made its way into her column. Eleanor told her readers that the more "you live in a 'goldfish bowl,' the less people really know about you."[146] In her correspondence with Hickok, she complained at the same time, "I must dress for the diplomatic dinner, a cozy party of 98! Gee, I'm sick of it."[147] Perhaps it was authenticity that enabled "My Day" to become an American institution. Eleanor certainly did not bare her innermost thoughts in public, but the column did give some insights into its creator. She established herself as both a "superwoman" who flew around the country and was attentive to family, friends, and worthy causes and a genuine individual who spoke the language of ordinary people. Not a sophisticated critic, she told readers the best-selling novel *Gone with the Wind* was "a book you would like to read straight through. . . . I can assure you, you will find Scarlet O'Hara an interesting character . . . circumstances mold even the little animal she seems to be."[148]

By 1938 some sixty-two newspapers, with a total circulation of

4,034,552, bought the rights to use "My Day," making Eleanor a popular columnist. She had more readers than political pundits like David Lawrence, although she lacked the appeal of the intellectual Walter Lippmann, who appeared in 160 newspapers with eight million readers.[149] The surface simplicity of the column concealed Eleanor's complex personality and the unusual nature of her marriage. The column was published six days a week, and Eleanor often hastily dictated it to Tommy while traveling in cars, planes, or ships. Spending about half an hour on each column, Eleanor determinedly met her deadline, rushing her copy marked "Press Rates Collect" to telegraph offices.

Sometimes the column provided comment on White House incidents that showed her annoyance. For example, when two high school students managed to crash the White House on New Year's Eve in 1938 to get the Roosevelts' autographs on a dare, Eleanor told her readers what happened and castigated the culprits. Their "rude and unmannerly behavior," she wrote, could have had unfortunate consequences.[150]

"My Day" gave Eleanor a legitimate claim to being considered a working journalist herself. She proudly joined the American Newspaper Guild, a union of newspaper editorial and business employees established under New Deal labor legislation that made it easier for workers to organize. Although she was not active in the union, which she joined in 1936 to show her support for organized labor, she attended some meetings of the Washington unit of the guild, knitting away while sitting in the front row, one veteran Washington correspondent recalled.[151] She told her press conference that she had no plans to strike or picket on behalf of the guild, but she was pulled into union politics in 1939 when the Denver chapter nominated her for national president.[152] She swiftly declined, but the effort gave rise to speculation that factions in the guild allied with Communists were trying to use her as a front.

She obtained union membership far more easily than membership in the Women's National Press Club, which accepted her as an active member by a divided vote in 1938 after she had written her column for two years. Nine members voted against accepting her because she did not earn most of her living from writing, which was supposed to be a requirement for membership. Doris Fleeson, a well-regarded political columnist for the *New York Daily News*, nominated her for membership, and Black and Furman seconded the nomination. Eleanor was admitted only after Black denied persistent rumors that she was the first lady's ghostwriter.[153]

The column served as a partial antidote to Eleanor's qualms about being first lady and as a measure of her own independence. When Eleanor was ill in September 1936, Franklin offered to write "My Day" for her, but she declined, saying, "if it once became the President's column we would lose our readers and that would be very sad."[154] Months before the election in 1936, Eleanor wrote Hickok that she was "so indifferent" to the outcome even though she planned to participate in the campaign.[155] In her response Hickok empathized with Eleanor's situation as a wife whose husband was surrounded by others: "A daily dose of Mac [Marvin H. McIntyre, the president's appointments secretary] and Missy [LeHand], along with all the fuss and pomp and adulation the man receives will distract anyone's view."[156] The month preceding the voting, Eleanor confided to Hickok: "Dear I realize more & more that FDR is a great man & he is nice to me but as a person I'm a stranger & I don't want to be anything else."[157]

After Franklin won reelection by a landslide in 1936, some of the women journalists who covered Eleanor continued to feel sorry for her. Hornaday recalled relatively little growth in Eleanor's leadership skills, remembering vividly "that nervous little laugh."[158] The English novelist Rebecca West attended one of Eleanor's press conferences in 1937 and described her as "always a little timid and tense," lacking "the peace of relaxation," even though she "gushed amiable enthusiasm."[159] Mildred Gilman, a reporter for the *Washington Herald*, recalled years later that Eleanor carried her head in front of her body, perhaps because she always appeared to be in a hurry.[160]

Their feelings of compassion lessened when the women saw the first lady as a professional rival, using "My Day" to circumvent their reporting. When Eleanor made inspection trips to District of Columbia institutions, she publicized her findings, which generally exposed disgraceful conditions, in "My Day" instead of reporting them to her press conference. At times she seemed uncertain which forum to use, the column or a press conference. In 1938 she hinted in "My Day" at deficiencies in Freedman's Hospital, a part of Howard University, before explaining them at a press conference. The resulting publicity helped the hospital gain funds for a $700,000 tuberculosis annex.[161]

After visiting the District's Gallinger Municipal Hospital the following year, she chose to publicize inadequate care there in "My Day" instead of reporting it to her press conference. When the women complained, she told them she could not take reporters with her "because I wouldn't be able to see the things I did see."[162] This included "totally inadequate" care by overworked student nurses.[163] Her explanation begged the question of why she had not presented her findings initially to her press conference group. It is likely she simply wanted to tell her story in her own voice. When reporters raised questions, Eleanor suggested that a congressional committee visit the hospital.

In an effort to compromise with the press women, Eleanor took Strayer with her on subsequent trips to the District home for the aged and an institution for juvenile offenders called the Children's Receiving Home. Strayer took notes in shorthand and reported to her colleagues on the poor conditions observed so they were prepared to question Eleanor at her press conference on her reaction. The arrangement left Eleanor free to write her own account in "My Day" and also maximized the publicity value of her inspections both in Washington and throughout the nation. Writing about these visits, Furman, who had launched a freelance feature service after leaving the AP, advised women in a Democratic Party publication to make similar inspection trips of public facilities in their own localities.[164]

"My Day" roamed widely from the concrete to the theoretical. Eleanor offered her own eclectic approach to political philosophy. On one hand she contended "hard times were not in vain" because they built individual character. On the other hand, in the same column extolling individual effort, she called for collective action, equating the heroism of pioneer days with attempts to unionize workers so they would "live decently in New York City."[165] Fascism interested her. In 1937 she took favorable note of Mussolini's reordering of Italian life to "allow women to enter any profession or business."[166]

Although always opposed to Hitler, in 1938 she went so far as to suggest Americans study a Nazi innovation to obligate every able-bodied man and woman to perform short-term national service.[167] Earlier she had faulted Nazi attempts to restrict women to child-bearing only, arguing that men and women alike should have access to "work which will produce at least a minimum of material security, love and faith."[168] She once told a friend she would have voted for the Socialist candidate, Norman Thomas, if her husband had not been running for president in 1932.[169] She even made a politically risky statement at one point that the ideals of communism were closer in spirit to democracy than to fascism.[170]

In 1938 she published a collection of excerpts from her "My Day" columns, which sold poorly, perhaps because the column's appeal lay mainly in its timeliness. Her personal accounts of White House life, which some political observers followed in an attempt to gauge administration morale, gave readers an immediate link to Washington that was missing in the book. Readers apparently found her daily schedule and mention of prominent people more interesting than her collected observations. Her son Elliott claimed that his mother hid her true personality in "My Day," painting a portrait of a contented woman instead of "the detached, harried, fault-finding wife and parent we knew."[171] Still, evidence of inner anxiety crept into the column. When she wrote, "I wish I could be three people [one] holding teas, luncheons. . . . [one sitting] at a desk eight hours a day . . . [and one] a wife, mother, grandmother and friend," she personalized the problem of fragmented lives faced by many women.[172]

If she compared herself to her husband, she usually put herself down. Following the 1937 inauguration, she mentioned, "Last night we saw a newsreel of the Inauguration and I must say I marvel at how well the President looks in all the pictures. I am correspondingly appalled at how funny I look."[173] A few days earlier she lamented being asked to pose in her inaugural gown, saying that she hoped it would be "the last posed picture I will have to have taken."[174] Obviously, she did not expect that Franklin would run for two more terms.

The column, as well as Eleanor's other writing, reflected the contradictory elements of her personality. Uncertain of herself in some ways, she nevertheless acted to make the White House into her own "bully pulpit," the phrase that her uncle Ted had used to describe the power of the president to influence public opinion.[175] A president could wield power by appealing directly to the public for economic and social changes. A first lady had no inherent power, but she did have access to the news media. Having started her career in the 1920s when women reformers were involved in "a domestication of politics" by advocating social welfare causes, Eleanor aspired to boost her network of women activists by publicizing their efforts. She wanted to showcase what they were doing by implementing and shaping social policies related to what historians now call the "maternalist" or "nurturant" political agenda that evolved into the modern welfare state.[176]

The names of the alphabet agencies that made up the core of the New Deal in Franklin's first term ran through "My Day," especially if they appeared to be part of the "maternalist" agenda. She wrote about the Civilian Conservation Corps (CCC), which put youth to work on flood control, forestry, and road building; the Federal Emergency Relief Administration (FERA), which sent money to state and local governments to address immediate needs for assistance and morphed into the Works Progress Administration (WPA), which put to work the unemployed by coordinating relief and construction projects; and the National Youth Administration (NYA), which helped young people stay in school or find jobs.

Her language lacked the strength of a masculine voice but conveyed a motherly tone. She referred to the CCC as an educational and uplifting operation, explaining that "it has taken boys who might have drifted into evil ways and kept them busy, it has given them better health and skill with which to face the world."[177] Another column praised the "WPA men and the CCC boys and NYA boys" for their roles in combating damage from a savage storm that hit New England in 1938.[178] Her references to males echoed the ideology of the New Deal, which subscribed to gendered and racial assumptions that focused on white male breadwinners and gave lesser amounts of aid to women and African Americans.[179]

Eleanor had a motivation for public communication beyond the purely political: She wanted to prove to herself that she could do something with a role that she initially feared would curtail her own self-development. In answer to a charge that she and her family were publicity hungry, she wrote in "My Day," "I have no illusions about being a great speaker or great writer, but I think in some of us there is an urge to do certain things, and if we did not do them, we would feel that we were not fulfilling the job which we had been given opportunities and talents to do."[180]

Nevertheless, she continued, she frequently stood back and viewed her own activities objectively, thinking of herself not as an individual, but as the personage she happened to be at this time of her life. She said she supposed this came from "having been a shy child . . . and having become accustomed to do things because they were expected of me and not because I wanted to."[181] Eleanor knew that Franklin used the image of "his Missus" for symbolic political purposes.[182] While she counted as a member of his New Deal team, Franklin generally left her to her own activities, enhancing her feelings of playing a role.

No doubt Franklin and Eleanor conferred on some of the contents of "My Day" at least during its first year. Before the 1936 Democratic national convention, Franklin asked her to include figures from a letter by Hickok reporting on unemployment in the steel industry due to automation by Republican industrialists. Eleanor quoted the material as though she had gathered it herself, writing Hickok, "I wanted to wait for your consent but Franklin won't let me. I think he wants me to be whipping boy and tho' he can't bring the question out he wants it out."[183]

When figures cited by Hickok were found to be incorrect, Eleanor tried to reassure her close friend, writing, "The fact of the whole business is all that matters and both F. and I looked on your letter only as an example to illustrate a subject vividly which needed to be discussed."[184] Three years later, Eleanor denied to her press conference that her husband ever tried to influence what she wrote: "He has never called me in and said he wished I had said this or that or the other thing."[185] Possibly at this time the communication gulf between Franklin and Eleanor had grown larger, and she had forgotten his earlier effort to use the column.

Eventually "My Day" became "required political reading for those seeking insight into administration policy," according to Arthur Krock of the *New York Times*.[186] Krock, one of the most authoritative Washington journalists, made his pronouncement in 1939 after Eleanor sat beside Franklin at a Hyde Park press conference and urged him to address cutbacks in WPA jobs that were aimed at reducing unemployment.[187] Since she previously had taken up the same issue in "My Day," Krock speculated that Franklin was following Eleanor's example. He declared the Roosevelts were "a political team," a new development in the history of the American presidency.[188]

Krock's comments followed a three-month appearance of "My Day" in the *New York Times.* The dignified *Times* surprisingly reprinted Eleanor's "My Day" columns on the visit of the King and Queen of England, even though they appeared first in the rival *New York World-Telegram*, which regularly bought the column. Eleanor's report on the visit, which captivated the American press, included numerous anecdotes, such as an account of how servants at Hyde Park tipped over a serving tray and "no one could think because of the noise of breaking china."[189] Next the hapless waiters dropped a tray of glasses and bottles, but, Eleanor assured her readers, "Their Majesties remained completely calm and undisturbed."[190]

Eleanor's ability to move from the comic to the serious helped endear the column to her readers. According to Carlin, her syndicate chief, "My Day" succeeded not because it was written by the president's wife, but because Eleanor transmitted her personal charm and eager spirit through the column. He called it "an honest projection of one of the great personalities of our own time; a woman great in her own right, and as a newspaper columnist, probably the best trouper of them all, never known to miss a deadline."[191]

"My Day" assumed special importance as a news vehicle in February 1939 when Eleanor announced in her column that she was resigning from an unnamed national organization to protest its refusal to rent a concert hall to a world-renowned singer. She couched her terse announcement in simple but indirect language: "They [the officers of the organization] have taken an action widely talked of in the press. To remain as a member implies approval of that action, and therefore I am resigning."[192]

Reporters immediately recognized she had withdrawn from the Daughters of the American Revolution (DAR) because the organization had forbidden Marian Anderson, the acclaimed African American contralto, to sing in Constitution Hall, then the largest venue for concerts in Washington and a tax-exempt public accommodation. The resulting controversy showed the first lady's ability to spotlight an act of racism. It ended on an uplifting note when Anderson sang before an integrated crowd of 75,000 on Easter Sunday at the Lincoln Memorial. Eleanor's action had obvious political significance, showing White House support for the equality of African Americans and enhancing her own stature among African Americans.

In fact, Anderson had sung at the White House in 1936 at Eleanor's invitation. By 1939 she had given some seventy concerts yearly throughout the United States. Yet, in keeping with the local custom of segregation in the city of Washington, the DAR, a patriotic organization then considered a potent political force among women, denied the famous singer use of its hall. By her resignation Eleanor focused attention on the organization rather than attacking local laws or practices, a more moderate stance than a direct assault on segregation.[193] She also dissuaded activists from picketing the DAR's annual convention in Washington.

Eleanor's resignation came a few months after she had refused to comply with an order to observe segregated seating at the founding convention of the Southern Conference on Human Welfare held in Birmingham. A crowd of about 7,000 persons, some 3,000 of whom were African American, filled Birmingham's Municipal Auditorium on 28 November 1938 when she addressed the conference.[194] Choosing a novel way to oppose the separation of the races required by local ordinance, she insisted on placing her chair in the center aisle between the two groups.[195] Her action brought an enthusiastic response from African Americans, even though she did not clearly condemn segregation, saying in answer to a question, "I could no more tell people in another state what they should do than the United States can tell another country what to do."[196] Nevertheless, Eleanor recognized that a first lady could oppose racial injustice by publicizing it.

The first lady may have played a behind-the-scenes role in arranging for Anderson's historic concert on 9 April 1939, although no written evidence exists to show that she did so.[197] The idea originated with Walter F. White, executive secretary of the National Association for the Advancement of Colored People (NAACP), and was approved by Harold Ickes, secretary of the interior, after checking with Franklin.[198] Although her name headed the list of distinguished sponsors, Eleanor did not attend the acclaimed event, which featured Anderson in a dignified program of arias and spirituals, after opening with the hymn "America."[199]

During the subsequent July Fourth weekend, after Anderson had sung for the King and Queen of England at the White House the preceding month, Eleanor presented her with the Spingarn Medal, the highest honor given by the NAACP. The ceremony took place at the NAACP's national convention in Richmond, once the capital of the Confederacy. Eleanor spoke on a coast-to-coast radio hookup in a symbolic gesture against racial discrimination.[200]

Eleanor's resignation from the DAR drew praise from a majority of Americans. A Gallup poll showed 67 percent approved while 33 percent, mainly in the deep South, disapproved.[201] It placed her in the forefront of a developing movement to combat racial injustice. After announcing her DAR resignation in "My Day," an act that generated headlines throughout the country, Eleanor said little about it at her press conference, having chosen not to denounce the DAR as militants had urged her to do. By this point her press gatherings had lost some of their significance. Eleanor had turned into her own publicist, writing chatty "My Day" columns akin to blogs today and giving frequent broadcasts. She continued her press conferences, but they no longer held center stage in her communication activities.

CHAPTER 5

REACHING THE DISPOSSESSED

"What we should strive to do is to accept the facts, face the truth, and make up our minds that we will try to keep ourselves and all the groups and people we can touch in the spirit of real trust, real democracy, and real charity toward all people."
Eleanor Roosevelt addressing a meeting of the National Conference of Christians and Jews in Washington, D.C., in 1939*

As first lady, Eleanor demonstrated an eagerness to learn about social conditions and do what she could to improve them that far surpassed the efforts of her predecessors. Literally all over the map in her travels, Eleanor reached out to various segments of the population—including women, African Americans, youth, the downtrodden, and refugees—attempting to use her access to political power to benefit those she believed needed her help. In doing so, she made the role of first lady an influential element in policymaking for the first time in American history.

Eleanor had Franklin's ear, if not always his agreement to act, on causes that particularly concerned her. According to columnist

* ERP, Speech and Article File, "Remarks of Mrs. Franklin D. Roosevelt at the Luncheon of the Washington Round Table of the National Conference of Christians and Jews," 13 April 1939, FDRL.

Harry Hopkins, head of New Deal relief efforts, addresses a meeting of state relief administrators at the Mayflower Hotel in Washington in June 1935 while Eleanor and Ellen Woodward, the director of women's relief programs, listen. Courtesy of the Franklin D. Roosevelt Library, Hyde Park, New York.

Raymond Clapper, Eleanor became a "Cabinet Minister without portfolio—the most influential woman of our times."[1] Working both publicly through her personal appearances and contacts with the media and privately through her own network of various New Deal officials, she tried to exercise leadership within the administration, even if she did not succeed.

In view of her unceasing activism in the White House, it seems surprising that Eleanor displayed reluctance to become first lady. Perhaps she disliked the thought of the move from New York, where she had established herself as a teacher and writer, to Washington, the site of her unhappiness after discovering Franklin's romance with Lucy Mercer. Along with these qualms over being again in the nation's capital, Eleanor obviously feared that she would be so engulfed by White House social events she would not be able to advance the liberal social agenda sought by women reformers with whom she had worked for a decade.

Eleanor committed herself to their agenda that called for government intervention to improve living and working conditions. After Franklin's election as governor of New York in 1928, she had resigned from the board of the women's division of the state Democratic Party and stopped overt political activity, in line with her repeated contention that she had entered politics to advance her husband's career.[2] Having discovered personal fulfillment in political organization, however, she pressed for the women who supported Franklin to be rewarded with political appointments.

Due in part to Eleanor's insistence, the Democratic National Committee named Molly Dewson to a full-time position as director of its women's division, a post she held from 1932 to 1934 before becoming chair of the division's advisory committee from 1934 to 1937.[3] Eleanor worked with Dewson in tandem to place women in prominent jobs, but as first lady saw her own political involvement as somewhat marginal. Guided by Louis Howe in the political realm and by Hickok in dealing with the press, Eleanor gradually refashioned her position into more than a ceremonial one, but she recognized that her own effectiveness rested on Franklin's prestige and power. She could speak up but not control the political process—and she paid a price for expressing her views.

Asked at one of her first press conferences if she got much "fan mail," she replied, "I get very little, but a great deal of critical mail. Because I make speeches, I am more in the press, I'm not dignified, I do something that isn't the proper thing to do."[4] Explaining that she answered the critical letters by saying she was sorry to have offended anyone, she said that "if I didn't do what I think is the right thing to do, I wouldn't be satisfied with myself. Everyone must live their own life in their own way and not according to anybody else's ideas."[5] Eleanor's first term as first lady was a search for what she thought was the right thing to do in an amorphous position that she ultimately shaped to her own character and personality. She knew she had to move carefully in the political arena, always conscious that Franklin, not she, had been elected.

Eleanor moved where Franklin both physically and politically could not go in terms of firsthand inspection trips, as well as pressing for controversial social reforms and civil rights.[6] Her traveling to see for herself conditions facing ordinary Americans was symbol-

Eleanor knits while seated in an airplane about 1936. This photograph was used by the airline industry to promote flying as an alternative to rail transportation. Eleanor liked to fly on her frequent fact-finding and lecture trips. Courtesy of the Franklin D. Roosevelt Library, Hyde Park, New York.

ized by a *New Yorker* cartoon of 3 June 1933, showing two miners looking up from their shovels and exclaiming, "For Gosh sakes, here comes Mrs. Roosevelt!"[7] It predated her actual descent into a mine by two years, but was indicative of her appearances in every state of the union except one, South Dakota, by 1940. During her first eight years as first lady she traveled some 300,000 miles, observing the lives of hard-pressed individuals in such diverse settings as Indian reservations, factories, migrant camps, poor neighborhoods, civil rights conferences, and federal relief projects. Determined to refuse Secret Service protection, she carried a gun in her glove compartment on vacation trips with Hickok in the summers of 1933 and 1934.[8]

It was not always clear when Eleanor acted with or without Franklin's support.[9] She personally sought more equality and economic redistribution than the New Deal embraced.[10] This gave Franklin the benefit of using her as an emissary to African Americans and other groups poorly represented in a Democratic Party heavily influenced by conservative Southerners and big city bosses.

It is impossible to know precisely what impact her ceaseless travels and meetings with persons in all walks of life had on the Roosevelt presidency. Faced with disastrous economic conditions, including a quarter of the population unemployed at the start of his presidency, Franklin and his advisors of necessity experimented with programs to salvage American industry and create a safety net to keep millions from destitution. Eleanor's reports and private conversations with Franklin constituted part of his intelligence gathering and decision making.

Similarly, Franklin drew on confidential reports written by Hickok, who went to work as the chief investigator of New Deal relief programs after leaving the AP in June 1933. Hickok sent the reports, written in a vivid, anecdotal style, to Hopkins, her immediate superior, with copies to Eleanor, who shared salient portions with Franklin.[11] In her daily letter to Hickok, Eleanor wrote in November 1933 that Franklin "always asks me if I have anything to read him from you."[12] Hickok's reports, utilizing her reportorial experience and contacts, advised the administration of bureaucratic and political incompetency in relief operations as when she exploded in one report, "Texas is a Godawful mess."[13] Seeking to reinforce Hickok's ego after the loss of her job as the top woman political reporter for the AP, Eleanor lavished praise on her work. Referring to her own dismay over routine tea-pouring and handshaking, Eleanor also told Hickok, "Your job is more stimulating than mine."[14]

The limitations of Eleanor's role appeared particularly in the area of civil rights for African Americans. As the first president's wife to engage markedly in public affairs, Eleanor displayed support for equal treatment of African Americans that far surpassed that of the New Deal in general.[15] She was one of the few White House supporters of legislation to combat lynching, the public torture and murder of individuals, usually African American men, by white mobs mainly in the South. This crude method of social control had increased during the Depression.

In 1933 the frequency of mob murders had quadrupled over the previous year, with twenty-four African American men lynched that year compared with six in 1932.[16] In the face of local officials who declined to take action against lynching, if not outright supporting it, the National Association for the Advancement of Colored People (NAACP) sought a federal antilynching law to end mob violence. Eleanor backed Walter F. White, the NAACP executive secretary who cultivated her assiduously, in efforts to get Franklin to support an antilynching bill introduced by two Democratic senators, Edward P. Costigan of Colorado and Robert F. Wagner of New York.

After White was unable to schedule a meeting with the president, Eleanor arranged for the two to talk face-to-face on the White House veranda in 1934. They met over the objections of two of Franklin's key aides, Stephen Early, press secretary, and Marvin McIntyre, who handled political appointments. When Franklin expressed fears that key senators would filibuster against crucial New Deal legislation if he supported a federal antilynching law, White answered his arguments so well that the president commented, "Somebody's been priming you. Was it my wife?"[17] Franklin never supported antilynching legislation, which came up repeatedly in Congress during the 1930s, and it did not pass.

In addition, Franklin curtailed Eleanor's public support for it. When White wanted her to speak at an antilynching rally in New York in 1934, following a particularly ugly lynching in Florida, she declined at Franklin's request. The next year she also declined to attend the opening of an art show against lynching in New York featuring works by famous artists, although she visited it unobtrusively.[18] Since Eleanor refrained from openly showing disapproval of Franklin's actions, she did not publically express support for antilynching legislation until 1939. It was only after his death in 1945 that she accepted a nomination to the board of directors of the NAACP.

Eleanor started her public career, as Cook put it, "steeped in the sensibilities of the Old South, filled with distorted and ugly images of blacks."[19] As a child Eleanor had been regaled with stories of idyllic plantation life by her great-aunt Annie Gracie King, the sister of Eleanor's paternal grandmother, Mittie Bulloch Roosevelt, who delighted in picturing loyal slaves serving the Bulloch family in Georgia.[20] As Eleanor broadened her life experience, she recognized the fundamental justice of African Americans' struggle for civil rights. Still, she sat up several nights in the White House enthralled with the sentimental picture of the Confederacy painted in *Gone with the Wind*.[21]

Eleanor remained part of a milieu in which white supremacy held sway, whether based on an elitist view toward African Americans as inferiors or on vicious acts to control them. Her friend Hickok quickly bought into the virulent racism of the South when she traveled there to investigate relief programs in 1934. She sent Eleanor and others in Washington bigoted accounts of illiterate African Americans as well as prejudiced comments on Indians and Hispanics.[22]

Eleanor's public statements on race relations both before and during World War II showed moderation. She counseled African Americans to show patience and to rally behind "educated Negroes who can become leaders among their people."[23] She wrote a woman who complained that African Americans were ruining her neighborhood "that it may take years to educate the great mass of colored people to be good in desirable neighborhoods, but we are largely to blame. . . . we have never given them equal chances for education, even after we emancipated them."[24] In common with other liberals of her day, she believed in the idea of social progress brought about by rational discussion.[25]

In general, the New Deal bowed to southern pressure and discriminated against African Americans. Still, Eleanor personified the interest of the Democratic Party in the growing black urban vote in northern cities and consequent need to reach out to African Americans in spite of segregationists. Those who clung to white supremacy hated the first lady as a symbol of social change. They circulated pictures of her in interracial settings, contending that she wanted to destroy the "southern way of life." They told wild stories

Eleanor visits the Vernon Nursery School in Los Angeles on 21 March 1938 and demonstrates her interest in African American children. Pictures of this type were widely circulated in African American newspapers. Courtesy of the Franklin D. Roosevelt Library, Hyde Park, New York.

that she sponsored fictitious "Eleanor Clubs" in the South to compel African American maids to leave the kitchens of white women. Rumors persisted to the point that the Federal Bureau of Investigation (FBI) launched an investigation into the "clubs" but found no basis in fact.[26] Eleanor's position on race may have helped lay the foundation for the later switch of white voters in the South from the Democratic to the Republican Party after passage of civil rights legislation in 1965.

Eleanor's alliance with White gave him a conduit to the White House at a time when her husband's advisors considered White a nuisance and political encumbrance. Uncomfortable at times with White's tactics that embraced public protests against segregation, Eleanor preferred less confrontational action, such as resigning from the DAR rather than denouncing the organization at a press conference after it refused to allow Marian Anderson to sing in Constitution Hall because of her race. Yet, the working relationship between White and Eleanor expanded her knowledge of racial issues and gave White hope that persons of goodwill could transcend racist thinking. Widespread prejudice during the 1930s, however, kept this goal from materializing in many New Deal projects, including one extremely close to Eleanor's heart. In spite of her best efforts, Arthurdale, the resettlement community for West Virginia miners to which she devoted considerable time and money, remained segregated.

Eleanor's interest in Arthurdale, which became her biggest and most controversial personal humanitarian project during the New Deal, initially stemmed from her intimacy with Hickok. Conditions in Scotts Run, West Virginia, northwest of Morgantown, appalled Hickok in her job as a confidential investigator of relief programs for the administration. She urged Eleanor to see for herself hundreds of beaten-down coal miners, some without work since an unsuccessful strike years before, who lived with their families in shacks without access to drinking water except what came from polluted gullies also used for sewage disposal. Driving alone to Scotts Run in August 1933, Eleanor met Hickok for a firsthand look at rural destitution. Guided by Hickok and representatives of the American Friends Service Committee (AFSC), an organization attempting to establish self-help programs for the miners and their families, she visited miners' families in grimy hovels without identifying herself.

Distressed by the misery she encountered, Eleanor told the story at a White House dinner of a pathetic little boy clutching a pet white rabbit that his sister said the family was going to eat.[27] It prompted William C. Bullitt, the administration's first ambassador to the Soviet Union, to send a check for $100 to keep the bunny alive.[28] While appreciating individual acts of kindness, Eleanor recognized they were insufficient. Her efforts to make permanent improvements in the lives of the miners and their families led to her involvement in the building of Arthurdale, the first of some fifty New Deal resettlement communities for those living in abject poverty.

The "back to the land" movement of the early twentieth century inspired these projects, designed to move families living in deplorable circumstances to planned rural communities. The movement attracted both Franklin and Eleanor as a way of allowing the poverty-stricken to escape from exploitive capitalism symbolized by absentee landowners. Advocates proposed to establish communities where subsistence farming, combined with jobs in small industries similar to Eleanor's Val-Kill furniture factory, would enable residents to improve their lives. Critics contended the program, which gave families on relief homesteads with housing and garden plots, smacked of communism.

Eleanor paid little heed to these objections. She took a maternal interest in resettlement projects as well as in the creation of planned communities known as greenbelt towns because they were built on unoccupied land near major cities. Only three greenbelt towns were actually constructed, the most noted of which was Greenbelt, Maryland, near Washington, where Eleanor made frequent trips, but dozens of resettlement communities came into existence in spite of protests from conservative business interests.

On her first visit to Scotts Run Eleanor discovered that efforts were under way by the Agriculture Extension Service of West Virginia University, located in Morgantown, to move the miners to a 1,200-acre farm, previously owned by the Arthur family, fifteen miles southeast of Morgantown. Eleanor told Franklin about the endeavor, which became the initial project of the Subsistence Homestead Division of the Department of the Interior.[29] The division, established in 1933, administered a revolving $25 million fund for homesteads slipped into key New Deal legislation, the National Industrial Recovery Act, which allowed industry to set prices to increase production and enhance buying power.

Howe, the gnarled newspaperman given the honorary title "Colonel," who served as Franklin's political guru and Eleanor's mentor, established a committee to develop a homestead project for the Scotts Run miners. Members included Eleanor and Clarence Pickett, the executive secretary of the AFSC, whose practical approach to social issues impressed both Roosevelts and led to Pickett being appointed assistant administrator of the Division of Subsistence Homesteads. Moving rapidly, the committee pushed the federal government to purchase the Arthur farm. On 13 October 1933 Secretary of the Interior Ickes announced that 200 miners and their families would be relocated there.[30]

Situated near the town of Reedsville, the project, named Arthurdale, became known as "Mrs. Roosevelt's 'Baby,'" since Franklin put her in charge of the new community.[31] Due to Eleanor's patronage, it was the most publicized of three resettlement communities in West Virginia, which Eleanor backed wholeheartedly. The other two, Tygart Valley, near Elkins, and Eleanor, named for her near Charleston, received less attention, although they, like Arthurdale, experienced administrative difficulties. In Arthurdale's case accusations of waste and good intentions gone awry dogged the project from its inception, stemming mainly from efforts to act rapidly without careful planning. Even as supportive a participant as Pickett questioned the haste involved. "The situation has been considerably complicated by the excessive interest of the President and Mrs. Roosevelt and Colonel Howe," Pickett wrote. "They want to establish one colony very quickly and have worked out some plans already, part of which are good and part of which are questionable."[32]

Arthurdale sprang into existence partly to counter fears that the Communist Party was gaining adherents among the most deprived segments of the population, like unemployed miners, and might serve as a catalyst for violence unless the government acted to alleviate distress. Political critics seized on blunders in its rapid development and ironically labeled it part of a "communistic" plot to subvert the economy of nearby Morgantown.[33] As Eleanor subsequently pointed out at her press conferences, this was an unfounded assertion, because the resettled miners had been unable to pay taxes or rent for years.

Intent on developing a model for all resettlement communities, Eleanor wanted Arthurdale to have modern homes, a progressive school system, an up-to-date public health clinic, cooperatives for both the production and consumption of goods, as well as programs to preserve Appalachian folk culture.[34] Investing herself heavily in the details of the project, she selected a school principal,

Elsie Clapp, a disciple of progressive educator John Dewey. Eleanor also hired Nancy Cook, her friend and partner in the Val-Kill furniture factory, to set up a center to preserve Appalachian handicrafts. She was able to inspire generous Democrats, like financier Bernard M. Baruch, to contribute to Arthurdale. She prevailed upon a well-to-do friend, Dorothy Elmhirst, a founder of the *New Republic* magazine, to donate funds for a small hospital and clinic and gave money of her own for them. Eleanor personally shopped for appliances and plumbing to install in Arthurdale homesteads.

Determined to resettle the miners before cold weather set in, the ailing Howe, described as "a man who sensed that he was in a race with death," hurriedly ordered fifty prefabricated houses.[35] Suitable for summer housing in New England, but not sturdy enough to withstand the cold of a West Virginia winter, the houses, which did not fit the foundations built for them, represented the first of a series of bureaucratic mistakes that beset the Arthurdale project. In defending the effort later, Hickok declared that "these house were infinitely better than the filthy, rat-ridden, tumble-down shacks in Scotts Run. Each family was given a cow, a pig, some chickens and seed to plant for a garden."[36]

Critics of Arthurdale complained that Eric Gugler, the Roosevelts' architect friend whom Eleanor consulted about redecorating historic rooms in the White House, received too much pay to modify foundations and upgrade the prefabricated houses.[37] Further unfavorable publicity resulted from the construction of 115 more substantial homes, which cost $10,000 a unit, far more than estimated. Their high price for the times stemmed mainly from Eleanor's insistence that the homes have electricity, plumbing, and refrigerators, even though many rural homes lacked these amenities in the 1930s. In addition, drilling to secure a supply of pure water proved expensive due to site topography.[38] Ickes, under whose domain Arthurdale fell, complained in his diary, "Mrs. Roosevelt took the Reedsville project under her protective wing with the result that we have been spending money down there like drunken sailors." He pointed out that the project had been attacked in magazines and newspapers, and that the administration was "distinctly on the defensive about it."[39]

In her championship of the relocated miners, Eleanor found herself forced to overlook their prejudices against sharing their new community with African Americans. White homesteaders displayed intense opposition to proposals to include African Americans even though they had worked in the mines alongside whites who had been resettled. In response Eleanor organized a White House dinner on 26 January 1934 with Pickett, White, and other prominent African American leaders to discuss New Deal racial policies. The meeting demonstrated Eleanor's personal commitment to equal participation by African Americans in federally funded programs, but it had no effect on Arthurdale itself. The new community remained segregated, a tacit admission of both the limitations of the role of the first lady and her forced acquiescence to political reality.

Attempts to attract industry for Arthurdale generated as much as or more opposition than the housing expenditures. Congressional critics, both Republicans and Democrats, complained bitterly that the administration was undercutting private enterprise by attempting to ensure that the relocated miners would be able to make their livelihood through a combination of subsistence farming and small-scale manufacturing. Their opposition defeated efforts by the Public Works Administration to allocate $525,000 to the U.S. Post Office Department to set up a factory in Arthurdale to produce post-office boxes and other postal equipment. William A. Wirt, an Indiana school superintendent who feared the Roosevelt administration was plotting a Communist takeover of the country, and a blind senator from Minnesota, Thomas D. Schall, joined forces to complain that the first lady was wasting $25 million in taxpayers' money to establish a "West Virginia commune."[40]

To help overcome opposition Eleanor called on Baruch, a wealthy Jewish speculator on Wall Street and her longtime acquaintance, to use his influence with Congress on behalf of the Arthurdale proposal. In World War I Washington, before Eleanor had sought a public career and overcome the common anti-Semitism of the day, she had found it distasteful to attend a party for Baruch. She wrote to Franklin's mother, Sara, "The Jew party [was] appalling. I never wish to hear money, jewels and . . . sables mentioned again."[41] By the time she reached the White House, Eleanor had broadened her outlook far beyond the narrow confines of her social class and developed alliances with those of different background.

She outgrew prejudices in part through her close association with Elinor Morgenthau, who sometimes accompanied Eleanor on visits to Arthurdale. The wife of Henry Morgenthau, who was Franklin's secretary of the treasury, Elinor had interests in social welfare similar to Eleanor's. The well-to-do Morgenthaus lived near Hyde Park on a cattle and apple farm and were the only Jewish family the Roosevelts were intimate with socially.[42] Elinor Morgenthau worked with Eleanor in the women's division of the New York State Democratic Party and was her frequent companion in Washington on early morning horseback rides in Rock Creek Park. The two women enjoyed going to the theater together in New York and often dined there at the exclusive Colony Club. When Eleanor proposed her friend for membership in 1937, both women were shocked when Morgenthau was blackballed because she was Jewish. Eleanor quietly resigned in protest.[43]

According to the Morgenthaus' son, his mother worked hard at maintaining her friendship with Eleanor. Commenting that both parents "retained footholds in the separate and sometimes rivalrous Roosevelt camps," Henry Morgenthau III attributed this to his mother's "diplomatic finesse."[44] Recognizing that Eleanor felt "trapped in the White House and was eager to roam the country in the mutually satisfying [to her and her husband] role of the president's eyes and ears," Morgenthau said that his mother was "ever enthusiastically available" to be Eleanor's companion, but that, unlike some of Eleanor's other intimates, she avoided being consumed by the first lady's need for emotional support.[45]

To some degree tensions in Eleanor's friendships stemmed not only from her emotional makeup, but from the fact that she was the president's wife and a conduit to the power of the presidency. If Eleanor used friendships to promote causes to which she was committed, like Arthurdale, some viewed the friends involved as acting from ulterior motives. This was true in the case of Eleanor's relationship with Baruch, who became a chief benefactor of Arthurdale.

After Franklin was elected president, Eleanor sought a political alliance with Baruch, whose hard-line conservative views gave him credibility with southern Democrats on Capitol Hill. Baruch and Franklin had a stressful relationship, based on both respect and distrust, but Eleanor and Baruch "needed, used and enjoyed each other," according to a Baruch biographer.[46] Two Roosevelt sons, James and Elliott, put it more uncharitably, claiming that Baruch's "infiltrating the White House" resulted from the fact that he "got to father through mother."[47] Baruch's involvement in Arthurdale served as one means for the financier, who yearned to be a presidential power broker and advisor, to retain his influence with the White House.

At Eleanor's invitation Baruch attended the official opening ceremonies on 7 June 1934 for both Arthurdale and Tygart Valley, a similar West Virginia homestead community, and told reporters on the train back to Washington about the "joyous faces" of the homesteaders.[48] His praise for the resettlement efforts helped create newspaper headlines like this one from the *Washington Herald*: "Homesteaders Wildly Cheer for First Lady."[49] When Congress did not appropriate funds to provide an industry for Arthurdale, Eleanor used Baruch's influence to get a General Electric subsidiary to open a vacuum cleaner assembly plant there. It did not succeed in obtaining orders and soon closed.

Baruch made generous contributions to Arthurdale's progressive six-building school complex, which included child-care facilities and a community center and lay close to Eleanor's heart. His financial support eventually diminished, as his doubts increased that the community would ever succeed economically. During World War II, however, he helped arrange for an aircraft factory to be located there. By earmarking earnings from her sponsored radio broadcasts for Arthurdale, Eleanor herself donated to both the school and the handicraft center that Cook had established.

In 1934 and 1935 Eleanor and Baruch together provided more than $50,000 for the school complex and $40,000 for the handicraft program.[50] However, by 1936, local authorities took charge of Arthurdale's schools, and the progressive experiment ended, partly because the high school had difficulty gaining state accreditation. In addition, Arthurdale residents were not attuned to progressive educational methods and wanted more traditional schooling for their children.

Eleanor herself never lost interest in the community, attending every school graduation there from 1935 to 1944 and persuading

Franklin to speak at the first commencement of the high school in 1938.[51] She invited Arthurdale residents to the White House and paid frequent visits to the community, "serving like a shot of adrenaline" according to a home economics teacher there, who remembered years later how the first lady had "frequently knitted when she attended an informal meeting or social gathering."[52]

In 1935 Rexford G. Tugwell, an economist who became head of the new Resettlement Administration that year, branded Arthurdale a financial failure in congressional testimony along with eight other subsistence homestead communities out of a total of thirty-seven. In contrast Eleanor refused to view Arthurdale in monetary terms. She could not understand why politicians, including Democrats, haggled over investments in people, especially since they spent so many millions to benefit industry, agriculture, businesses, and the military.[53]

Arthurdale consisted of some 165 homes and related community facilities when the government sold it, mainly to residents, in 1947 at a loss of $2 million.[54] Calling attention to Arthurdale's development into a middle-class community today, Cook argued that Eleanor's interest in human goals led her to spurn a "cost-accounting approach" in favor of government-assisted human development.[55] Arthurdale represented the first effort by a president's wife to become intimately involved in a tax-supported effort for social betterment, although critics ridiculed the attempt.[56]

Eleanor's interest in social conditions placed her in the forefront of liberals seeking to improve the segregated city of Washington comprising the District of Columbia surrounding the White House. Less than a week after moving into her new home, Eleanor took a tour of the capital's notorious alley dwellings. Charlotte Hopkins, a Washington society figure who had crusaded for two decades against unsanitary housing mainly occupied by African Americans, showed Eleanor vile tenements that lacked access to running water, indoor plumbing, and garbage collection.[57] As first lady Eleanor tried as best she could to eliminate these disease-breeding slums.[58]

Named honorary president of the Washington Housing Association, she worked for better housing with existing organizations, including the National Capital Park and Planning Commission, chaired by Frederic A. Delano, Franklin's uncle.[59] Franklin himself declined to support a bill to do away with alley dwellings in 1933 as inconsistent with his financial program. A subsequent bill did gain administration approval "in accordance with Mrs. Roosevelt's suggestion."[60] Still, the effort to replace Washington's alley slums with decent housing lagged for years.

Eleanor crossed the barriers that separated the nation's capital into two cities—one white and one black. She spoke at Howard University, an African American institution, and at African American churches. She participated in a rally for the March of Dimes, an effort to raise money to fight infantile paralysis, at the segregated Lincoln Theater, center of Washington's "Black Broadway" district.[61] She toured the Industrial Home for Colored Children at Blue Plains as well as the Industrial Home in Georgetown, which was limited to white children, in her attempt to call attention to deplorable conditions at public homes and hospitals.

After a visit to Freedmen's Hospital, the teaching hospital for Howard University Medical School, she reported to her press conference on 14 February 1938, "Like so many other things in the District, the physical equipment is very poor, with the result that when the physical equipment is poor in Gallinger Hospital [for white patients], it's too bad for the District. But when it is poor in Freedmen's Hospital, it's too bad for the country at large." She pointed out that Howard University had one of only two "adequate" medical schools for African Americans in the nation and that "fifty percent of the Negro doctors and nurses throughout the country" received their training at Freedmen's.[62] Her support for Howard helped secure more appropriations for the private university, which receives federal funding.

Eleanor's interest in the improvement of District facilities led her to back local self-government (termed home rule). She argued against the unfair treatment of District of Columbia residents who paid taxes but lacked voting rights or representation in Congress. She recognized the inherent problem of having residents governed by a board of three commissioners appointed by the president and dependent on the mercy of a Congress that controlled the District's budget and took little interest in the welfare of residents, even though some worked as domestic servants for congressional families. Eleanor's efforts to focus attention on the District of Columbia's underfunded and neglected institutions led her to become the first president's wife to actually testify before Congress, after initially hesitating to do so. In 1934 she told a Citizens Committee on Old-Age Security, "I could not possibly accept invitations to testify before congressional committees," but as time went by, she reversed her stand.[63]

On 10 February 1940, wearing what her journalist friend Ruby Black described as a "dashing hat with a curled and trailing green ostrich plume," Eleanor took the witness chair before a subcommittee of the House District Committee examining public institutions to argue that voting rights for Washington residents would lead to civic improvements.[64] Newspapers quoted her as saying that home rule was essential to bringing the city's "long-neglected institutions up-to-date."[65] Since men selected by Franklin ran the District government, she avoided direct criticism of it. Franklin himself had little interest in local concerns and opposed home rule.

In her autobiography Eleanor expressed annoyance at Franklin's refusal to act on behalf of African Americans, even though he personally favored both the antilynching bill and legislation to remove the poll tax, widely used in the South to keep African Americans from voting. Yet, she did not think it her place to openly counter his views. She wrote, "I felt he was in a position to evaluate the essentials of his program and that I had no right to endanger that program by any action of mine."[66] Franklin clearly stayed in charge, and Eleanor accepted his decisions even when they met with her disapproval.

In 1935, as Franklin prepared to run for a second term the following year, Eleanor sent Hickok, who frequently critiqued her magazine submissions, a manuscript that explored the question of whether a woman could be elected president. Eager to meet a deadline at *Cosmopolitan*, then a general-interest women's magazine, she submitted the article to the editors before Hickok could respond.[67] "The feminists will be down on me and a lot of people will say it is camouflaged political partisan material and in a way it is!" she told Hickok.[68] Her conclusion—that women needed more experience before aspiring to the highest office—did not resonate well with many of her friends.

After detailing virtually superhuman attributes needed by a successful president, Eleanor stated in the article, "I am enormously interested in the contributions which women can make to the advancement of the world, but this does not blind me to the fact that there are things so far which men have been better trained to do by custom and experience."[69] She called on women to continue to network to gain experience in public life and declared that they should not take positions "before they are prepared to fill them. . . . We will not do well to rush unprepared into action."[70] Speculation that she harbored ambitions to run for the presidency herself may have led her to write the article, which presumably squelched such reports.[71]

The article also implied her opposition to the Equal Rights Amendment sought by the National Woman's Party. If women were not ready to vie directly with men for high political office, it followed that they had need of protection. As Eleanor put it, both men and women still felt that "man is the natural defender and the natural bearer of burdens."[72] She could not reconcile her view of women's special status with a proposed constitutional amendment that required legal equality.

Her conviction that women workers deserved protective legislation led her to oppose the reappointment of Doris Stevens, a member of the National Woman's Party, to the Inter-American Commission of Women in 1939, although Eleanor took no responsibility for Stevens's ouster. When the *New York Times* claimed that Eleanor had been behind the replacement of Stevens with Mary Winslow, a member of the Women's Trade Union League (WTUL), a strong backer of protective legislation, the first lady told her press conference, disingenuously, "It is my practice never to propose anybody for anything," although she admitted passing on suggestions for appointments that came her way.[73]

Even in matters of women's representation Eleanor clung to a public fiction that her opinion carried little weight. She presented her frequent travels to the public as fact-finding trips for a president so incapacitated, as well as busy, that it was difficult for him to leave Washington, but she never presented herself as a decision maker in the administration. Perhaps she considered it impolitic to claim influence under any circumstance. Most Americans at the time appeared to agree with Eleanor when she contended in *It's Up to the Women* that "women are different from men. . . . Their physical functions in life are different and perhaps . . . the contributions which they . . . bring to the spiritual side of life are different."[74] She seemed to hold to the idea that women were separate—and perhaps morally better—than men, but she did not present them as equals.

In reality, Eleanor separated Franklin as a husband and father from the role of heroic statesman that her article claimed a president should be. Furious with him for bringing their eldest son, James, into the White House in 1937 as his secretary and advisor following the death of Howe, Eleanor foresaw accusations of nepotism, which soon occurred. She also feared that James, not yet thirty years old, would flounder in his new responsibilities, an assessment that proved accurate when James left the post in 1938 following surgery for stress-related ulcers. In addition, James's wife, Betsy Cushing Roosevelt, flirted outrageously with Franklin and ignored Eleanor, further upsetting the dynamic between the president and first lady.[75] Holding her tongue, Eleanor sometimes took refuge in icy coldness, but said she did not express herself openly to her husband.

Writing Hickok, to whom she had expressed disappointment in 1935 when Franklin's proposed Social Security and WPA legislation discriminated against African Americans, Eleanor burst out, "I know I've got to stick. I know I'll never make an open break and I never tell FDR how I feel. . . . I blow off to you but never to F! . . . I'm never likely to fight with F. I always 'shut up.'"[76] She compensated for her frustrations by using her position as first lady to carry on her own career as a writer and public commentator while she advocated for the causes in which she believed.

On ceremonial occasions and holidays, particularly Christmas, she presented herself as a traditional wife and mother in the White House. In common with Franklin, she loved Christmas, which the Roosevelts made a three-day festival highlighted by Franklin's reading of Dickens's *Christmas Carol* to his family on Christmas Eve.[77] All year long, Eleanor stocked up on Christmas presents for friends, family, and employees, keeping them in a special closet. Christmas meant a fresh spruce tree lit by real candles, at Franklin's insistence, and parties for staff and Secret Service personnel including their families. Eleanor found time to sing carols at a communal Christmas tree set up in the Washington slums and noted that "as I looked at the poor people about me I could not help wondering what Christmas could mean to those children."[78]

Franklin and Eleanor celebrate Christmas at the White House in 1939 with members of their multigeneration family who have joined them for the holiday. This picture, taken on Christmas Day, shows from left to right (seated): Eleanor; Sara Delano Roosevelt, Franklin's mother; Ethel de Pont Roosevelt, wife of son Franklin D. Jr., holding Franklin D. III; Franklin; daughter Anna Roosevelt Boettiger, holding her son John; Elizabeth R. Roosevelt, the widow of Franklin's half-brother, James "Rosy" Roosevelt; Anna Roosevelt, wife of son John; (standing): son Franklin D. Jr., son John, son-in-law John Boettiger. Seated on floor: granddaughter Eleanor "Sistie" Dall, Anna's daughter; Diana Hopkins, daughter of Harry Hopkins, then living at the White House; and grandson Curtis "Bussie" Dall Jr., Anna's son. Courtesy of the Franklin D. Roosevelt Library, Hyde Park, New York.

Eleanor's recognition of flaws in the Social Security Act that Franklin signed into law on 14 August 1935 increased her determination to speak up for deprived groups. Because large categories of workers, including agricultural and domestic employees, were not covered, 80 percent of African American women and 60 percent of African American men were excluded from old-age pensions and unemployment benefits along with 60 percent of white women.[79]

Although women, particularly Frances Perkins, played major roles in the creation of Social Security legislation, the sexist premise that men constituted primary breadwinners and women secondary wage earners, who did not need as much coverage, underlay the new law. While praising Social Security as a major step forward taken largely through the efforts of women activists, Eleanor urged the broadening of benefits in her speeches and newspaper columns.[80] She recognized that politics sometimes meant taking gradual steps toward desired goals.[81]

Although she subordinated herself to Franklin's leadership, Eleanor became the first president's wife to be acknowledged in public as a significant political player by journalists and political figures, if not by herself. Clearly recognizing that her husband, not she, had been elected to office, she exercised influence through her access to administration decision makers and her opportunities to sway public opinion via mass communications. Drawing on her background in politics in New York State, Eleanor maneuvered her way among Franklin's advisors in Washington who subscribed to her point of view.

In doing so she kept in frequent contact with a network of women activists, spearheaded by Molly Dewson in her role as director of the women's division of the Democratic National Committee at the time of Franklin's first inauguration. Dewson relied on Eleanor to act as an intermediary with the men who controlled patronage, particularly James Farley, who served as postmaster general during Franklin's first two terms.[82] Dewson's successors, Carolyn Wolfe, women's division director from 1934 to 1936, and Dorothy McAlister, director from 1936 to 1940, also counted on Eleanor's assistance. After Dewson stepped down as director, she remained head of the women's division advisory committee until 1937.

As first lady, Eleanor occupied the central place in a sisterhood of Washington politics that included a closely knit group, many of whom had backgrounds in the woman suffrage campaign and social welfare work along with a history of loyalty to the Democratic Party.[83] Some twenty-eight of these talented, well-educated women, many related by marriage or birth to male political figures, held positions in the administration and the Democratic Party in the 1930s. Secretary of Labor Perkins stood out as the first woman cabinet member. Lesser-known individuals included Josephine Aspinwall Roche, appointed assistant secretary of the treasury in 1934, where she oversaw the U.S. Public Health Service, then part of the treasury department, and Jo Coffin, assistant public printer, a member of the WTUL, who had helped Eleanor set up a center for unemployed women in New York City in 1932–1933.[84]

Among the sisterhood Eleanor's old friend, Mary Harriman Rumsey, was appointed chair of the consumers' advisory board of the National Recovery Administration (NRA) in 1933. Declared unconstitutional two years later to the chagrin of New Deal advocates, the NRA promoted economic recovery through government/business cooperation that created industry-wide codes to fix prices. Rumsey headed the board charged with protecting consumer interests. Sue Shelton White served as assistant chair, a position secured after Dewson appealed to Eleanor to find a place for White, a lawyer, who had worked in the women's division of the Democratic Party.[85] Another assistant, Emily Newell Blair, a veteran Democratic Committeewoman, had worked in Franklin's 1932 campaign.

A railroad heiress who had cofounded the Junior League, a social service organization for debutantes, Rumsey, a widow, shared a house with Frances Perkins in Washington. Both of them served on the National Emergency Council, a coordinating body for New Deal agencies. Recognizing the potential for industry to advance itself at the expense of the public, Eleanor took a personal interest in strengthening consumer representation in the NRA. Her efforts prompted Rumsey to write to her, "I wish I could tell you or that *you knew* how much you have helped the whole range of consumer problems and policies."[86]

The ties between the two women went back many years. As a young woman Rumsey had brought Eleanor into the Junior League. Under its auspices she had taught calisthenics and dancing at the Rivington Street settlement house on New York's Lower East Side during the winter of 1903–1904, before her formal engagement to Franklin. Although her death following a fox-hunting accident in 1934 cut short Rumsey's Washington career, she brought her brother, Averell Harriman, a former schoolmate of Eleanor's brother Hall, into the NRA as an administrator. He became one of FDR's inner circle, serving as an envoy to England and ambassador to the Soviet

Union during World War II. Eleanor's warmth toward Harriman cooled after he developed a friendship with Harry Hopkins at a time when Eleanor thought Hopkins had deserted social welfare goals to push military aims, but the family connection remained in place.

Perkins saw to it that another friend of Eleanor's was appointed to an NRA advisory board. Rose Schneiderman, president of the WTUL, served on its labor advisory board, which oversaw the efforts of unions to organize in industries covered by NRA codes. Schneiderman also accompanied Eleanor and Hickok on their 1934 trip to Puerto Rico and the Virgin Islands to inspect labor conditions there, especially among women needleworkers. In the 1920s Schneiderman had introduced Eleanor to working-class issues and organized labor. Franklin too expanded his horizons due to contacts with Schneiderman and her friend, Maud Swartz, another WTUL leader, who frequently visited Eleanor. In fact, Perkins attributed Franklin's knowledge of the union movement to "the knowledge he had gained from these girls."[87]

In her NRA post Schneiderman represented women workers, calling her service there "the high spot" of her career.[88] This referred to the fact that the NRA codes required minimum hourly wages that benefited women workers, who traditionally received lower pay than men. Written into the Fair Labor Standards Act of 1938, after the NRA went out of existence, these provisions remained in force. The 1938 act also outlawed child labor, a goal of Eleanor and other women activists for many years.

Under Perkins other New Deal women held significant jobs in the Department of Labor. Mary LaDame, an industrial researcher, was made associate director of the U.S. Employment Service and special assistant to the secretary. Clara M. Beyer became associate director of the Division of Labor Standards. In the 1920s she had worked with Dewson at the National Consumers' League, an organization that investigated the working conditions of laboring people. Eleanor had joined the league before her marriage and subscribed to its principles even though her activism centered on other organizations. But Perkins declined to appoint an African American woman, as Eleanor requested, to a position in the Women's Bureau, which was in the Department of Labor, citing the prevailing climate of prejudice.[89]

The daughter of a Wisconsin senator, Katharine Lenroot took over as chief of the Children's Bureau in 1934 following the departure of Grace Abbott, a Republican who had been considered sympathetic to the New Deal, although she had been appointed in the Harding era. Taking a special interest in child welfare, Eleanor invited the field staff of the Children's Bureau to the White House. Lenroot sent her a thank-you note: "The opportunity for informal discussion of problems with Mrs. Roosevelt following the delightful tea was the highlight of the conference."[90]

The political sisterhood also included women connected with the National Woman's Democratic Club (NWDC), organized in Washington in 1922 to bring together Democratic women. Eleanor had been a charter nonresident member and as first lady served as the honorary president. The club's cofounder, Florence ("Daisy") Jaffrey Harriman, the widow of a cousin of Averell and Mary Harriman, was named U.S. minister to Norway from 1937 to 1941, even though she had not supported Franklin in 1932. Another club founder, Marion Glass Banister, was appointed assistant treasurer of the United States in 1933, remaining in that post until 1951. The NWDC published the *Democratic Digest*, a magazine for Democratic women, until 1935, when the publication was taken over by the women's division of the Democratic Party. Eleanor wrote frequently for the magazine, which had a paid circulation of 20,000 by 1938, and it highlighted her activities.

Eleanor quickly learned that being the president's wife gave her a platform to advocate for both individuals and causes in which she believed. She used her position behind the scenes to recruit women for the administration and to insist that their voices be heard by male superiors. With their backgrounds in suffrage and reform efforts, many of Eleanor's women acquaintances gained jobs in New Deal agencies set up to alleviate social distress. These included the Federal Emergency Relief Administration (FERA), the Works Progress Administration (WPA), and, from 1935 on, the Social Security Administration (SSA). Jane Hoey, a social worker, organized the Bureau of Public Assistance of the SSA, where she worked from 1936 to 1953. Eleanor helped see to Molly Dewson's appointment to the Social Security Board in 1937, although ill health forced her resignation after one year. Another member of the women's network, Lucy

Somerville Howorth, a Mississippi lawyer, was named to the Board of Appeals of the Veterans Administration, where she served from 1934 to 1950.[91]

In addition, Eleanor represented a friend in high places to political women who already had established themselves in Washington. Ruth Bryan Owen, who had served two terms in Congress, was selected as minister to Denmark in 1933, making her the first woman to hold a major diplomatic post. Daughter of the famed orator and unsuccessful Democratic presidential candidate William Jennings Bryan, Owen had hoped to be appointed secretary of the interior.[92] Eleanor, who had sought to place her in an important position, hosted a dinner for 800 in her honor after she received the diplomatic assignment as a consolation prize.[93] Mary Anderson, a Republican who headed the Women's Bureau of the Department of Labor from 1920 to 1944, recalled that "during the years of the Roosevelt administration, I felt much closer to the White House [than before] because of Mrs. Roosevelt's interest and friendship."[94] Eleanor and Anderson first had become acquainted through their mutual involvement in the WTUL.

Speaking at the Democratic national convention in 1936, Congresswoman Mary T. Norton of New Jersey, another member of the network, emphasized that the administration had given women "a new freedom because a just President in appointing them to high offices and places of distinction has given them more courage and faith in themselves."[95] While this may have been true, it obscured the fact that the group faced formidable obstacles in a male-dominated political world. Impressive in terms of background, education, and commitment to social welfare, New Deal women still represented a small number of individuals in policymaking roles.

As a group, the women pushed two particular causes. They opposed the Equal Rights Amendment advocated by the National Woman's Party because they supported protective legislation for working women. Since the National Woman's Party, an outgrowth of the radical wing of the suffrage campaign, had relatively little influence in Congress in the 1930s, the women found it reasonably easy to block this proposal.

A far greater challenge was defeating Section 213 of the 1932 National Economy Act, which barred both husband and wife from working for the federal government, in effect forcing the resignation of women because they made less money than their husbands. It resulted in the ouster of 1,600 married female government workers from 1932 to 1937, over the objections of the Government Workers' Council, which comprised many of the New Deal women who appealed to Franklin without success to back repeal of this legislation.[96] A disappointed Dewson wrote Eleanor in 1936, "poor harassed man he has let me down."[97] Section 213 finally was repealed in 1937. The slowness of the repeal effort demonstrated the difficulties New Deal women faced within the Democratic Party itself, even though they worked hard in Franklin's reelection campaign of 1936. Like Eleanor herself, they realized they remained secondary players in politics.

Within nine months of entering the White House, Eleanor used what clout she had as first lady to call attention to the plight of unemployed women. Her first official White House Conference, designated a Conference on the Emergency Needs of Women, held on 2 November 1933, featured speeches by Hopkins and his assistant, Ellen Woodward, who had been put in charge of women's relief programs at Eleanor's urging. As one of her first acts Woodward, who had met Eleanor in 1932 when she was Mississippi's national committeewoman for the Democratic Party, called on Eleanor to host the conference and Eleanor responded.[98]

At the White House gathering Hopkins promised that some 300,000 women would be placed in work projects by the year's end, but there were no guarantees of equality.[99] Projects often involved traditional female tasks such as sewing and canning for which women received less pay than men employed in relief jobs, on grounds that men were breadwinners. After Eleanor pointed out in December 1933 that women on relief received less for skilled work in sewing, nursing, and teaching than men doing unskilled labor, reporters questioned Hopkins about women's pay. He replied, "Yes, I know it's lower. We think that's right."[100]

Although disappointed when Franklin did not move as far as she thought he should on social welfare projects, Eleanor realistically knew that it was better to do what she could than to insist on all or nothing. From the 1933 conference onward until 1938, when Woodward left the WPA, which succeeded FERA, Eleanor backed Woodward's efforts to broaden women's relief projects. They eventually enrolled nearly 470,000 individuals at their peak in 1936.[101]

About half of the women were placed in libraries, museums, schools, and other sites of professional activity, while the other half were assigned to sewing rooms and training programs for housemaids. Both Eleanor and Woodward championed training for domestic workers because they wanted to see the occupation of maid turn into a skilled one.[102] Since 1928 Eleanor had been honorary chair of the National Committee on Household Employment, which tried to elevate domestic service.[103] Woodward considered Eleanor jointly responsible with her for women's relief programs, even though disparities remained between men and women in qualifications and compensation. In later years Woodward wrote Eleanor, "You deserve the major credit."[104]

In addition, Eleanor showed special interest in projects to save American handiwork in line with her efforts at the Val-Kill furniture factory and to back the arts in general. Through Eleanor's patronage in 1936 Woodward was given charge of a special Four Arts program for writers, artists, musicians, and actors, in which women were well represented. The previous year Eleanor had helped convince Hallie Flanagan, founder of an experimental theater at Vassar College, to head the Federal Theatre Project (FTP) of the WPA. The FTP put actors to work performing creative entertainment, including Living Newspaper documentaries dealing with Depression conditions.[105]

Conscious of the blatant discrimination by the WPA against African American women, who were underrepresented both in relief jobs and as supervisory personnel, Eleanor and Woodward joined forces in 1938 to make New Deal agencies more aware of the needs of minority women. They acted at the request of Mary McLeod Bethune, a New Deal appointee and president of the National Council of Negro Women, who was Eleanor's closest African American woman advisor. Eleanor invited some fifty representatives of Bethune's organization to meet with administration officials at a White House Conference on Participation of Negro Women and Children in Federal Welfare Programs on 4 April 1938.[106]

To their disappointment little resulted from the conference because by that time congressional budget-cutters were chopping away at New Deal programs.[107] The conference had been a partial follow-up to a similar one held the preceding year on the Problems of the Negro and Negro Youth. Although it did not meet in the White House, Eleanor had been the keynote speaker. When Bethune presented the conference report to Franklin, she said that the first lady's presence represented the first time the federal government had shown significant concern for African American citizens.[108]

Her comment illustrated the way in which both Eleanor and Franklin depended on each other's strengths as communicators to project symbolic messages that affected the lives of ordinary Americans through the political process. With his jaunty manner and insistence that all the nation had to fear was its own fear of the future, Franklin, forced by his own physical disability to develop optimism in order to lead a productive life, worked to restore confidence in democracy. Eleanor, the product of a troubled childhood who felt betrayed by her husband, identified with those in need and pushed Franklin toward social reforms. Tugwell, the presidential advisor, recalled, "No one who ever saw Eleanor Roosevelt sit down facing her husband, and, holding his eye firmly, say to him, 'Franklin, I think you should . . .' or 'Franklin, surely you will not . . .' will ever forget the experience. . . . It would be impossible to say how often and to what extent American governmental processes have been turned in new directions because of her determination that people should be hurt as little as possible."[109]

Franklin served as a father figure to a nation desperate for reassurance. Eleanor, with her talent for communicating with average individuals, presented a motherly image of caring for the unfortunate. Her skill in forming coalitions, particularly among women and African Americans, complemented Franklin's leadership, while her abilities at gathering information and reporting what she learned from her frequent travels provided him with a fresh pair of eyes and ears. In short, she proved herself an indispensable element of the New Deal presidency.[110]

In accustoming herself to being first lady and deciding where to concentrate her efforts, Eleanor drew on personal relationships with those outside her family, as she built her own career from a White House platform. Although she maintained extensive networks of women in politics, social reform, and journalism, she depended heavily on a few intimate friends in Washington—among them Tommy, her loyal secretary; Hickok, her chief confidante in the early days of the New Deal; and then Joseph P. Lash, a radical young graduate of Columbia University who stimulated her interest in leftist student movements in the late 1930s. Although close to Hopkins when he oversaw relief efforts during Franklin's first two terms, Eleanor, unlike Franklin, had no formal advisors, with the exception of Howe. Eager for affection, she was guided by her individual associates, as well as her own predilections, in selecting programs that drew the greatest share of her attention.

Long before she developed an intense friendship with Lash, the leader of left-wing student movements who eventually became her biographer, Eleanor used her White House platform to assist young people, both men and women, who faced economic hardship. Her concern represented a logical extension of her long-standing leaning toward social work, as well as her recognition of the social dynamite posed by millions of youth both out of school and out of work. "I have moments of real terror, when I think we may be losing this generation," she told the *New York Times* in May 1934, explaining, "We have got to bring these young people into the active life of the community and make them feel that they are necessary."[111]

As the primary ambassador of the New Deal, Eleanor visited Civilian Conservation Corps camps, popular relief efforts to put unemployed young men to work on tree planting and other conservation projects in the countryside. Eleanor thought them too militaristic, because they were run by the army.[112] Although she sought somewhat similar opportunities for young women in the interest of fairness, her real passion lay in a broader program for all needy youth that would be similar to a national service corps. She was seen as the guiding spirit behind creation of the National Youth Administration (NYA), set up in 1935 as part of the work-relief program of the WPA, the New Deal's main relief agency.

Before the NYA existed, to support relief for young women, Eleanor hosted a White House Conference on Camps for Unemployed Women. This conference, held on 30 April 1934, helped push through Congress a proposal for what became known as "she-she-she" camps. In advocating the camps, Eleanor worked with Hilda

Worthington Smith, a FERA official and former head of the Bryn Mawr Summer School for Women Workers, where Eleanor's friend, Marion Dickerman, had taught in the 1920s.[113] Constrained politically by traditional ideas of preparing young women for marriage, women's camps offered only brief stays for limited vocational guidance, in contrast to CCC camps, which provided jobs and education.

Eleanor picked out one women's facility, Camp Tera in New York near Bear Mountain, as her favorite cause and donated money and materials to it. By 1936, ninety camps served some 5,000 women under the umbrella of the NYA, a much more ambitious program, but all women's camps were closed in 1937 due to budget cuts.[114] By contrast the CCC camps enrolled half a million men at their peak in 1935 and lasted until 1942.

Eleanor's name long has been attached to the NYA, although historians disagree on precisely what part she played in its creation. Franklin himself called it the "Missus organization."[115] Eleanor was certainly involved in planning for it. The NYA offered work-study grants to young people in high school or college so they could remain in school and aided those who had dropped out with relief jobs that aimed to provide training of lasting value. Eleanor stated in her autobiography that she presented the idea to Franklin at the request of Hopkins, who by that time had become head of the WPA, and Aubrey Williams, the associate director, a liberal Alabama social worker with whom she had spoken repeatedly about the plight of unemployed youth.

Hopkins and Williams apparently feared that a targeted youth program would be politically unpopular in view of youth organizations being set up in Germany by Hitler. Unwilling to approach Franklin directly on the issue, they asked Eleanor to intercede for them with her husband. To gain his approval, Eleanor wrote, "I waited until my usual time for discussing questions with him and went into Franklin's room just before he went to sleep." According to her, Franklin asked, "Do you think it is right to do this?" When she replied affirmatively but pointed out possible political pitfalls, she said he simply answered, "If it is the right thing to do for the young people, then it should be done."[116]

Some scholars of the NYA claim that this account is too simplistic—

that Franklin was committed to a youth program before Eleanor talked to him and that he had received plans for it from Williams, a social worker who became its first head.[117] Regardless of Eleanor's exact role in the formation of the NYA, she and Williams worked together as a team, corresponding frequently about the agency. Williams, who called Eleanor "the greatest person I have ever known," responded positively to her involvement, which included recommendations for hiring and establishing contacts with members of its national advisory board.[118] A well-received program that eventually touched the lives of some five million young people before its end in 1943, when there were more jobs than workers to fill them during World War II, the NYA nevertheless faced opposition from critics who disliked its liberal racial policies.

The association between Eleanor and Bethune turned the NYA into one of the few New Deal agencies that made a sustained effort to address the plight of African Americans.[119] Through her NYA position, which she owed to Eleanor, Bethune established a reputation as one of Eleanor's close political associates. Bethune was considered the most influential African American woman in the United States for three decades mainly as a result of her connection with the Roosevelt administration.[120]

The two women had become acquainted at a luncheon for women leaders hosted by Sara Roosevelt in 1927 at her home in Manhattan. At the time Bethune had been invited as president of the National Association of Colored Women. The head of what became Bethune-Cookman College in Daytona Beach, Florida, which she transformed from an institute teaching skills to African American girls into an accredited four-year coeducational college, Bethune founded the National Council of Negro Women in 1935. That same year Eleanor arranged for her to serve in an unpaid position on the NYA national advisory committees. The position allowed Bethune to develop a political partnership with the first lady that sensitized her to African American issues.

In 1936 Bethune took a paid job in charge of activities for African Americans in the youth agency. Three years later, as the NYA geared up to prepare young people for jobs in defense industries, Bethune was named director of the division of Negro affairs. She was the highest-ranking African American in the New Deal.[121]

The relationship between Eleanor and Bethune, one of seventeen children of an illiterate South Carolina sharecropper, symbolized Eleanor's commitment to civil rights in the face of New Deal inaction. Bethune, a charismatic personality who exercised powerful leadership, fought for more jobs and opportunities for African Americans in the NYA. While she gained the adoption of nondiscriminatory policies, the proportionate amount spent on African Americans still remained less than that spent on white youth.[122]

Through Eleanor, Bethune cultivated a friendship with Franklin, making her the only African American leader other than Walter White, executive secretary of the NAACP, who had access to the White House. As such Bethune formed the Federal Council on Negro Affairs, commonly known as the Black Cabinet, which met at her home. Made up of some two dozen African Americans who worked as administrators in cabinet departments and agencies, the council tried to sensitize the New Deal to the needs of African Americans and served to make African Americans more aware of the importance of the federal government.[123] Bethune stood out in the group not only for her gender—she was the sole woman—but also because of her dark complexion. Unlike White, who could have passed for Caucasian, and many other members of the Black Cabinet, Bethune had dark skin.

In part because of her skin color, Bethune enabled Eleanor to project an image of interracial cooperation that testified to the first lady's interest in African Americans and helped convince them to leave the Republican "Party of Lincoln" for the Democratic fold. Pictures of the two women visiting NYA sites, which often ran in African American newspapers, sent powerful messages in a period when many Caucasian politicians avoided being photographed in the company of African Americans.[124] Bethune accompanied Eleanor to the founding meeting of the Southern Conference on Human Welfare in Birmingham in 1938, where Eleanor refused to sit in a segregated section and placed her chair squarely in the aisle separating the races.[125]

Eleanor herself considered her friendship with Bethune a culminating moment in overcoming her own prejudices. Eleanor believed she had reached this point when she felt comfortable giving Bethune a kiss on the cheek like she gave her Caucasian friends.[126] To spare

Bethune embarrassment, after a White House gardener called her "Auntie," a term commonly used for African Americans in the South instead of "Miss" or "Mrs.," Eleanor would wait in the White House foyer for Bethune when she was scheduled to visit. When she appeared on the walkway, Eleanor would run to embrace her and escort her into the White House.[127]

Like Walter White, Bethune represented an older generation of African American leaders who had learned to accommodate themselves to the white world even as they pressed for equality. A younger African American who also influenced Eleanor's position on civil rights took a more militant stance. Pauli Murray, who had been excluded on grounds of race from the University of North Carolina, copied Eleanor on an angry letter she sent to Franklin in 1938 following his address there praising the university for its liberalism.[128] Moved to respond, Eleanor, who counseled Murray not to "push too hard," invited Murray to Hyde Park and learned from her that African American youth did not intend to put up with the injustices that had been inflicted on their parents.[129] Murray, who went on to have a distinguished career as a writer, legal scholar, and theologian, became Eleanor's lifelong friend. A leading women's rights advocate in the mid-twentieth century who later became an Episcopal priest, Murray was a founder of the National Organization of Women (NOW).

Eleanor's desire to reach out to Murray paralleled her response to leftist students like Joseph Lash who claimed the NYA offered only a Band-Aid for the wounds inflicted by the evil capitalist system. Instead of being offended by students who behaved discourteously, she sought to convince them to trust a reform-minded democratic government in place of radical ideologies and models from other nations. Eleanor found in Lash, an intellectual who was the son of Russian Jewish immigrants, a young man whose fundamental beliefs about economic and political justice strengthened her own interest in effecting social change. As their friendship developed over a period of years, Eleanor found in Lash a kindred spirit whose devotion surpassed that of her own sons.[130]

Lash, who earned a master's degree in literature and philosophy at Columbia University, had found it difficult to gain employment during the Depression and questioned the capitalist system. After a stint as secretary of the Socialist Party's Student League of Industrial Democracy, he served as national secretary of the American Student Union (ASU) from 1935 to 1939. During the late 1930s, he brought Eleanor into contact with the thinking of Communists and Socialists. Her long-standing concern for peace as well as economic and racial justice predisposed Eleanor to take seriously the ideas of the radical student movement, influenced by Marxist and pacifist teachings as well as liberal democratic thought. Like many idealists of her generation, her pacifist leanings stemmed from a conviction that World War I had been a disaster resulting from militaristic buildups.

Lash initially came to Eleanor's attention during the time that she and Bethune were visiting black communities together to inspect NYA projects. Eleanor first met him in January 1936 at a White House tea attended by representatives of the American Youth Congress (AYC), a broad-based group that included the ASU, as well as the Young Communist League and the Young Women's Christian Association. That event, subsequently labeled the "Red Tea" by her critics, led to charges that she was associating with Communists. When the "Red Tea," along with subsequent contacts with radical youth, came up at her press conference in 1939, she said that the youth she knew "as individuals . . . are not Communists." But, she said, there was "no reason" why Communists "should not be among a group who might come to tea," adding that "I frequently have Republicans to tea."[131]

Ironically, the AYC leadership had arrived in Washington to protest that the NYA, so closely associated with Eleanor, did not offer sufficient resources to aid young people. Instead, they proposed the American Youth Act, a $3.5 billion youth unemployment relief bill far more sweeping and expensive than the NYA.[132] The ASU, which mobilized 500,000 students for massive peace demonstrations in 1936 and 1937, exercised considerable influence in the AYC, with both organizations having a substantial number of Communist Party members in leadership roles. It took Eleanor several years, however, to realize that radical youth leaders concealed their Communist Party membership in their dealings with her.

The commitment to peace by the ASU and the AYC changed dramatically in 1937 after Joseph Stalin mandated the concept of the Popular Front. This called for democratic and Communist nations to unite against fascism in Europe. As a result leftist youth organizations sent members to fight in the Abraham Lincoln Brigade, which backed the Loyalist government in Spain as it tried unsuccessfully to defeat fascist rebels under General Francisco Franco from 1936 until 1939. Eleanor passionately supported the Loyalist side.[133] She advocated lifting the arms embargo that restricted shipment of U.S. weapons to the Loyalist government.

Endeavoring to work out an alliance with the militant students, by 1938 Eleanor was heavily involved with leftist activists. She addressed the World Youth Congress meeting in 1938 at Vassar College in Poughkeepsie, New York, only a few miles from Hyde Park. The conference brought leftist groups closer to the New Deal, which was looking for additional supporters in the face of conservative congressional opponents, who were eager to slash the budget for the NYA and other social programs.[134] Eleanor emerged as a significant link between the Left and the New Deal, although critics contended that she was advancing the Communist cause.[135]

Eleanor was perceived as heading a group of left-wing New Dealers, including Hopkins, Aubrey Williams, and Charles Taussig, head of the NYA national advisory committee, who were interested in preventing radicalism by democratic means. Her advocacy for the ASU and the AYC enhanced the stature of these organizations, as testified to by the fact that after she disavowed them, they quietly faded away. At the same time as she supported the controversial youth organizations, she grew more radical in her other associations, supporting left-wing groups such as the National Negro Congress, the Southern Tenant Farmers Union, and the Southern Conference for Human Welfare.[136]

Eleanor's most publicized assistance to the youth leaders occurred in November 1939 after she met Lash and other youth leaders by chance on a train ride from New York to Washington. When she learned they had been summoned by the House Un-American Activities Committee (HUAC) to answer charges that their movement was Communist-dominated, she offered her support. In her autobiography she wrote that she attended their HUAC hearing because she had heard that the committee engaged in hostile questioning of witnesses who lacked influence or backing. "When the questioning seemed to me to be particularly harsh, I asked to go over and sit at the press table. I took a pencil and a piece of paper, and the tone of the questions changed immediately. . . . my action had the effect I desired," she noted.[137] Concern about what she might say in her "My Day" column apparently made HUAC members tone down their questions.

Four months before the hearings, the Popular Front had fallen apart when the Soviet Union signed a nonaggression pact with Nazi Germany that disillusioned liberal opponents of fascism. After Germany and the Soviet Union invaded Poland in September 1939, Britain and France declared war on Germany, and World War II officially began, with the United States attempting to maintain neutrality. Following the Communist Party line, some leaders of the ASU and AYC turned against the New Deal and supported the nonaggression pact. Lash, who previously had been an admirer of communism's opposition to Franco, changed his position and became a leading non-Communist within the student movement.

Called upon to testify at the HUAC hearing, Lash evaded questions and gave flippant replies, disassociating himself from the nonaggression pact but not willing to publicly break with other youth leaders who falsely testified that their organizations were not controlled by Communists.[138] Eleanor sympathized with his predicament and invited him and other witnesses to the White House after the hearings. She gave special attention to Lash, urging him to use her Val-Kill cottage while he made plans for the future. He subsequently directed the youth division of Franklin's 1940 reelection campaign and worked as general secretary of the International Student Service, which sponsored student exchange visits, from 1940 to 1942. Eleanor hosted that organization's leadership training workshop in 1941 at the Roosevelt summer home on Campobello Island.

The friendship between Eleanor and Lash deepened, possibly because she saw Lash as a melancholy young man who needed her.[139] Lash himself explained: "Perhaps my miseries . . . reminded her of her own when she was young. Insecurity, shyness, lack of social grace, she had to conquer them all, and helping someone she cared about do the same filled a deep unquenchable longing to feel needed and useful."[140] She used her attachment to him as a stimulus for devotion to the cause of young people facing uncertain futures. It also met her emotional craving for a few intimate friends on whom she could lavish attention.[141]

Similar to her association with Hickok, Eleanor's relationship with Lash, whom conservatives considered a dangerous radical, raised eyebrows. False rumors of a salacious affair between the two spread during World War II and appeared in Eleanor's FBI file held by J. Edgar Hoover.[142] According to India Edwards, executive director of the Women's Division of the Democratic Party in the 1940s, "When Lash moved into the bedroom at the White House next to Eleanor's room that had been occupied by Lorena Hickok, there was gossip about an affair," which Edwards discounted.[143] Hickok had stopped staying at the White House before her work for Hopkins ended in 1936 and she became a publicist for the New York World's Fair. She moved back to the White House in 1941 when she took a job as executive secretary of the Women's Division of the Democratic Party, but she stayed in Louis Howe's old room, maintaining a fiction that she lived at the Mayflower Hotel where her office was.[144] By this time, Eleanor had grown far closer to Lash than to Hickok.

While Eleanor naïvely continued to support the radical student movement in the months ahead, Lash helped her understand the way Communists operated. When the AYC conducted a demonstration in Washington in February 1940 to demand U.S. neutrality, Eleanor maintained that the group acted from motives of pacifism rather than serving as puppets of the Soviet Union, which had joined Germany in overrunning Eastern Europe. She arranged for Franklin to speak to the group, which assembled on the White House lawn. When he appeared, after the crowd had been kept waiting in a soaking rain, he administered a "verbal spanking," lecturing the students on their opposition to an American loan to Finland, which was trying to stave off a Soviet takeover.[145] Although Eleanor was appalled when the crowd booed the president, she met with them for two more days, patiently defending her husband's policies and gaining a standing ovation herself. According to the *Baltimore Sun*, she won a debate between "a President's wife and a critical, not to say hostile, auditorium full of politically-minded youth of all races and creeds."[146]

By this time Eleanor had moved toward an internationalist stance personally, calling for the United States to oppose expansion by the Axis powers of Germany, Italy, and Japan.[147] As World War II loomed closer and closer to the United States, changing the character of the New Deal, she backed Franklin's efforts to assist nations allied against fascism. She favored the draft that took effect in 1940. Fearful of the threat posed by Hitler's Germany, she backed Lend-Lease, an administration effort to give military assistance to countries endangered by the Axis. When King George VI and Queen Elizabeth of England visited the United States in 1939 to seek support, Eleanor made it plain she sided with them against Germany.

Her final break with the radical student movement took place in the summer of 1940 when Eleanor told a group of leaders whom she had invited to Hyde Park that she could no longer work with them, although she would contribute to their project to aid sharecroppers. In response some of the youth, who accused her of having been "sold down the river to the capitalists," picketed the White House.[148] A year later when Germany invaded Russia in June 1941, the Communist Party line changed again and so did the AYC. This time it supported U.S. mobilization against Germany.

The AYC sent her a telegram saying, "Now we can work together again," but Eleanor no longer was interested. "I never worked with the Youth Congress again," she stated. "I could not trust them to be honest with me."[149] Her determination to meet with the students for as long as she did represented a continuation of the concern she had shown for unemployed young people since the beginning of her tenure as first lady. If she were gullible in her contacts with them, she acted from compassion for those confronting economic and political dislocations that made them question traditional democracy. After leaving the White House, she regarded her interaction with the militant students as preparation for her later career in which she dealt with Communists outside the United States.

"I have never felt the slightest bitterness toward any of them and, as a matter of fact, I am extremely grateful for my experience with them," she wrote while she was U.S. delegate to the United Nations. Enumerating what she had learned from the students—how organizations could be infiltrated and made subject to methods of objection and delay—she said, "My work with the American Youth Congress was of infinite value to me in understanding some of the tactics I have had to meet in the United Nations!"[150] Her experience with the students led her to delve more deeply into international issues at a time when both fascism and communism were on the march and it was only too obvious that the United States soon would be drawn into World War II. It now appeared that she would remain first lady far longer than she had anticipated.

CHAPTER 6

BACKING THE WAR EFFORT

"People can gradually be brought to understand that an individual, even if she is a President's wife, may have independent views and must be allowed the expression of an opinion. But actual participation in the work of the government, we are not yet able to accept."

Eleanor Roosevelt, explaining her resignation as assistant director of the Office of Civilian Defense in "My Day," 23 February 1942

As the presidential election of 1940 approached, Eleanor found herself in a far different situation than she had been at the start of Franklin's first term. Although the clouds of World War II appeared on the horizon, her ability to humanize administration actions made her a reassuring presence to millions of Americans. Nervous and ambivalent about her role in 1932, she had emerged as one of the strongest and most popular voices in Washington in spite of critics who derided her nontraditional activism and alleged meddling in political matters. In 1938 she had adjusted sufficiently to her role to write Hickok, "I am not unhappy." But it was a qualified statement, followed by "Life may be somewhat negative with me, but that is nothing new."[1] The responsibilities of the position of first lady, combined with her own desire to pursue a career, fueled her pursuit of activities that masked a tendency to depression in the midst of public acclaim.

When the Gallup poll asked Americans in January 1939, "Do you approve . . . of the way Mrs. Roosevelt has conducted herself as first lady," 67 percent said "yes," while only 58 percent approved of her husband's actions as president.[2] Featured on the cover of *Time* magazine in April 1939, a rare achievement for a woman of her era, Eleanor was referred to as "an oracle to millions of housewives" and "the world's foremost female political force" due to her own hold on public opinion, not simply her relationship to the president.[3] Through her press conferences, which continued to generate news stories, her lectures, magazine articles, voluminous correspondence, and most important of all, her "My Day" column, Eleanor kept in contact with ordinary Americans.

Even when critics called into question her judgment, they pictured her as a motherly figure led astray by others. For example, in commenting on her appearance on behalf of the radical American Youth Congress when its leaders testified before the House Un-American Activities Committee, the conservative *New York World-Telegram*, which carried her "My Day" column, editorialized that she had been "deceived by devious-minded followers of the party line."[4] Since she was a wife, not an elected official, she was excused for efforts, however ill advised, to help others. Dorothy Thompson, the most acclaimed woman political columnist of the 1930s, called the youth congress Communist-dominated and attributed Eleanor's support of it to her innate goodness: "She never suspects anyone of ulterior purposes."[5]

At this point Eleanor had become an expert in handling her own press relations and managing her press conference group. On one occasion she showed irritation when newspaper coverage pictured her behind political appointments even when it appeared very likely that she was. She introduced Mary Winslow at a press conference in 1939 as the newly appointed U.S. representative to the Inter-American Commission of Women. A member of the Women's Trade Union League, which Eleanor long had supported, Winslow, like other WTUL members, favored legislation to protect women workers and was opposed to the proposed Equal Rights Amendment. She replaced Doris Stevens, a staunch backer of the Equal Rights Amendment and a member of the National Woman's Party, who unofficially had been the representative for ten years, in what one male journalist ridiculed as a big "fight in Washington."[6]

Winifred Mallon, a veteran *New York Times* reporter who covered Eleanor's press conferences, published a subsequent story claiming that Eleanor had been behind the Winslow appointment as well as responsible for the appointment of two men, one favored by her friend Aubrey Williams, to the Interstate Commerce Commission. According to Bess Furman, the journalists at Eleanor's next press conference were fearful of antagonizing the first lady by raising questions about the Mallon article until "somebody finally got up the courage" to do so. Using what Furman called her "sweetest public speaking voice," Eleanor denied that she had proposed "anybody for anything," although she admitted passing on suggestions for nominations, which might be construed as the same thing. Looking directly at Mallon, Eleanor rebuked her for "printing mere rumor."[7]

Discrediting Mallon's story by a reference to "clearing away the gossip," Ruby Black, Eleanor's most admiring journalistic supporter, asked Eleanor if she had sent cables to a meeting of the Inter-American group to urge protective legislation.[8] Eleanor replied that she had not, but said, "I did discuss the matter in small groups."[9] She proceeded to tell the reporters that she had expressed her opposition to a resolution for equal rights introduced at a conference in Peru because she considered Latin American women even less ready for equal rights and loss of protective legislation than women in the United States.

The press women let the matter rest at this point, moving on to traditional women's page subjects like questions of etiquette arising from handshaking with visiting dignitaries and lore about Lincoln's ghost in the White House. Their orientation toward women's page feature material made them as, if not more, interested in human interest details than probing into an inter-American commission. They did not want to offend the first lady, whom they viewed as a valuable news source as well as a fallible human being. They recognized she was increasingly becoming deaf and dependent on Thompson to repeat their queries. Eleanor benefited from their lack of follow-up questions, which made it easy for her to take refuge behind a façade of political innocence.

Since the press conference group served her in many ways, including as a source of information that influenced her own activities, Eleanor did not want to directly antagonize it. A month before the furor over the Winslow appointment, she had cancelled an appearance in Alexandria, Virginia, at one of many balls scheduled on Franklin's birthday to raise funds to combat infantile paralysis. She declined to go after learning at her press conference that if she went, she would have to cross a picket line of striking waitresses protesting their pay of only fifty cents a day plus tips. "I won't go through the picket line," she told the group. "Minimum wage standards should not include an allowance for tips."[10]

When Eleanor turned to issues of war and peace, she described herself as simply presenting a woman's point of view. Occasionally, her comments ran contrary to official U.S. policy of neutrality toward conflict in Europe. At her press conference on 7 February 1939 she spoke out against the "vindictiveness" of the dictatorial terms imposed by Gen. Francisco Franco on the democratic forces overturned in the Spanish Civil War.[11] Earlier in her "My Day" column she had written that she was sickened by motion pictures showing the bombing of Barcelona and declared, "Why the women in every nation do not rise up and refuse to bring children into a world of this kind is beyond my understanding."[12] When asked if she had read in the *New York Times* of German press disapproval of her comments against dictatorships, she brushed off the question by saying, "I didn't even know the German newspapers were interested in, or paid any attention to a woman. I thought their attitude was one that the women didn't count."[13]

She maintained that her views were merely her personal opinions and had no relationship to official policy.

Eleanor's public comments on the visit to the United States of the King and Queen of England in June 1939 highlighted her ability to connect with the public and handle sensitive subjects with diplomatic skill. They showed how a president's wife could deflect attention from the growing horror of aggression in Europe by humanizing a state visit of two attractive young monarchs desperately seeking assistance. While King George and Queen Elizabeth came to cement ties for an inevitable war, in concert with the rest of the administration, Eleanor maintained the illusion they were on a ceremonial pleasure trip. Although numerous members of European royalty engaged in hat-in-hand visits to the United States, none of the other sovereigns received the same flattering attention as King George and Queen Elizabeth due partly to publicity generated by Eleanor herself.

For weeks the women at Eleanor's press conferences asked question after question about the British monarchs' tour. Society and women's page reporters filled their columns with accounts of ceremonial etiquette and royal customs followed by details of their majesties' itineraries, wardrobes, and entertainments. Eleanor's close friends among her press corps got a peek at preparations for the couple's state dinner, and a day later all of the women journalists were invited to meet the king and queen. No doubt, the visit caused extra work for Eleanor as an official hostess. According to Margaret Truman, "The imminent arrival of these ultimate royals touched off a frenzy of activity in the White House." Truman, who did not condone Eleanor's lack of interest in domestic details, wrote disapprovingly that "Eleanor Roosevelt's interest in decorating was minimal and the place badly needed an overhaul. Rugs and wallpaper were replaced or dry-cleaned and the staff waxed floors and dusted furniture until everything gleamed."[14]

Eleanor's own journalistic career benefited from the visit, with her syndicate offering subscribers "an exclusive report from the First Lady on an important and national event."[15] A total of sixteen daily newspapers in England, Canada, and the British empire, as well as a number of major U.S. newspapers that did not normally carry "My Day," including the prestigious *New York Times*, published the column during the king and queen's eight-day stay. Eleanor used the column to defend herself against accusations that she had imperiled the dignity of the nation by serving hot dogs, along with other typical American food, to their majesties at a picnic at Hyde Park.[16]

Most press attention focused on the king and queen as representatives of a nation that had laid the foundation for American democracy. It played up the cultural similarities of the two nations, countering isolationist sentiment in the United States that called for strict neutrality in European conflicts. Eleanor's portrayal of the monarchs stressed their humanity and their belief in the same values as Americans in the face of fascism. Asked at a press conference if Americans were not afraid that European democracies might draw the United States into war, she answered, "I don't quite see why the people of the United States should be afraid of European democracies. If they are, they have little realization of the history of the past few years." She said Americans should follow a policy "aimed at least to prevent wars before wars begin."[17] Her answer reinforced the administration's effort to convince Americans that this nation needed to show support for England even though public opinion as well as official policy favored neutrality.

In her autobiography Eleanor devoted a chapter of sixteen pages to royal visitors, describing humorous incidents, such as accidents by awestruck servants, during the stay of King George and Queen Elizabeth at the White House and Hyde Park. She also included a nine-page itinerary of the monarchs' visit with lists of those persons presented to them. This material previously had charmed her "My Day" readers and spoken to the American public's fascination with crowns and castles. As she put it, "Even in this country, where people had shed their blood to be independent of a king, there is still an awe of and an interest in royalty and in the panoply which surrounds it."[18]

The lighthearted autobiographical chapter ended on a somber note. Eleanor recalled that her heart was heavy when she watched the royal couple leave Hyde Park because of the "clouds that hung over them."[19] By this time Eleanor's own interest in pacifism had been shaken by the realization that a full-scale war was about to break out and threaten the United States. Conscious of the forthcoming presidential election, she expressed her support for embattled European democracies very carefully, holding out hope that the United States could remain aloof from the conflict.

When Germany invaded Poland in September 1939, three months after the visit of the English monarchs, Eleanor told her press conference that she supported amending the Neutrality Act. Proposed amendments to this legislation, designed to keep the United States out of war, would permit the sale of weapons to England and France, which had declared war against Germany after the invasion. Critics charged that it would lead to U.S. involvement in the conflict. By adding that the question of the amendments "is up to Congress, and I don't think my opinion is that much important," Eleanor downplayed her own change of position.[20] Two years before, under the auspices of a committee of isolationists, she had spoken up much more forcefully. In a radio broadcast from the White House, she had endorsed the concept of "No Foreign War."[21]

Remarkably, the women journalists at her press conferences seemed to accept her self-effacement and did not point out the shifts in her own position regarding neutrality. In her United Press dispatch Ruby Black soft-pedaled Eleanor's statement on amending the Neutrality Acts. Black began her article, "While President Roosevelt's press conferences are dominated by subjects connected with the European war, Mrs. Roosevelt's press conferences are chiefly concerned with how to make peace, and what a war situation does to White House customs."[22]

As Franklin turned his attention to military preparedness, Eleanor sought the continuation of New Deal social programs. In 1938 when European nations appeased Hitler at Munich, she wrote to Grace Howe, the widow of Louis Howe, "For a little while Franklin thought of nothing but the imminence of war. I do not feel the danger is over permanently but we have a breathing spell at least."[23]

The efforts of the women journalists to confine Eleanor's comments on neutrality to a noncontroversial middle ground minimized the significance of her role in the administration, perhaps because Black and other admirers sought to protect her from critics of her activism. On the other hand, perhaps Eleanor preferred to distance herself from what she saw as the gendered world of war, hoping that the "breathing spell" would last for a while longer. During Franklin's first term, she had been an adamant pacifist in line with her views on women's place in society. In *It's Up to the Women*, she referred to men's proclivity to wage "war as a means of settling disputes between nations." She claimed masculine discourse held that it was human nature for men "to always feel that they must fight."[24] Women, she contended, should look for alternatives.

During the 1920s, Eleanor had been one of the most prominent members of the women's peace movement spearheaded by Carrie Chapman Catt, who had led the successful call for adoption of the woman suffrage amendment to the U.S. Constitution in 1920. Eleanor enthusiastically endorsed the Women's International League for Peace and Freedom (WILPF), an outgrowth of the Woman's Peace Party founded by Catt, Jane Addams, and other prominent women during World War I. When Catt organized her first conference on the Cause and Cure of War in 1925, Eleanor had been on hand for the event, which was held in Washington. Two years later Eleanor hosted a women's peace movement conference at Hyde Park with Catt as the keynote speaker. Eleanor subsequently contributed a chapter on the obscenity of war to Catt's book, *Why Wars Must Cease*, published in 1935 on behalf of her Cause and Care of War organization.

That same year, shortly before Addams's death, Eleanor held a White House reception to celebrate the twentieth anniversary of the WILPF. She also hosted a radio broadcast, "Women Want Peace," sponsored by the National Council for the Prevention of War.[25] As late as 1937 Eleanor contended in a radio address that when enough women organized to seek peace, wars would end, because a "woman's will is the strongest thing in the world."[26] It was hard for her to understand Franklin's position that domestic isolationist sentiment meant the administration could not press strongly for U.S. participation in the Permanent Court of International Justice, known as the World Court, which she viewed as a necessary force for peace. In 1934 she wrote her friend Esther Lape, with whom she had lobbied for the World Court during the preceding decade, that administration officials did not want the court issue to "come up until after the next election."[27]

The advent of hostilities in Europe caused Eleanor to rethink her commitment to pacifism. She was outraged by the bombing of civilians in the Spanish Civil War, which she attributed to Franco's forces allied with fascism. Her outspoken support for the Loyalist government brought condemnation by Catholics, an important political group who favored Franco, as well as U.S. pacifists. Acting informally, Eleanor sympathized with groups, particularly the American Friends Service Committee and the Joint Committee for Spanish Children, that organized relief efforts to aid refugees from the brutal conflict.

She moved cautiously because of her position in an administration officially committed to neutrality and continually assailed by isolationists, including the powerful Hearst media interests. As international turmoil mounted, however, Eleanor did not believe that the United States could or should remain totally aloof. In 1937 she wrote an associate in the WILPF that she rejected the position of Rep. Jeannette Rankin, a Montana Republican who was the first woman elected to Congress and the only member of Congress to oppose U.S. entry into both World Wars I and II. Eleanor called "rather impractical" Rankin's plan to protect the United States from overseas aggression by reliance on submarines and coastal defenses.[28]

Eleanor expressed her changing views on pacifism in *This Troubled World*, a forty-seven-page book that she published in 1938. It addressed issues of war and peace in a simple style easily understood by readers. A call for people to band together and work for peace, the slender volume broadened the discussion of pacifism to include international efforts by nations to settle disputes among countries through united actions such as the imposition of economic boycotts and, if necessary, military force against aggressors.[29] Reviewers said her arguments were not original, but they praised the book because it spoke directly to individuals.[30]

As German and Italian fascism continued to produce refugee crises in Europe, particularly affecting Jews, Eleanor, working mainly behind the scenes, became an advocate for increased immigration of refugees, especially children. She supported the Emergency Rescue Committee, which tried to expedite the admission of refugees to this country, and was honorary chair of the U.S. Committee for the Care of European Children.[31] She sought passage of the Wagner-Rogers bill of 1939 to allow 20,000 German refugee children, most of whom were Jewish, into the United States. She gave permission at her press conference to be quoted directly when she said, "I hope the Wagner Act on Refugees will pass. Other nations take their share of the child refugees, and it seems a fair thing to do."[32]

According to Furman, this was the first time that Eleanor made a press conference endorsement of pending legislation.[33] The bill was withdrawn, however, in the face of strong political opposition to immigration from patriotic groups like the American Legion and the Daughters of the American Revolution. In large measure this reflected national prejudices against Jews. Franklin himself did not think it politically wise to support the bill, since congressional forces were arrayed against it, arguing that the German situation was overdramatized.

In 1939 and 1940 Eleanor worked more openly for the Children's

Crusade for Children, a nonpartisan organization, headed by Dorothy Canfield Fisher, a well-known novelist, which collected donations from American schoolchildren to help refugee children. In contrast to the position taken by some members of the administration, particularly the anti-Semitic Breckinridge Long, assistant secretary of state in charge of issuing visas, Eleanor was regarded as a friend of refugees who lobbied her husband on their behalf.[34] She intervened with Franklin when Long cut the operating funds of the President's Advisory Committee on Political Refugees, forcing Long to apologize.[35]

At the request of Clarence Pickett, executive secretary of the American Friends Service Committee, in 1940 she convened a meeting of the U.S. Committee for the Care of European Children, which tried to address the growing emergency. She sought to bring 5,000 French children, mostly Jews, to the United States, although the effort failed because of stalling by the German puppet Vichy government in France. She also intervened with Franklin to obtain visas for French Jews aboard the ship *Quanza*, so the refugees would not be denied entry to the United States, as were the passengers on an earlier ship, the *St. Louis*, which was forced to return to Europe.[36]

Yet these were relatively minor acts of mercy in a horrendous situation. Much controversy has arisen in recent years over the Roosevelt administration's policy toward Jews fleeing Hitler's persecution. While Franklin may have been restricted by both existing immigration laws and popular sentiment against admitting refugees, there is ample evidence he did relatively little to allow Jews to enter the United States, even though Hitler encouraged their emigration from Germany until 1941. Eleanor herself did not speak out against Hitler's atrocities against Jews when these first came to her attention in the 1930s, although she aided individual Jews in the United States and spoke at meetings of Jewish organizations. Eleanor did not respond to reports of atrocities between 1933 and 1938.[37]

Eleanor's silence may have reflected political considerations: Franklin needed votes from those of German background as well as votes from southern Democrats and Catholics, groups likely to harbor anti-Semitism inflamed by Nazi propaganda.[38] Perhaps she thought it best to remain quiet because Franklin, unlike his predecessors, had appointed well-qualified Jews to high-level positions at a time when prejudice often barred Jews from private employment, leading bigots to refer to the "Jew Deal."[39] Eleanor's two closest Jewish friends, Elinor Morgenthau and Bernard Baruch, did not encourage her to speak up during this period, perhaps fearing that United States protests against Hitler would increase domestic hostility toward Jews. Such hostility was undeniable. Public opinion polls confirmed that the majority of Americans, while opposed to Hitler's treatment of Jews, were unwilling to lend assistance, particularly if it meant the additional immigration of Jews into the United States.[40]

Eleanor first learned of Nazi persecution of Jews from Dr. Alice Hamilton, a physician who was the first woman professor at Harvard Medical School, at a dinner in 1933. The event, also attended by Jane Addams, was held at the home of Lillian Wald, like Addams a settlement house pioneer and peace activist. Afterward Eleanor arranged for Hamilton, who had returned from a trip to Germany, to visit Hyde Park so she could inform Franklin directly about Hitler's cruelties. The next year Eleanor received a report from Pickett, just back from touring Europe, on Hitler's persecution of the Jews, but when she referred to Pickett's trip in her column for the *Women's Democratic News*, she did not mention this subject.[41] If she had done so, she would have violated State Department opposition to public censure of Hitler's politics.

Even after the horrors of Kristallnacht, the night of 9–10 November 1938, when German mobs killed Jews and burned synagogues, Eleanor still seemed unable to divorce herself totally from the anti-Semitism that pervaded the era. Shockingly, especially in view of her later fervent support for the state of Israel, on 6 September 1939 she wrote a German friend from her Allenswood days, Carola von Schaeffer-Bernstein, who was a Nazi sympathizer, that it was possible to rationalize action against the Jews. While she pointed out that Americans were unable to understand how "one man and his storm troopers" could countenance the horrors in Germany, Eleanor added, "I realize quite well that there may be a need for curtailing the ascendancy of the Jewish people, but it seems to me it might have been done in a more humane way by a ruler who had intelligence and decency."[42]

From 1939 on, however, Eleanor worked both publically and privately to aid Jewish refugees. She served as honorary chairwoman of

Youth Aliya, which encouraged settlement of Jewish children in Palestine. She attempted to help Varian Fry, an editor who went to France in 1940 on behalf of the newly formed Emergency Rescue Committee to save Jewish artists and intellectuals from the Nazis. At Fry's request she forwarded a message to Franklin in the summer of 1940 asking him to appeal to the governments of Latin America for asylum for European refugees, mainly Jews. Subsequently she wrote Fry that "the President. . . . will try to get the cooperation of the South American countries in giving asylum to the political refugees."[43]

She also used her long-standing friendship with Undersecretary of State Sumner Welles to support Fry's effort to allow the culturally elite into the United States using emergency visas. Welles, considered the author of Franklin's "Good Neighbor" policy toward Latin America, had been a page boy at the Roosevelts' wedding in 1905 and moved in the same social circles as the Roosevelt family. He virtually ran the State Department, which he had joined in 1915, due to his long experience and deep understanding of foreign relations. Because of Eleanor's long association with Welles, she was able to work through him to foster more departmental compassion for the plight of refugees. For example, when he responded in bureaucratic language to a letter from her criticizing British refusal to let Jews enter Palestine, Eleanor told him tersely that the United States had to take action.[44] But she could only do so much.

As Lash pointed out, from a list of 576 refugees submitted to the State Department in August and early September 1940, only about forty visas had been issued by late September.[45] In November Eleanor, after prodding Franklin to intervene, wrote Welles, "Is there anything you can do to hasten the process so that the [Emergency Rescue] Committee will have assurance that the visas are cabled as soon as possible?"[46] Nevertheless, only a trickle of refugees gained entrance.

When the State Department dropped its emergency visa program in the summer of 1941, Eleanor bowed to administration policy.[47] Writing Fry's wife, she said, "I think he will have to come home because he has done things which the government does not feel it can stand behind."[48] The program folded because Franklin, preoccupied with keeping subversive agents out of the United States, objected to liberalizing the nation's extremely restrictive immigration laws.[49]

The general indifference of the American public to the plight of the refugees also influenced policy decisions.

After the United States entered World War II in 1941, Eleanor stood out as the most conspicuous figure in the administration to protest Hitler's program to exterminate the Jews. In April 1943 she wrote touchingly in "My Day" of Ben Hecht's cantata, "We Will Never Die," a pageant viewed by more than 100,000 Americans that portrayed Holocaust victims.[50] Yet, she did not call for specific action to end the Holocaust.[51] Eleanor subscribed to the Roosevelt administration's view that winning the war took precedence over efforts to rescue the Jews, such as bombing concentration camps. In a statement on 29 October 1943 to the Emergency Committee to Save the Jewish People of Europe, she said: "The best way is to win the war as rapidly as possible and that the allied armies throughout the world are achieving."[52]

In a "My Day" column in 1943 Eleanor said she did not "know what we can do to save the Jews in Europe and to find them homes, but I know that we will be the sufferers if we let great wrongs occur without exerting ourselves to correct them."[53] She proceeded to describe Jews in a manner intended to counter prejudice, but extremely offensive today. She wrote, "Largely because of environment and economic conditions, there are people among them who cringe, who are dishonest, who try to take advantage of their neighbors, who are aggressive and unattractive."[54]

In 1944 the Roosevelt administration's policy toward the Jews changed. Elinor Morgenthau's husband, Henry, the secretary of the treasury, condensed a report prepared by his general counsel, Randolph Paul, "On the Acquiescence of This Government to the Murder of the Jews," and presented it to Franklin. It charged the State Department with willful failure to act. Within a week Franklin, after years of relative inaction, established the War Refugee Board to rescue persecuted "minorities" from the Nazis.[55] Cynics said he acted in view of the upcoming 1944 election since public sentiment, as reflected in congressional debate, was mounting to aid refugees. The board set up a "free port" in Oswego, New York, which accommodated 987 refugees from Europe. Eleanor certainly supported such efforts, but John Pehle, director of the board, described them as too little and too late, although they saved some Jewish lives.[56]

When Franklin made his unprecedented bid for a third term as president, Eleanor realized that the goals of the New Deal were threatened by the increased emphasis on military preparedness in the United States. A significant indication of the gulf between the two was the fact that neither discussed the prospect of a third term with the other, although Eleanor wrote later she eventually recognized the fact that there was no one else who could carry the nation through a wartime crisis.[57] Still, she did not want the ideals of the New Deal to die. In May 1940 Eleanor had been honored by the *Nation* magazine for her work in civil rights and fighting poverty. One thousand people attended a dinner in New York to praise her efforts. "I suppose she worries about Europe like the rest of us," one speaker, Stuart Chase, said, but "she does not allow this worry to divert her attention from the home front. She goes around America, looking at America, thinking about America . . . helping day and night with the problems of America."[58]

Due to the deteriorating international scene, Eleanor no longer had Franklin's undivided attention for reports on social and economic conditions she observed on her travels as she had during the height of the Depression. Now when she returned from inspection trips, she found Franklin dining with Harry Hopkins, far more interested in defense strategies than welfare programs. Replacing the strong tie between Hopkins and the first lady in their joint desire to alleviate poverty, a close relationship had developed between Franklin and Hopkins, who moved into the White House with his six-year-old daughter, Diana, after the death of his wife, Barbara. Feeling excluded from their conversations, Eleanor coped with depression by spending more and more time away from the White House. She told Frances Perkins, who thought she should stay home more, "He [Franklin] doesn't need my advice any more. He doesn't ask it. Harry tells him everything he needs to know."[59]

Yet Franklin depended on Eleanor, if somewhat reluctantly. When delegates at the Democratic national convention balked at the prospect of nominating the idealistic Henry A. Wallace for vice president, as Franklin wanted, it was Eleanor who flew to Chicago to calm the raging delegates. Wallace, the liberal secretary of agriculture, was a former Republican, had relatively little personal following, and, like Franklin himself, was perceived as an internationalist, but Franklin made it plain he would decline the nomination if Wallace were not his running mate. He prepared a statement saying that if Wallace were rejected, it would mean the Democratic Party remained controlled by "the forces of conservatism, reaction and appeasement."[60]

Franklin declined to attend the convention. According to Eleanor, he initially told her, "it might be very nice for you to go, but I do not think it is in the least necessary."[61] She decided otherwise after receiving phone calls from Farley, acting as chairman of the Democratic National Committee, and Hickok, then employed as a committee publicist, who insisted she was needed to deal with the tense situation.

Eleanor started her trip from an airport near Hyde Park, where she had been enjoying a visit from Joe Lash. She flew in a private plane provided by C. R. Smith, the head of American Airlines, who was Eleanor's good friend. An early devotee of aviation, she happily noted in her autobiography that the pilot "allowed me to fly the plane for a while" on the way to New York City, where she met Smith and her son Franklin for the flight to Chicago.[62] Arriving at the convention, she learned to her dismay that Franklin had not told Farley whom he wanted for vice president. After she arranged for the two men to confer by telephone, Farley reluctantly agreed to back Wallace instead of rival candidates representing the conservative wing of the party. Farley then persuaded Elliott Roosevelt, attending the convention as a member of the Texas delegation, not to embarrass his parents by nominating Jesse Jones in place of Wallace.

In the midst of a turbulent convention scene, Eleanor suddenly found herself called on to speak. In her brief extemporaneous address she did not mention Wallace by name, but aimed, as she put it, "to persuade the delegations in the convention to sink all personal interests in the interests of the country and to make them realize the potential dangers in the situation we were facing."[63] She explained that her husband could not campaign because he needed to stay on the job and that if he wanted a particular person to help him, the convention should accede to his wishes.

"This is no ordinary time, no time for weighing anything except what we can best do for the country as a whole," she told the delegates eloquently.[64] The tumultuous crowd of 50,000 listened in si-

Eleanor gives an eloquent speech at the Democratic national convention in Chicago on 18 July 1940, stressing, this is "no ordinary time" and securing the nomination of Henry A. Wallace as Franklin's vice president for his historic third term as president. Courtesy of the Franklin D. Roosevelt Library, Hyde Park, New York.

lence and proceeded to nominate Wallace. Leaving the convention immediately thereafter, Eleanor received telephone calls from both Franklin and Hopkins as her plane was taxiing from the gate. They praised her for doing a good job. She soon found herself back in Hyde Park "just as though the last eighteen hours had not seemed the longest I had ever lived through."[65]

Eleanor's appearance on behalf of Franklin concealed her own ambivalence about remaining in the White House another four years. "It's hell," she told Bess Furman, after describing what it was like to be the wife of a public man, which included doing "what you're told to do as quickly as possible" and remembering to "lean back in a parade, so that people can see your husband."[66] She told members of her press conference that she envied them during the visit of the King and Queen of England because "you can write what you want to write—I have to be very careful."[67] The pressure of being a hostess as first lady never let up. In 1939 Tommy reported, "Mrs. Roosevelt had 4,729 for meals, 323 house guests, 9,211 tea guests, and she received 14,056, which means a total of 28,319 [persons entertained that year]."[68] Balancing her White House duties with her own career, Eleanor drew on what seemed to observers to be an inexhaustible supply of energy.

After the convention the election appeared almost anticlimactic. In August 1940 Franklin endorsed a controversial move for a peacetime draft, the first in the nation's history. In "My Day" and her magazine columns Eleanor argued for a broader form of national service, one that would include both men and women and carry out New Deal ideals by fighting against poverty and uplifting community life. After she wrote a "My Day" column trying to explain why young people opposed the draft, May Craig, an influential member of her press conference, told her, "Reporters commented you were bucking the old man."[69] Eleanor immediately made it clear that she did favor the draft and differed sharply with the American Youth Congress, which opposed it.

The Republican Party, which had chosen Wendell Wilkie, a liberal former Democrat, as its presidential candidate, sought to capture the isolationist vote by portraying Franklin as a prowar candidate, a charge it had made for some months and that Eleanor had joined in refuting. Prior to the election she held to the official administration policy that the United States would be able to avoid direct participation in war, although it needed to strengthen its defenses. She insisted at her press conference on 10 October 1939 that making democracy work at home served as "one of the ways to keep us out of war." Asked for reaction to being called a "warmonger" for favoring defense measures, she replied, "the only way to keep peace is to keep peace as a whole in the world."[70] It was a repudiation of isolationism, but it was not an endorsement of American intervention. In "My Day" she emphasized the fact that warfare in Europe and Asia had not spread to the United States: "The fact is before you that in a world of war we are still at peace."[71]

Following institution of the draft, Wilkie began climbing upward in the polls and Franklin made an ill-advised campaign promise to American mothers and fathers: "Your boys are not going to be sent into any foreign wars."[72] Eleanor tried to hedge on the meaning of what he had said. In "My Day" two days later she wrote, "All any human being can do is to promise that he will do his utmost to prevent this country from being involved in war."[73] She told her press conference following the election, "[In] most of the things I have read and remembered hearing him say, he has always said 'unless we are attacked.' I don't see how anyone understood it any other way."[74]

Even though Eleanor obviously supported Franklin, she refused to let the campaign destroy her friendship with Isabella Greenway King, who had been one of her bridesmaids and served as Arizona's first congresswoman. Although a Democrat, King, who retired from Congress in 1936, decided to back Wilkie in hopes he would solve problems of unemployment. After receiving a letter from King giving her reasons for favoring Wilkie, Eleanor replied it was "difficult" for her to understand "why you think that Mr. Wilkie can accomplish the things which he promises," but, she concluded, "As far as I am concerned political differences never make any difference in one's own personal feelings."[75] She continued sending Christmas presents to her old friend as usual and inviting her to lunch.

Republicans tried to make Eleanor and the Roosevelt children into campaign issues with little success. While being attacked for her nontraditional stance as first lady, Eleanor gained some favorable publicity from publication of her first biography, a highly laudatory work written by Ruby Black. Published on 11 October 1940, Eleanor's fifty-sixth birthday, it received mixed reviews, in part because of the sentimental tone. Black pictured Eleanor as a political partner with Franklin. The book came close to being an official biography. Black submitted questions to Eleanor through Tommy and incorporated the first lady's answers in the manuscript, allowing Eleanor to approve content in advance. Black gained permission to discuss Eleanor's problems with her mother-in-law, but was told not to call Eleanor "Mother of the NRA," so she used the term "Inspiration of the NRA" instead.[76]

Political opponents accused both Eleanor and her children, whose multiple divorces created tabloid headlines, of profiting from their family name. After quitting his White House post in 1938, James, "Jimmy," the eldest son, had become a Hollywood movie executive, persuading his mother to read the prologue of an English anti-Nazi film that he distributed. He went on active duty with the U.S. Marines the same month Franklin won reelection and eventually was promoted to colonel.

Cynics said Anna and her husband, John Boettiger, had been employed to run Hearst's *Seattle Post-Intelligencer* newspaper only because of her father's position, giving Hearst an opportunity to both embarrass the administration and keep in contact with it. Elliott, who had refused to attend college, had gone through a series of jobs in the 1930s, including being vice president of a Hearst radio chain. In the 1940 campaign he was criticized for obtaining a captain's commission in the air force, a charge Eleanor believed particularly unfair because he held a civilian pilot's license.[77]

The waspish columnist Westbrook Pegler derided Eleanor and her children unmercifully in his syndicated column, "Fair Enough," distributed, like "My Day," by United Features. Although he had called Eleanor "the greatest American woman" in 1938, he subsequently berated her social activism and ridiculed her involvement in the American Newspaper Guild, the newspaper union she joined in 1936.[78] An early guild member himself, Pegler resigned in 1937, attacking the guild for being "run by Communists" and declaring that it ought to "get rid of ineligibles," starting with the first lady.[79] In response, Eleanor announced that she intended to attend guild meetings to vote Communists out, if they were there, and subsequently described in "My Day" how her ivory knitting needles clicked away while she endured long-winded speeches.[80] While Eleanor resented the attacks on her children, she claimed she was merely amused when Republicans passed out large campaign buttons saying WE DON'T WANT ELEANOR EITHER.[81]

Voters decided otherwise. An electoral vote of 449 for Roosevelt overwhelmed the 82 given Wilkie. Franklin took 54.7 percent of the popular vote, while Wilkie gained 44.8 percent, but the Roosevelt landslide of 1936 was not repeated.[82] Lash, on the scene at Hyde Park for the election returns, found Eleanor a detached rather than elated participant. Nonetheless, she told Lash that in her own desire to leave the White House she had "underestimated the importance of the president's reelection."[83]

As the third term got under way, Eleanor's insistence that the social goals of the New Deal continue to be pursued spurred her into taking the position of assistant director of the Office of Civilian Defense (OCD), a post that made her the first president's wife to actually hold a federal appointment. While she received no pay, the appointment had to be officially approved by the president. She served from 22 September 1941 until 20 February 1942, when she was forced to resign due to unfavorable publicity.

In an account of Eleanor's performance, Margaret Truman offered an unflattering, if not malicious, assessment, probably reflecting the Truman family's negative view toward Eleanor but also drawing on contemporary criticism of Eleanor's OCD activity. While Mayor Fiorello La Guardia of New York, the head of the agency, was an old friend of Eleanor's, Truman asserted: "he and the first lady soon fell to quarreling because Mrs. R. had a bad habit of appealing to the president when she did not get her way."[84] According to Truman, "FDR, up to his eyeballs in trying to organize a major war, had no time for minor ones. He solved the problem by putting the agency under the supervision of a New Dealer, who said yes to everything Mrs. Roosevelt wanted to do. La Guardia resigned with a farewell blast at the first lady."[85] In actuality, the "New Dealer" was James Landis, Harvard Law School dean, who was brought in to straighten out the situation. La Guardia then resigned but without criticizing Eleanor. Landis next accepted Eleanor's own resignation.

Truman contended that when members of Congress discovered Eleanor had hired two old friends who were getting the same pay as Gen. Douglas MacArthur, then fighting the Japanese in the Philippines, "a firestorm of negative publicity broke out in the media. The friends resigned and a humiliated Eleanor Roosevelt soon followed suit." Truman found this to be proof of the unseemliness of a first lady moving into an official position.[86]

A more nuanced version of Eleanor's tenure showed her in a less unfavorable light, although her appointment ultimately raised questions about both her judgment and the propriety of a president's wife serving as a public official. Eleanor saw civil defense as an instrument for the continuation of progressive social legislation, which she feared would be forgotten in the present emergency. Moved by the work of Lady Stella Reading, who headed the women's civil defense operation in England, Eleanor wanted to involve women in building a new social order.

When Franklin issued an executive order creating an Office of Civilian Defense in May 1941, he set up a broad-based agency under La Guardia to bolster civilian morale by overseeing volunteerism, civilian protection, and communities' needs related to the newly created defense program. That same month Eleanor started writing her own question-and-answer page, "If You Ask Me," in the *Ladies' Home Journal*, following a format she had used in the *Democratic Digest*. In launching the page, she proposed conscripting young women, as well as young men, for a year of national service.[87] Eleanor soon criticized La Guardia's agency because it ignored women.

In September she reluctantly accepted the position of assistant director at the urging of both Hopkins and Anna Rosenberg, a key La Guardia aide, to deal with volunteers, many of whom were women. In her autobiography she said she feared that taking the position would give "ample opportunity for faultfinding" to critics of the administration, which turned out to be the case.[88] Although Eleanor held that Franklin was neutral on whether she should take the post, Rosenberg asserted, "He was glad to channel her energies into one area so that she would leave him alone in other areas. He knew that she felt frustrated because many of the liberal programs had to be put aside."[89]

Busy running for reelection, the mayor dismissed most volunteer efforts other than those of air raid wardens and firefighters, leaving Eleanor with "every activity which Mayor La Guardia did not want in his part of the program . . . thrust into my division."[90] The agency's press releases said she would take charge of "fortification in recreation, health, welfare, family security, education and other types of public and private community services."[91] Press attention, however, centered less on the duties she was given than on the spectacle of a president's wife holding an official appointment.

Eleanor began her new duties against a background of family losses. Franklin's mother, Sara, died at Hyde Park on 7 September 1941, just two weeks before her eighty-seventh birthday. Venting some of her personal feelings in "My Day," Eleanor referred to her mother-in-law as a "grande dame," but said, "She was not just sweetness and light, for there was a streak of jealousy and possessiveness in her where her own were concerned."[92] In a letter to Joe Lash, she wrote more plainly: "It is dreadful to have lived so close to someone for 36 years & feel no deep affection or sense of loss. It is hard on Franklin however."[93]

Recognizing Franklin's grief, which stemmed from his exceptional closeness with Sara, Eleanor initially made an effort to give him more companionship. Their son Jimmy wrote that Eleanor showed Franklin "more attention during those days than at any other time I can recall."[94] Yet Eleanor always surrounded herself with others, those referred to by a distant Roosevelt cousin, Margaret "Daisy" Suckley, in her diary as "the splendid people who are trying to do good and improve the world, 'uplifters,' the P. [president] calls them."[95] The unmarried Suckley, who herself had a crush on Franklin, wrote a year later that Franklin missed his mother, "as his wife is here so rarely—always off on a speaking tour, etc."[96]

The death of his mother, for whom the president donned a black armband of mourning that he wore for more than a year, came three months after Missy LeHand was stricken at a White House dinner party. A stroke left her partially paralyzed with little ability to speak. After extensive hospitalization including treatment at Warm Springs, LeHand was taken to the home of her sister in Massachusetts, where she died in 1944. Her illness deprived Franklin of the woman who made sure he relaxed at the end of the day and sat patiently by his side while he pored over his stamp collection. The flirtatious Princess Martha of Norway, a refugee from Hitler living in the Washington area, sometimes substituted as a dinner partner during Eleanor's frequent absences. Yet Franklin, deprived of both his adoring mother and devoted secretary, found himself left alone more than ever before.[97]

Less than a month after Sara's death, Eleanor's brother, Hall Roosevelt, died at Walter Reed Hospital in Washington. His death from cirrhosis of the liver on 25 September affected Eleanor deeply. All her life she had tried to look after Hall, who was seven years younger, attempting with Franklin's help to find employment for him and endeavoring to assist his family. A Phi Beta Kappa graduate of Harvard University, Hall had not lived up to his early promise, had two failed marriages, could not keep a job, and ended up living in an outbuilding on the Roosevelt estate at Hyde Park. According to his daughter, Eleanor "felt she had failed him, that it was somehow her fault he was addicted to drink."[98] Eleanor and Franklin held his funeral at the White House and buried him on 27 September at Tivoli, New York, where he and Eleanor had lived as children with their grandmother Hall.

Immediately after returning to Washington on 29 September, Eleanor reported for work at the OCD, walking nearly a mile from the White House to DuPont Circle, where the office headquarters were located. When she arrived at ten minutes after nine on her first day on the job, some reporters accused her of being tardy. "First Lady Is Late for New Job," blared headlines in the *Washington Times-Herald*, an anti-Roosevelt newspaper.[99] Even favorable reports gave the impression she was dabbling in government business. In her United Press stories Ruby Black quoted Eleanor as saying she would "really work" but could not observe regular hours because of other commitments.[100]

No doubt she did work. She wrote later that she tried to "numb" her feelings over Hall's death by throwing herself into her new responsibilities.[101] White House staff reported to Franklin that the lights stayed on all night in her room as she sat up dealing with civilian defense matters as well as her mail and career commitments. These now included a series of thirteen Sunday evening radio broadcasts billed as news commentaries and sponsored by the Pan-American Coffee Bureau, a trade association of Latin American coffee growers.

Aided by Elinor Morgenthau as her unpaid assistant, Eleanor attempted to coordinate volunteer civil defense activities with state and local defense councils that drew on existing governmental resources, a complex and thankless undertaking as nonprofit groups, agencies, bureaucrats, and military officials fought among themselves. Friction arose with Mayor La Guardia. She contended he made rushed decisions and showed more interest in "dramatic aspects" than in "building morale."[102] La Guardia, as a part-time civilian defense director, sought to concentrate on specifics, such as plans to fight fires in case of bombings, while Eleanor envisioned civil defense as a way of mobilizing communities to offer an array of social services, including maternal health and child-care programs. Her broad-brush approach emphasized physical education as a way of strengthening America physically and mentally. Eager for her staff to keep fit and set an example, she instituted lunchtime dancing on the roof of civilian defense headquarters. This, like some of her appointments, engendered embarrassing ridicule in the face of actual war.

When the Japanese attacked Pearl Harbor on 7 December 1941, Eleanor, not Franklin, first addressed the nation. She spoke to the American people a few hours after the attack on her scheduled radio program, telling the audience in her high-pitched patrician voice, "We know what we have to face and we know that we are ready to face it."[103] She appealed particularly to women and youth to back the war effort, a theme repeated on the Pan-American Coffee Bureau broadcasts that continued until the end of her contract in April. On 8 December she accompanied Franklin to the Capitol, where he gave his famous "live in infamy" speech to Congress, referring to the date of 7 December.[104] She listened as he asked for the formal declaration of war that brought the United States into immediate conflict with Japan, Germany, and Italy and thought about her "four sons of military age."[105] All four subsequently saw active duty in war zones and won decorations. Her son-in-law, John Boettiger, also joined the military.

From Capitol Hill Eleanor rushed to the airport to accompany La Guardia on a trip to the West Coast designed to alleviate public fears that a Japanese attack would occur momentarily. Traveling from San Diego to Seattle in a train with concealed lights, she found very little evidence of civilian defense preparation. She returned to Washington convinced that La Guardia's inept management called for him to be replaced, a conclusion reached by other officials, including Harold Smith, director of the budget.[106] On 12 December she broadcast to the American people seeking donations for the American Red Cross, of which she as first lady was the honorary vice chair.

In public appearances Eleanor spoke up for civil liberties in the midst of war. While on the West Coast, she posed with Japanese Americans in photographs distributed by the AP that illustrated her unpopular stand of tolerance toward those of Japanese background. In her "My Day" column of 16 December 1941, she told readers that fair treatment of minorities represented "perhaps the greatest test this country has ever met."[107] Much of the public and press, however, reacted to Pearl Harbor with more fear than reason and saw civilian defense in a far different light than Eleanor.

Although La Guardia was reluctant to leave the top civilian defense position, in January 1942 Franklin named Landis, who already was serving as New England regional civil defense director, the executive officer of the OCD, an appointment favored by Eleanor. Jonathan Daniels, later editor of the *Raleigh News and Observer*, was made executive aide. This took administrative control away from the mayor, whom Franklin told to go on speaking tours to get away from Washington, and strengthened operations. It also helped the administration deal with questions about Eleanor's own efficiency as an administrator, which had become the target of embarrassing attacks.

Criticism of Eleanor was exacerbated by a comment made in her "My Day" column for 24 December 1941 when she noted she had been late arriving at the OCD because the president "finally decided to tell me that British Prime Minister, Mr. Winston Churchill, and his party were arriving sometime in the late afternoon or evening."[108] The first of nine meetings between Franklin and Churchill during World War II, the visit called into question Eleanor's duties as first lady. By all accounts Churchill was a trying guest. He kept Franklin awake far into the night so that he needed "several days to catch up on his sleep after Mr. Churchill left," Eleanor wrote later.[109] An upsetting aftermath even occurred several years later. Louis Adamic, an author whom Eleanor had invited to a dinner for Churchill, wrote an unflattering account of the evening in a book, *Dinner at the White House.* It so enraged Churchill he sued Adamic for libel in England.

Eleanor's own comment on her tardy arrival at her civil defense office, in an era when punctuality was important, added to the newspaper outcry against her government appointment. A week earlier, the influential Walter Lippmann, writing in the Republican *New York Herald Tribune*, attacked her for "sugar-coating" civil defense with "all manner of fads, fancies, homilies, and programs which would have been appropriate to the activities of an excited village improvement society." He contended that a first lady had no business being "a subordinate official in a subordinate department of the government which her husband administers."[110]

The civil defense reorganization with Landis in charge occurred as congressional critics tried to push through legislation to put civil defense under the army, a move Eleanor publically opposed as contrary to her concept of civil defense for social betterment. She disappointed feminists by declining to press for women as army volunteers. She said at a press conference, "If you need them, I think it should be possible to use them; but I don't believe in obliging women to do things when it isn't necessary for them to do them."[111] She also drew hostility from segregationists who objected to her plans to allow African Americans to participate in civil defense programs. In a "My Day" column in which she called for fair treatment toward minority groups, she wrote, "if we cannot keep in check anti-Semitism, anti-racial feelings as well as anti-religious feelings, then we will have removed from the world, the one real hope for the future."[112]

Within a month of Landis's appointment, La Guardia resigned. He was replaced by Landis, who saw to Eleanor's own resignation on 20 February 1942. Previously Landis had demanded the resignation of Eleanor's most controversial appointee, Mayris Chaney, a ballroom dancer who had originated the "Eleanor glide" in the first lady's honor. Eleanor had hired her at a salary of $4,600 annually, more than an army colonel's pay, to develop a children's recreational program in bomb shelters.[113] An enraged House of Representatives banned the use of civilian defense money for dancing instruction, deemed frivolous at a time when the nation desperately needed bombers and armaments.

Eleanor left her civilian defense post after a barrage of criticism in Congress and from the press for allegedly harboring friends who were Communist sympathizers in civilian defense posts. These included Joseph Lash, an unpaid member of the youth advisory committee, and Melvyn Douglas, an actor considered politically radical, on the arts council. His salary was $8,000 annually, more than the pay of General MacArthur, who was leading forces under attack in the Philippines. One popular columnist, Raymond Clapper, who was considered nonpartisan, complained, "How can you have any kind of morale with a subordinate employee, who happens to be the wife of the President of the United States, flitting in and out between lecture engagements to toss a few more pets into nice jobs."[114]

As a federal official Eleanor had no longer been able to restrict press conferences at the Office of Civilian Defense to the women reporters who attended her White House gatherings. Although it was a woman journalist, Christine Sadler of the *Washington Post*, who first reported the Chaney appointment, Eleanor was subjected to tougher questioning at the civilian defense press conferences than at her women-only gatherings. For example, asked several times at a press conference on 9 February 1942 what Chaney was doing and why she was chosen for her job, Eleanor referred questions to John Kelly, national physical fitness director, and said Chaney had "brought a plan for this type of thing," but did not tell what it was.[115] Following the questioning on Chaney, Eleanor moved her press conferences back to the White House and closed them to men except on special occasions.

On 5 January 1942 she denied defensively that she and Mayor La Guardia would resign, although both departed in the next few weeks, and became flustered when asked if she had rehired assistants whom the mayor had fired.[116] Another awkward press conference moment came a week later when a reporter called attention to congressional charges that she was "too busy" to handle the job, and she responded, "What do people consider too busy. . . . What is a full-time job? How many hours does that mean?" She added that she could not estimate how much time she actually put in her office on civilian defense work because she spent "a good deal in other places . . . 12 hours a day." A skeptical reporter replied, "You do?" and Eleanor modified her comment by saying there were "certain days" when she did not do any civil defense work at all.[117]

In her autobiography Eleanor wrote that she resigned because "the mounting wave of attack in Congress finally convinced me that I was not going to be able to do a real job in the OCD."[118] While she said she did not mind criticism of herself "much," she was upset by criticism of her friends, particularly Chaney, who she said was targeted "entirely unjustly." Eleanor saw the attacks as purely political, commenting, "I offered a way to get at the president . . . the episode was short but it was one of the experiences I least regretted leaving behind me."[119]

Making use of both her radio broadcast and newspaper column, she assailed her critics. In a 22 February 1942 broadcast for the Pan-American Coffee Bureau, she called her detractors "the same group which has felt that everything which was done to make life pleasanter and easier for the people as a whole, was in some way useless, and therefore, should be branded as boondoggling." Naming names, which she rarely did, she said that arrayed on one side were her attackers, the "virtuous Westbrook Peglers," and on the other "the boondogglers, so-called. . . . It is a question of privilege or equality."[120] In "My Day" she avoided the issue of her own performance in the OCD and portrayed herself as the victim of being first lady, contending the nation was not yet ready to accept "actual participation in the work of the government" by a president's wife.[121]

In an apparent response to Eleanor, Pegler, by this time a Pulitzer prizewinner for exposing wrongdoing in organized labor, ridiculed Eleanor's efforts to do good works in a rapier-sharp parody of "My Day." Using her own conversational tone, Pegler mocked the wide-ranging enthusiasms, reports on frequent travels, and chats with those she met along the way that often marked the column. The parody began, "Yesterday morning I took a train to New York and sat beside a gentleman who was reading the 1937 report of the international recording secretary of the World Home Economics and Children's Aptitude and Recreation Foundation of which my very good friend, Dr. Mary McTwaddle . . . is the American delegate."[122]

Yet, even in his effort to humiliate the first lady, Pegler unintentionally pictured her as well-meaning. After her departure from the Office of Civilian Defense, journalists more favorable to the Roosevelt administration consciously adopted this position toward her. *Time* called her "a kind lady" giving the nation "a lesson in good manners" by resigning.[123] The *New York Times* declared that the resignation did not reflect on her "ability, her goodwill, and her unselfish devotion to the general welfare."[124]

Very likely, Eleanor was more upset by the criticism than she acknowledged. With Franklin warning her not to get into a "bad smells contest" with Pegler, she rarely responded directly to his attacks.[125] Behind the scenes she acted differently, asking the FBI under J. Edgar Hoover to investigate Pegler on possible charges of sedition linked to his column. This attempt proved that Eleanor did not always revere First Amendment rights.[126]

When the war effort geared up, Pegler targeted attacks on Eleanor as a champion of organized labor, arguing that she refused to recognize problems of racketeering that impeded the manufacturing of war materials. With Franklin's blessing she sought an investigation of a Pegler column of 28 November 1942 in which he quoted an obscure worker in a Philadelphia tank factory who complained that union regulations were hampering production. The Roosevelts apparently thought the column revealed that Pegler might be in league with Nazi sympathizers undercutting the war effort.

Franklin made political use of the FBI in World War II by ordering sedition investigations of anti–New Deal newspaper publishers, including Hearst. Eleanor, on the other hand, has been pictured as upholding free speech. In this case, however, she zealously sought action against Pegler. When the initial investigation proved nothing, Eleanor prodded the Bureau to continue.[127]

In violation of confidentiality, Eleanor forwarded the initial FBI report to Josephine Truslow Adams, a left-wing activist, who carried on her own investigation that disagreed with the FBI findings. Eleanor subsequently forwarded Adams's report to Hoover, but again the FBI concluded that no sedition case could be made.[128] The incident revealed that Eleanor was willing to use her White House influence to silence her most vociferous critic.

As Eleanor was making the crucial decision to leave the OCD, Franklin took an action of which she disapproved strongly. On 19 February 1942 he signed Executive Order 9066 in reaction to hysterical reports, later proven false, of alleged spying and treachery by Japanese Americans on the West Coast. Military authorities and press campaigns of vilification against the Japanese led Franklin to a decision that tore thousands of innocent people from their homes and livelihoods, giving those who envied Japanese Americans' success as small-scale farmers a chance to profit from their misery.

Franklin's order authorized the designation of military zones from which persons could be excluded. It set in place a process by which more than 100,000 persons of Japanese extraction on the West Coast and in Arizona were forced to go to makeshift shelters, in such places as stockyards and racetracks. From there they were dispersed to ten relocation centers, which resembled concentration camps with barbed wire and guard towers, in Utah, Arizona, Colorado, Arkansas, Idaho, California, and Wyoming.

Eleanor tried to convince Franklin of the injustice of this policy, to no avail, allying herself with Attorney General Francis Biddle, the only member of the administration to oppose this obvious violation of civil liberties. "These people are good Americans," Eleanor told

Franklin, "and have the right to live as anyone else."[129] Yet, once she realized that the decision had been made she did not speak out against it. She told her radio listeners, "It is obvious that many people who are friendly aliens have to suffer temporarily in order to insure the safety of the vital interests of this country while we are at war." She also assured her audience that the removal of the Japanese was "going to be done so that they will not waste their skills."[130] In letters to personal friends, on the other hand, she expressed outrage, writing Flora Rose, the head of Cornell University's Home Economics Department, for example, "This is just one more reason for hating war—innocent people suffer for a few guilty ones."[131]

Viewing Eleanor as friendly to their situation, individual Japanese Americans sought her aid in ameliorating their situation and she tried to help. She intervened with the War Relocation Authority (WRA), established to oversee the internment, when she received reports of mistreatment in relocation camps. For example, in response to a letter from a San Jose, California, woman protesting camp living conditions, Eleanor replied that she had brought the complaint to the attention of Milton L. Eisenhower, head of the WRA.[132] She also called on the Justice Department to investigate claims of discrimination against the few Japanese Americans allowed to remain in California.

Her most extensive inquiry into the situation came in 1943 when Franklin asked her to visit the Gila River Camp in Arizona on her way home from a Phoenix vacation in view of disturbances there. Her report on 23 April 1943 described the valiant efforts of the internees to aid the war effort and make the best of their environment, while noting that family structures were under great strain and advocating a relaxation of the ban on letting the Japanese return to the West Coast. In "My Day," she called attention to the camp's desert location and said that when the internees arrived, the place was "not only uncomfortable but very chaotic." She praised the Japanese for having shown "endurance and willingness to cooperate, or they would have despaired of ever making life livable, and have become useless burdens on the Government."[133]

Franklin subsequently approved efforts to allow individual internees to leave the camps if they had guarantees of employment. The internment centers themselves remained in operation until after he was reelected in 1944, and it was not until 17 December 1944 that the WRA began to shut the camps down. The last residents were released in 1946.

No evidence has come to light on why Eleanor remained silent concerning Japanese American internment, although Franklin probably demanded it.[134] One rationalization can be gleaned from a heated reply that Eleanor made to Pauli Murray, a young African American friend. Murray wrote an impassioned letter to Franklin regarding the evacuation of the Japanese Americans on grounds, frequently given in the press, that it was for their own protection from mob action. She said that African Americans were watching Franklin's Republican rival Wendell Wilkie "campaigning on the race question" and that she hoped the president would take "a more forthright stand on this whole problem of color."[135]

Eleanor's reply expressed exasperation. To Murray's suggestion that the president also "evacuate Negro citizens from 'lynching' areas in the South," Eleanor seemed astonished at drawing parallels between the two groups. "How many of our colored people would like to be evacuated and treated as through they were not as rightfully here as any other people?" she wrote. Although she was "deeply concerned that we had to do that to the Japanese who are American citizens," she justified internment because "we are at war with Japan and they have only been citizens for a very short time. We would feel a resentment if we had to do this for citizens who have been here as long as most of the white people have." Turning to Wilkie, Eleanor pointed out that he had no official position so he could "say whatever he likes," whereas Franklin had to take Congress into consideration. As for herself, she said, "I can say just how I feel, but I could not say it with much sense of security unless the President was willing for me to do so."[136] Eleanor proceeded to emphasize creation of the Fair Employment Practices Committee (FEPC, later the Fair Employment Practices Commission), set up by the administration in 1941 to provide equal employment in defense industries. Eleanor herself had played a part in setting it up, serving as an intermediary among Franklin, Walter White, and A. Philip Randolph, president of the Brotherhood of Sleeping Car Porters, who had threatened a massive march on Washington to protest discrimination. She told Murray that the FEPC might not be able to do as much as its backers desired, but that government could not move faster than citizens wanted it to.

To sympathetic observers Franklin's willingness to let her speak out more forcefully on racial issues than he did indicated his basic agreement with her statements. The more cynical contended that Franklin benefited from her comments without having to take any action of his own. African American voters assumed he supported their struggle for more equality, but since he took little action on their behalf he did not confront the southern bloc in Congress determined to maintain segregation.

Murray's letter had been occasioned by the Odell Waller case, which had a powerful influence on the African American community. Waller was a young Virginia sharecropper sentenced to death in the electric chair after being convicted by an all-white jury of murdering his white landlord in a dispute over a crop. Long concerned about the plight of sharecroppers and tenant farmers in the South, Eleanor tried to intervene after receiving a note written by Waller in his prison cell, referring to her as "a nice lady" and saying that he had shot the landlord "to keep him from hurting me not meaning to kill him."[137]

Eleanor appealed to Franklin, who declined to appoint a presidential commission, but did send a personal letter to Virginia governor Colgate Darden urging him to commute the death sentence. This was in line with a national campaign for clemency waged by the Workers Defense League, which included Randolph and other civil rights leaders with Murray as field secretary. When Darden did not give in, Randolph led a delegation of civil rights leaders, including Mary McLeod Bethune, to Washington the day before the scheduled execution, hoping to persuade Franklin to intervene, not knowing he was at Hyde Park.

Eleanor tried to telephone Franklin on their behalf, but was told repeatedly by Harry Hopkins that the president was unavailable. Finally Franklin took the phone to tell Eleanor personally that he planned to take no action. Eleanor called Randolph at NAACP headquarters to break the news as Murray and nine other people listened to the conversation on extension phones. Murray recalled in her autobiography that Eleanor's voice trembled as she said, "I have done everything I can possibly do. . . . It is in Governor Darden's jurisdiction and the President has no legal power to intervene. I am sorry, Mr. Randolph, I can't do anything more."[138]

Waller was executed on 2 July 1942. Eleanor's efforts on his behalf were leaked to the press, enhancing her reputation among African Americans while adding to the outcry against her from southern conservatives. Eleanor herself became totally disillusioned with Hopkins, who she thought had deserted her and liberal principals to seek influence as Franklin's close advisor. Against her better judgment, Franklin asked Hopkins to bring his second wife, Louise, to live in the White House where Eleanor had been looking after Hopkins's daughter, Diana. Franklin also invited Hopkins to be married at the White House, leaving Eleanor to plan the ceremony, which took place the same month as Waller's execution.

Eleanor resented the presence of the apolitical, ultrafeminine Louise, and the Hopkinses finally moved out of the White House in December 1943, leaving Franklin bereft of the constant companionship of his trusted aide. Eleanor saw Louise Hopkins as akin to the female admirers who surrounded her husband in the absence of Missy LeHand: Princess Martha, Margaret Suckley, and another middle-aged cousin, Laura Delano. In particular, the new Mrs. Hopkins offended Eleanor by assuming some of the prerogatives of the first lady, such as arranging seating at dinner parties.[139]

As marked by the telephone conversations with Hopkins, the Waller case put extra stress on the tangled marital affairs of Franklin and Eleanor. It manifested their differences as Eleanor sought increasingly to be her own person. She accompanied Franklin partway, at his request, on a two-week nationwide inspection tour of factories and military installations during September 1942, paying special attention to the women, both white and black, who had been recruited into defense plants, but left the tour to fulfill other commitments. On the trip, according to their son James, Franklin asked Eleanor to stay with him more in the White House and to resume her role as a wife.[140] Eleanor promised to think it over while she flew to the West Coast to visit her daughter Anna. Back in Washington she declined indirectly, telling Franklin that she wanted her own war-related responsibilities.

On the southern part of the trip with Franklin, Eleanor ran into numerous stories of the fictitious "Eleanor Clubs," which African

American domestic servants supposedly were forming to demand better pay and more equality. At a 1942 press conference she reported the FBI could find no evidence that any such clubs existed "despite a great sweep of rumors."[141] She also used her press conference to deny a rumor that she had brought "colored guests" to Washington hotels, which were segregated in common with other public facilities in the capital, a false report she declared "of value to the Nazis."[142]

Such rumors stemmed from the fact that before and during World War II Eleanor became increasingly outspoken on the racism that pervaded American society. Interviewed in 1939 for *An American Dilemma*, a monumental study of U.S. race relations by Gunnar Myrdal, a Swedish sociologist, she criticized those "guilty of writing and speaking about democracy and the American way without consideration of the imperfections within our system with regard to its treatment . . . of the Negro."[143] In a short book, *The Moral Basis of Democracy*, published in 1940, Eleanor called for attention to Christian principles and boldly stated that racial prejudice and poverty continued to enslave American Negroes and American Indians.[144] Reviewers generally endorsed the work, with one saying it was better than the "banalities and trivia" of "My Day."[145] Another reviewer commented that naïveté and lack of development of themes kept the book from being a major achievement.[146]

While widely attacked by segregationists, Eleanor avoided a radical stand on civil rights. In the 11 May 1942 issue of the *New Republic* she acknowledged the injustice of asking black Americans to be patient, but contended, "that is what we must continue to say in the interests of our government as a whole and of the Negro People," although, she added, "that does not mean that we must sit idle and do nothing."[147] The next year she contributed an article to the "If I Were a Negro" feature in *Negro Digest* asserting that if she were black, she would have both tremendous bitterness and patience.[148] Eleanor wrote, "I would not do too much demanding. I would take every chance that came my way to prove my quality and my ability and if recognition was slow, I would continue to prove myself, knowing that in the end good performance has to be acknowledged."[149]

She urged African Americans to support the war and "accept every advance that was made in the Army and Navy, though I would not try to bring those advances about any more quickly than they were offered."[150] Her controversial article, which offended some African Americans as well as white supremacists, boosted circulation of the new publication to 100,000, making it the foundation of the Johnson Publishing Company in Chicago, the nation's largest black-owned publishing firm. John H. Johnson, the owner, credited Eleanor with helping ensure the success of his operation.

The *Negro Digest* article appeared the same year that Eleanor was blamed for a race riot in Detroit in which thirty-four persons, twenty-five African Americans and nine whites, had been killed. It broke out in June 1943 when tensions peaked over the move of African American defense workers into the 200-unit Sojourner Truth housing project built with federal funds. As a strong proponent of public housing, Eleanor had encouraged Clark Foreman of the Federal Works Agency to develop the Detroit project to provide permanent housing for black workers in an integrated setting over the objections of other housing officials who pushed for temporary worker housing, segregated by race.

She lobbied Franklin to approve the project in spite of opposition against it in Congress, contending that leading white politicians like Walter Reuther of the United Auto Workers favored integration.[151] White workers, who wanted the Sojourner Truth housing for themselves, did not. They reacted furiously when the first tenants tried to move in during 1942, causing the city to delay occupancy until April 1943, when African Americans families entered the project under state police escort. Segregationists claimed Eleanor's racial liberalism fomented violence between the races. After the Detroit outbreak, the *Jackson* (Mississippi) *Daily News* proclaimed, "It is blood on your hands, Mrs. Roosevelt."[152]

During the period of the Detroit riots, disturbances also broke out in Los Angeles, brought about by cultural clashes between white servicemen and Latinos. Mobs of sailors and marines targeted Mexican American youth considered unpatriotic because they dressed in "zoot suits," consisting of wide-brimmed hats, broad-shouldered coats, peg-legged trousers, and dangling chains.[153] Police, influenced by a press hostile to Mexican Americans, did not intervene as the servicemen beat Latinos and tore off their clothes in a weeklong riot that included attacks on African Americans and Filipinos.[154]

After military authorities restored order, the Los Angeles City Council, siding with the rioters, banned the wearing of "zoot suits" as evidence of hoodlumism.

Expressing her views on the situation, Eleanor attributed the violence to racism. "For a long time I have been worried about our attitude toward the Mexicans," she said in Washington.[155] "We have in this country a very serious race problem and we've got to solve it. We'll have it in the world after the war." Her prophetic words fell on many deaf ears. The *Los Angeles Times* on 18 June 1943 headlined her remarks, "Mrs. Roosevelt Blindly Stirs Race Discord," while its editorial page accused her of Communist leanings.

Tensions at home, the lack of a concrete job to do following the civil defense fiasco, and limited rapport with Franklin and key aides all entered into Eleanor's desire to travel overseas during World War II, as well as her interest in finding new material for her journalistic pursuits. When she told Franklin in the fall of 1942 that she wanted to serve as a roving representative of the administration, he agreed to let her make a long-sought visit to American troops in England, even though he previously had asked her to spend more time with him in the White House. Accompanied only by Tommy, she flew to Great Britain on a three-week inspection trip as the guest of Queen Elizabeth, who invited her to stay for two nights at chilly Buckingham Palace, which bore the scars of German bombing. In London she met her son, Elliott, on duty there before leaving for action in Africa, who teased her that after staying in an enormous suite in the palace her White House bedroom would never again be adequate.[156]

From 21 October to 17 November 1942, Eleanor worked to help cement the Anglo-American alliance. Although never in doubt, it had become somewhat frayed during the preceding year. Some Americans, Eleanor among them, feared that Winston Churchill intended to use American participation as a way of restoring the British empire at the war's end, whereas she was committed to a nonimperialistic world based on a new international organization. She and Churchill clashed at a dinner party in London over the Spanish Civil War, with Eleanor objecting to his comments that seemed to favor the dictator Francisco Franco. Nevertheless, when she left to go back to the United States, Churchill sent her a handwritten note saying that "you certainly have left golden footprints behind you."[157]

Eleanor's visit had a twofold purpose—to see how the British were coping with the war and how American troops were faring. In addition to dining with royalty and dignitaries, her trip included tours of bombed-out sections of London along with stops at hospitals, military facilities, and defense plants staffed by women war workers. She talked for hours to American service personnel, including African American troops, who were better accepted by the English than by some white Americans, although Franklin apparently cautioned her not to comment on their treatment for fear of arousing southern hostility, and she did not.[158] She broadcast to the British people over the BBC and she filed her own "My Day" columns daily, praising the fortitude of the English people in the midst of war and envisioning a new and less class-conscious nation emerging after the war ended.

Eleanor also reported on her conversations with American troops, both publically and privately. "Every soldier I see is a friend from home, and I want to stop and talk with him whether I know him or not," she wrote in "My Day."[159] As an unofficial representative of the American Red Cross, she investigated the quality of services at its canteens and recreation centers. While praising the organization openly, on her return she privately told Franklin and Norman Davis, the Red Cross head, that officers were unfairly receiving better recreational benefits—such as more movies—than enlisted personnel.[160]

Eleanor's trip did not receive unanimous approval at home. Pegler and other critics claimed she was taking advantage of her position to make useless junkets at taxpayers' expense, while ordinary Americans had to endure rationing and limit their own travel. Segregationists resented her picture being taken with African American soldiers. Eleanor paid little attention to this criticism.

She continued to advocate that African American troops have equal access to recreational facilities and transportation, writing so many letters on the subject to Gen. George Marshall that he had to assign two staff members to answer them.[161] The War Department finally gave in on 10 March 1943, when all commands were forbidden to use racial designations in facilities intended for the welfare of soldiers, a prelude to desegregation of the military. Similarly, Eleanor pushed military authorities to allow African American pilots who had been trained at Tuskegee Institute to actually engage in combat

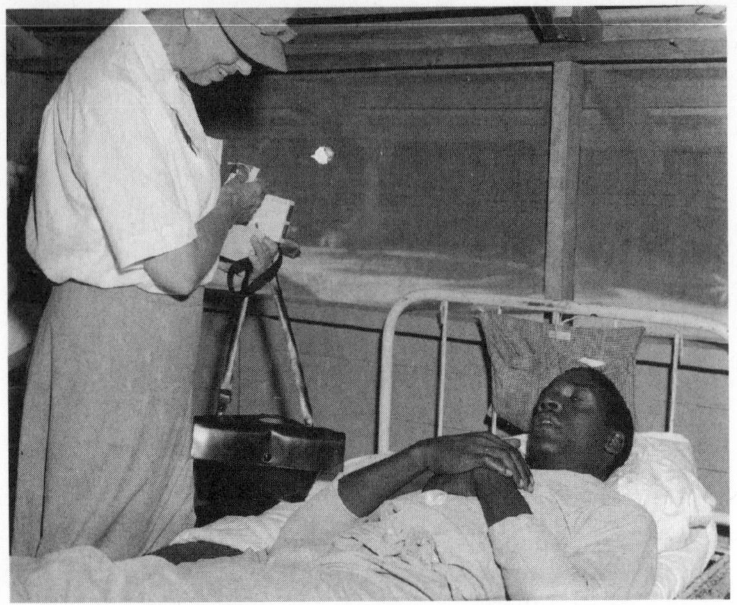

Wearing a Red Cross uniform, Eleanor visits wounded World War II troops on a tour of battlefield sites in the Southwest Pacific during August and September 1943. Courtesy of the Franklin D. Roosevelt Library, Hyde Park, New York.

as did white pilots, which they finally did in the spring of 1943. In answer to a question of whether African Americans should be admitted to the air corps without segregation, she spoke out firmly: "Negroes should be admitted anywhere other Americans are admitted."[162]

The excellent performance of the Tuskegee airmen, who formed the 99th Pursuit Squadron and won a hundred Distinguished Flying Crosses, did not diminish racial ill will directed at Eleanor as a champion of equal opportunities. "I suppose when one is being forced to realize that an unwelcome change is coming, one must blame it on someone or something," Eleanor wrote Jonathan Daniels.[163] Yet Eleanor stopped short of advocating total equality. "I have never advocated social equality or intermarriage," she wrote a white Southerner in 1942.[164]

Perhaps because the administration wanted to get Eleanor out of the country following the Detroit race riots, less than a year after her trip to England, she took off on a more extended and controversial journey—flying more than 25,000 miles on a five-week mission to inspect troops in the South Pacific. From 17 August to 24 September 1943 her plane landed on seventeen small islands as well as in Australia and New Zealand. Her stops included Guadalcanal, Bora Bora, Samoa, Fiji, New Caledonia, and Christmas Island.

Wearing the uniform of the American Red Cross, Eleanor spent time at military facilities, hospitals, and Red Cross canteens, where she saw an estimated 400,000 servicemen and -women. Typing her column herself, she reported on her experiences to "My Day" readers and in an article for the *Ladies' Home Journal* that ran in its December issue. She donated the proceeds to the American Red Cross, perhaps to defuse criticism that she had no right to wear its uniform since she had not taken the required training for volunteers.

Eleanor's motivations for the exhausting tour, during which she lost thirty pounds, were mixed. As a goodwill ambassador, Eleanor expressed the desire of the administration that the troops in the remote Pacific receive the same treatment as those in Europe. Meeting with women's groups, she helped repair relationships among New Zealand, Australia, and the United States, strained over accusations of anti-Americanism displayed toward American troops. Having engaged in numerous conversations with U.S. military personnel in hospitals, mess halls, and camps, Eleanor recalled, "I carried away an endless number of names of mothers, wives, sweethearts and sisters to whom to send messages when I got home."[165]

Perhaps the most extraordinary feature of the trip was a surprise visit to Guadalcanal, where her close friend, Joseph Lash, whom she always called Joe, had been assigned to a weather forecasting station. She insisted on traveling there, although the island still was subjected to Japanese air attacks, and spent time alone with Lash in between greeting troops, who were astonished to see the first lady in their midst, and touring hospitals and a cemetery. Her desire to converse with Lash may have been a primary factor in her decision to make the trip. Certainly she treasured their time together—which might have been the reason he was on Guadalcanal to begin with.

Years later Lash speculated that his weather unit might have been sent there to remove him from Eleanor's presence. His speculation revolved around the fact that Eleanor had visited him at weather forecasting school in Illinois, where the two occupied adjoining hotel rooms on two separate occasions. Suspecting Lash of being connected with a Communist conspiracy, the Army Counter-Intelligence Corps (CIC) kept him under surveillance in 1943 and bugged his hotel room in Urbana, Illinois. Learning that Eleanor and he planned to meet at Chicago's Blackstone Hotel, they also bugged Eleanor's room there in March 1943. Tipped off by a hotel employee, Eleanor complained to Harry Hopkins, who took the incident up with army general George Marshall. When word reached Franklin, he ordered the CIC disbanded, but Lash's unit soon found itself in the South Pacific.

Recordings made from the bug came into the possession of J. Edgar Hoover, who placed them in a confidential file. The discredited head of the CIC, however, spread a story around Washington that the recordings picked up sounds of sexual relations between Eleanor and Lash. This charge was vehemently denied by Lash, although he admitted that the recordings contained evidence of sexual encounters between him and Trude Pratt, secretary of the International Student Service. She was a married woman about to leave her husband for Lash with Eleanor's full knowledge of the affair.[166] Eleanor, then fifty-eight years old, never seemed concerned about the propriety of her intense friendship with Lash, then thirty-three years old, or the appropriateness of their spending two weekends in adjoining hotel rooms. Her devotion to Lash highlighted her correspondence with him. The day after leaving Guadalcanal, she wrote him, "It was so wonderful to be with you, the whole trip now seems to me worthwhile."[167]

The public and press were less enthusiastic, although Eleanor had supporters, who thanked her for visiting their loved ones, as well as detractors like Pegler, who claimed she had no right to use scarce resources of fuel and manpower for her travels. Both Eleanor and the American Red Cross received hundreds of letters complaining that she had donned a volunteer's uniform without fulfilling training requirements. Back at the White House Eleanor fell into a deep depression, which she tried to evade through more rounds of ceaseless activity, spelling out a program for the postwar world in columns and speeches. She stressed education for veterans, exchange visits by young people, a permanent peace-keeping international organization, and a worldwide relief agency.[168]

Perhaps as a result of criticism of her use of a Red Cross uniform in the South Pacific, Eleanor did not wear one or even mention the Red Cross in her "My Day" columns on her next major overseas trip.[169] This one took place from 4 March 1944 to 28 March 1944 when she traveled 10,000 miles to visit military installations in the Caribbean. After her return, a Gallup poll in May showed her trips were not popular with the public. The poll showed 45 percent opposed them on grounds that she claimed travel privileges denied to others and 6 percent had no opinion, while 13 percent said the trips were none of their business, and only 36 percent were clearly in favor of them.[170]

Conservatives called her a "female-dictator" and urged her to "keep Franklin company (as a real good woman should do)" and "tend to her knitting."[171] Eleanor shrugged off such unfavorable comments. In a *Ladies' Home Journal* article called "How to Take Criticism," she wrote, "Life would become unbearable if you thought about it all the time, so you have to ignore the critics."[172] While the murky role of first lady did not make plain what she was to do, she wanted and needed to believe in the importance of what she did. In fact, the war left her freer to travel than she would have been otherwise, since White House social activities were severely curtailed after the Pearl Harbor attack.

As commander-in-chief, Franklin traveled outside the United States during the war, going to Casablanca to meet Churchill and French general Charles de Gaulle in January 1943 and to Cairo, where he met Generalissimo Chiang Kai-shek of China, and on to Teheran in November 1943 to confer with Churchill and Joseph Stalin. Eleanor pleaded with Franklin to take her to Teheran, eager to be of help, but he said no, although he had invited their sons Elliott and Franklin Jr., as well as his son-in-law John Boettiger, to join him. According to Lash, "In continuing to serve him she walked a lonely path."[173]

In 1944 the Roosevelts' daughter Anna and her youngest son, John Boettiger, moved into the White House to provide company for the war-weary president. Anna acted as a buffer between her mother, who continued to press Franklin for action on causes in which she believed, and her father, whose health was declining markedly. Since Eleanor often was away from the White House, Franklin asked Anna if he could invite his old friend Lucy Mercer

Eleanor attends a Women in the War luncheon sponsored by an organization of advertising women in New York City on 19 October 1943. Seated at the head table with her are, from left, Anne O'Hare McCormick, New York Times *columnist; Caroline Hood, a publicist for the Rockefeller Center; and Mabel Flanley of the Institute of Public Relations. Courtesy of the Franklin D. Roosevelt Library, Hyde Park, New York.*

Rutherfurd to an occasional dinner and Anna agreed. It was a secret they kept from Eleanor.

Many of Eleanor's activities during the war were directed at other women whom she tried to mobilize for the war effort. On lecture and inspection trips from one end of the United States to the other she encouraged housewives to endure rationing willingly and to conserve food. As first lady she posed for pictures showing her and the White House housekeeper, Henrietta Nesbitt, taking a consumer pledge for defense promoted by the Office of Price Administration, which administered rationing.

Eleanor paid particular attention to women war workers, symbolized by the mythical figure of Rosie the Riveter. She praised the patriotic efforts of women induced by government publicity campaigns as well as good wages to leave their homes for defense jobs. Concerned that women workers also were burdened by home and family responsibilities, Eleanor advocated daycare programs and communal kitchens to provide take-home meals. Perhaps most importantly, she called for equal pay for equal work. A "My Day" column urging Congress to continue subsidies for food to combat inflation drew a rebuke from George Carlin, her syndicate head, responding to complaints from one newspaper client regarding her "political speech."[174] Carlin preferred she simply chronicle her activities.

At press conferences, and in her writing and lectures, she spoke up for women in the military. She wrote the army to urge the use of women doctors and asked why army nurses were not allowed to marry.[175] She advocated that women military personnel be made part of the regular armed forces, a step taken when the Women's Auxiliary Army Corps (WAACS) became the Women's Army Corps (WACS) in 1943.[176] One noteworthy conference, which resulted in headlines like "Mrs. Roosevelt Assails Stories about Waacs," produced a firm denial of a whispering campaign, which Eleanor blamed on the Nazis, that servicewomen engaged in widespread immorality.[177]

As first lady, Eleanor interacted continually with women's organizations, including her own press corps, which had organized itself as Mrs. Roosevelt's Press Conference Association. Continuing to introduce notable guests to the women who covered her, Eleanor invited Madame Chiang Kai-shek, wife of the Chinese leader, to appear at her press conference on 24 February 1943. Asked to give her views on the proposed Equal Rights Amendment pending in Congress, Madame Chiang said, "I have never known brains to have any sex."[178] Reporters, who usually were barred from using direct quotations, were allowed to quote this sentence directly. Although a definite supporter of protective legislation for women and consequently not an ERA supporter at this time, Eleanor was well aware that in the 1944 presidential election campaign both Democrats and Republicans included a pro-ERA plank in their platforms.

Madame Chiang spoke to the press conference a few days after delivering a well-publicized plea to Congress for more assistance to the Chinese government in its battle against Japanese. Initially, Eleanor spoke very favorably of her guest, who had a lengthy White House stay following hospitalization in New York, even though she demanded imported silk sheets that had to be changed throughout the day and summoned her servants by clapping her hands. Eleanor's opinion began to change when Madame Chiang refused to address a mass meeting of the National Association for the Advancement of Colored People, effectively divorcing herself as an Asian from the struggle of colored people in the United States. Eleanor shared with her press conference Madame Chiang's insistence on her sheets being removed "seven times a day or something," one journalist, Esther Van Wagoner Tufty, recalled later.[179] She said Eleanor's comments were similar to hints of displeasure she previously had dropped about her mother-in-law, but that the press women did not consider them suitable for publication.

Republicans tried to make Eleanor a factor in the 1944 election. They applauded Frances Hutt Dewey, the wife of the GOP candidate, Thomas E. Dewey, as a traditional wife who believed a first lady "should pretty largely stay put in the White House."[180] Eleanor realized that she was a target for critics. To Lash, she complained that Franklin urged her to tone down public comments on racial issues: "He feels he must not irritate the southern leaders as he needs their votes for essential war bills. I am not sure they could be much worse than they are."[181]

Possibly for that reason Eleanor answered a letter from a southern white woman denying that she believed in social equality and ending with a statement that implied racial bias. She wrote, "We made a grievous mistake in bringing the Negroes here and we cannot undo that."[182] When the letter was circulated, the African American press tried to minimize its importance, with the *Baltimore Afro-American*, for example, writing, "This reply is evidently composed by a secretary," and characterizing it as an obvious bid for southern white votes in 1944.[183]

Newspapers that opposed the Roosevelt administration looked hard for perceived flaws in Eleanor's performance as first lady. The anti-Roosevelt *New York Daily News* accused her of injudiciously benefiting from her position. Ruth Montgomery, who became head of Mrs. Roosevelt's Press Conference Association in 1944, faulted the first lady for behaving at the conferences with "giddy informality," offering rambling statements and introducing women guests who were relatively low-level government employees.[184] In her memoirs Montgomery gave an example of Eleanor answering a press conference question: "'Did Mrs. Roosevelt think it was right for her to accept an $11,000 mink coat during wartime, a gift from the Canadian mink ranchers?' Mrs. Roosevelt assured us that she did, since there were no legal restrictions against a President's wife receiving presents."[185]

Other women journalists at the conferences continued to write glowing articles on Eleanor. Her old friend, Bess Furman, who was hired by the *New York Times* Washington bureau in 1943, focused on Eleanor's humanitarian dreams of a peaceful postwar world.[186] Eleanor's travels and comments on social issues became relatively routine to many journalists as the war went on, a "diminishing novelty," as one put it.[187]

Eleanor used her press conferences, however, to reassure voters concerning what was perhaps the most significant issue in the election—Franklin's health. She told the women that there were no physical reasons why he could not continue in office and that he was looking much better than previously, six months before the election.[188] Perhaps this was because Franklin's doctors did not communicate to her in detail the severity of Franklin's heart condition.[189] Perhaps it was because she herself almost never suffered from physical ailments and lacked understanding of those who did. And perhaps she simply refused to see what was obvious to others close to Franklin—that his health was failing.

In terms of her own election role Eleanor's behind-the-scenes participation lessened. She argued strongly, but unsuccessfully, that the liberal Henry Wallace should stay on the Democratic ticket as the vice presidential candidate, but Franklin was unwilling to fight to keep Wallace, who was feared by party conservatives, on the ticket and readily agreed to his replacement with Harry S Truman. Democratic leaders refused to heed the desires of Eleanor's friend, Walter White of the NAACP, to put a strong civil rights plank in the platform.

Franklin himself did not appear at the Democratic convention in Chicago, giving an acceptance speech from San Diego before leaving for Hawaii on an inspection tour that took him to Alaska before he returned to the White House. Possibly he used wartime censorship to cover up his declining health. He certainly relied on it to avoid public notice of his train stopping in New Jersey en route to Hyde Park in 1944 so he could see Lucy Mercer Rutherfurd at her estate, concealing his visits from Eleanor as well as the rest of the country.[190]

When Franklin himself showed little interest in campaigning, Eleanor urged him to do so, aware that Dewey was moving up in the polls. Ed Flynn, the Tammany Hall politician who engineered Franklin's 1944 campaign, was shocked by his appearance and begged Eleanor to keep him from running again, but she did not do so. She wrote Lash that she feared Dewey's leadership of the country, although for herself "four more years in the White House is almost more than I can bear."[191] In September 1944 she accompanied Franklin to a second Quebec conference for a seventh summit with Churchill to make plans for the postwar world, including economic aid to England, since German forces were expected to collapse imminently. After the conference Churchill and his wife, Clementine, visited the Roosevelts in Hyde Park for two days. Eleanor told Joe Lash that she resented being "a glorified housekeeper" for the occasion, complaining, "if I were not a well-disciplined person I would go out and howl like a dog!"[192]

Back in Washington Eleanor supported Franklin's decision to go on the campaign trail, starting 23 September with a speech to the Teamsters Union in Washington to put to rest rumors that he was too ill to continue in office. Giving one of his greatest addresses, Franklin used his little dog, Fala, as a foil to chastise Republican opposition. Braving icy winds and rain, Franklin spoke to thundering applause that fall whenever he appeared. He easily won reelection, although by a smaller margin than in 1940, getting 53 percent of the popular vote and 432 electoral votes, while Dewey won 46 percent of the popular vote and 99 electoral votes. The Democrats had become the party of labor, immigrants, African Americans, big-city politicians, Catholics, and Jews.

Shortly after Franklin's inauguration for the record-shattering fourth term, he was off on his last major trip. In January 1945, he journeyed to Yalta in the Soviet Crimea, for a final meeting with the leaders of the Grand Alliance, Churchill and Stalin. He took along Anna, not Eleanor, a blow to his wife's feelings. The Big Three discussed the United Nations, the new world security organization, as well as how to treat a defeated Germany. Franklin returned in poor health. On a vacation trip to rest at the Little White House in Warm Springs, Georgia, he died unexpectedly on 12 April 1945 of a cerebral

Eleanor and Clementine Churchill, wife of Prime Minister Winston Churchill of England, address the people of Canada over the radio from Chateau Frontenac during the second Quebec conference of Franklin and Churchill during World War II. The conference, held 11–16 September 1944, aimed to plan for the postwar world. Courtesy of the Franklin D. Roosevelt Library, Hyde Park, New York.

hemorrhage. A nation had lost its leader, and Eleanor had lost her husband after forty years of marriage.

The complicated dynamics of their relationship still pose problems for historians. In the midst of the war Eleanor had forwarded ideas to Franklin that seemed utterly implausible, such as dropping hornets, bees, and wasps on enemy lines.[193] In his desk Franklin kept a copy of a satirical poem, "The Lady Eleanor," which ended with "And despite her global milling, / Of the voice there is no stilling, / With its platitudes galore, / As it gushes on, advising, / Criticizing and Chastising, / Moralizing, patronizing / Paralysing—ever more / Advertising Eleanor."[194]

Yet Franklin allowed no one to criticize her and tolerated her causes.[195] Perhaps he saw in her a force that had greatly enhanced his presidency, even though the two moved on separate tracks.

CHAPTER 7

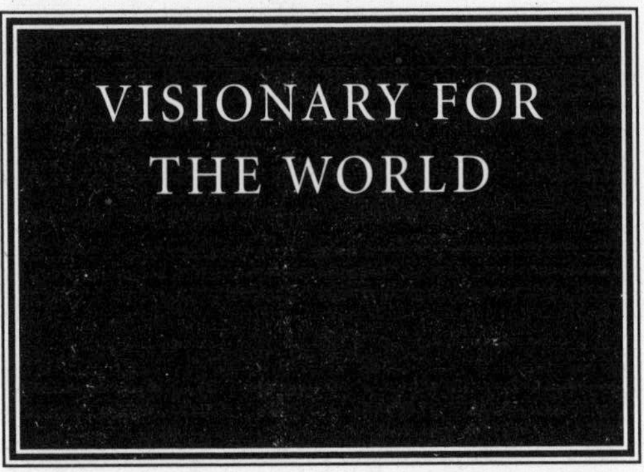

VISIONARY FOR THE WORLD

"For it isn't enough to talk about peace. One must believe in it. And it isn't enough to believe in it. One must work at it."

Eleanor Roosevelt in a broadcast on the work of the United Nations over the Voice of America, 11 November 1951*

By coincidence on the day that Franklin died, Eleanor held what was to be the last of her White House press conferences. It seemed to be a relatively routine morning event with Eleanor urging the public to suspend judgment on the treatment of defeated Germany until the U.S. government could provide more information for international consultation on postwar conditions. Even though Japan had yet to be vanquished, she was looking ahead to the forthcoming organization of the United Nations, set to take place at a conference in San Francisco on 20 April. Eleanor planned to accompany Franklin there. She spoke about the importance of the new international organization—how it would empower nations to work together. "We have got to get over a habit of ours for many years, to consider

* ERP, Speech and Article File, script for "The United Nations Today," Voice of America broadcast, November 1951, FDRL.

only what we will do," she told the group. "We will have the United Nations Organization so all the world's opinion will have a clearing place."[1]

A minor flap developed when questions arose concerning a column by Drew Pearson on 8 April 1945. In it he had asked whether "the honeymoon" was over between Eleanor and her press conference. Pearson charged that Malvina Thompson had "doctored" a press conference transcript so Eleanor could claim being misquoted in news reports saying she saw no reason for the United States to feed Europe, at that time facing mass destitution. Off the record, Eleanor replied that Pearson's "question did not merit an answer."[2] Her friend Furman suggested the matter be referred to the press conference association, little imagining that it was about to go out of existence, since Bess Truman, who succeeded Eleanor as first lady, declined to hold press conferences.

While Eleanor was attending a benefit that afternoon at the exclusive Sulgrave Club, she received a message to return immediately to the White House, where Steve Early and Dr. Ross McIntire, the president's primary physician, told her that Franklin had died. Eleanor changed from her red suit into a black dress, cabled the news to her four sons in uniform, sent for Vice President Harry S Truman, and waited for him with Anna in the first lady's sitting room. When Truman arrived, she said simply, "Harry, the President is dead."[3] Stunned, Truman remained speechless for a moment before asking if he could do anything for her. She replied: "Is there anything we can do for you? For you are the one in trouble now."[4] At 7 p.m. that night members of the Cabinet gathered at the White House to see Truman sworn in as the thirty-third president of the United States. Immediately after the ceremony Eleanor left by plane for Warm Springs to begin facing the difficult days ahead.

Arriving at Warm Springs about midnight, Eleanor immediately asked Franklin's two cousins, Laura Delano and Margaret Suckley, who had gone with him to Warm Springs, as well as Grace Tully, who had taken over as Franklin's chief secretary after Missy's illness, for a full account of Franklin's last hours. At that point she learned from Delano that Franklin had collapsed in the living room of his cottage where he had been sitting with Lucy Mercer Rutherfurd having his portrait painted by her friend, Elizabeth Shoumatoff. After hearing this unexpected and emotionally devastating news, Eleanor walked alone into Franklin's bedroom to see his body. Emerging dry-eyed five minutes later, she asked for more details about Lucy's visits to Franklin. She found out that Lucy had frequently visited Franklin at the White House with Anna's knowledge.

Giving no sign of her distress, Eleanor carried on in her first lady's role as the nation's chief mourner. She selected the clothes for Franklin's burial and accompanied his coffin as it was transported by train from Warm Springs to Washington, making a slow eight-hundred-mile journey with the casket visible to the thousands of mourners who lined the tracks along the way. "I lay in my berth all night with the window shade up, looking out at the countryside he had loved and watching the faces of the people at stations, and even at the crossroads, who came to pay their last tribute all through the night," Eleanor remembered.[5]

Following what she said were Franklin's wishes, she did not allow his body to lie in state in an open coffin in the Capitol. She accompanied the funeral procession with its horse-drawn caisson from the railroad station to the White House, where grieving crowds massed outside the entrances. The coffin was placed in the East Room and opened at her request only once—when she went into the room alone for her personal farewell.[6] Unfortunately, the closed coffin gave rise to rumors, which persisted for years, that Franklin had not really died, a reflection of the public's shock at the death of a man who had defined the decades of the Depression and World War II.[7] Immediately afterward, she confronted Anna about the presence of Rutherfurd at the White House. When Anna acknowledged the meetings between Franklin and his old love, Eleanor became intensely angry, but she maintained her composure for the funeral. At the 4 p.m. service in the East Room she remained dry-eyed in the midst of sobbing family members and friends, longing for three of her sons whose military service precluded their attendance.

Reboarding the funeral train for Hyde Park, she took charge of arrangements for Franklin's burial on 15 April in the rose garden of his beloved family home as he had requested. She recorded in her autobiography that she and other members of the funeral party "watched out of the windows of the train the crowds of people who stood in respect and sorrow all along the way."[8] When the caisson was brought to the garden, cannons boomed and West Point cadets stood at attention as the assemblage of dignitaries gathered, led by President Truman and members of the Cabinet. Looking back, Eleanor recalled, "At the time I had an almost impersonal feeling about everything that was happening."[9]

Reflecting on her years in Washington, she wrote that when she first entered the White House, "I felt sure that I would be able to use opportunities which came to me to help Franklin gain the objectives he cared about—but the work would be his work and the pattern his pattern."[10] Of her husband she said, "I sometimes acted as a spur, even though the spurring was not always wanted or welcome. I was one of those who served his purposes."[11] She did not add that she had drawn on her position as first lady to serve her own purposes, using it to enlarge opportunities to speak, write, and express herself through the media. She concluded by saying she had lived her White House years impersonally, "almost as though I had erected someone a little outside of myself who was the president's wife. I was lost somewhere deep down inside myself."[12]

After the burial, Eleanor moved as quickly as she could from the White House, leaving in less than a week. She resumed her "My Day" column on Monday, 16 April, just four days following Franklin's death, referring to Franklin as a leader who showed others the way to world peace. She concluded that peace could not be the work of one leader, "so, when the time comes for people to assume the burden more fully, he is given rest."[13] Two days later in "My Day" she announced that she planned to become more outspoken, stating, "Because I was the wife of the President certain restrictions were imposed on me. Now I am on my own and I hope to write as a newspaperwoman."[14] On 19 April 1945, her last full day in the White House, she repeated this intention, but refused permission to be quoted directly, at a farewell tea attended by all the fifty-seven women who belonged to her press conference association in 1945. She told the women that Franklin's home, the Big House at Hyde Park, would be turned over to the U.S. government, in accordance with his wishes, if her children agreed, as they soon did. She herself planned to live in her Val-Kill cottage and in New York City.

While overseeing the packing and sorting of family possessions during her final week in the White House, she found time to give a tour to Bess Truman and her daughter Margaret, who were dismayed at what they saw.[15] The Roosevelt family pictures had been taken down from dust-streaked, faded walls that badly needed painting. Shabby furniture, carpets, and drapes testified to the fact that Eleanor had been too occupied with various activities during the war years to spend $50,000 allocated by Congress for White House upkeep and repair. According to the White House butler, Alonzo Fields, "Mrs. Roosevelt was more concerned about people being swept under the national rug due to injustice than she was about someone finding dirt under the White House rug."[16]

On Friday, 20 April, she left Washington for her New York apartment on Washington Square. Reporters waited outside the door, but Eleanor maintained she had nothing to say and announced, "The story is over."[17] It was a poor prophecy.

To a large extent a substantial part of her career, which continued until her death in 1962, lay before her.[18] She remained a power in the Democratic Party, and the nation's "Most Admired Woman," as reflected in public opinion polls, during most of the remaining years of the twentieth century.[19] Her appointment as U.S. representative to the United Nations from December 1945 until January 1953 led to her leadership of the Human Rights Commission, which produced the Universal Declaration of Human Rights, one of the most important documents of the twentieth century.

Eleanor's immediate tasks after Franklin's death were to deal with innumerable details involving the settlement of his estate as well as to acknowledge the public outpouring of grief at the loss of a great man. President Truman arranged for a White House secretary, Dorothy Dow Butturff, to go to Hyde Park to help Eleanor deal with thousands of letters of sympathy. Eleanor felt a sense of relief when the last pile was read at the end of August 1945, noting, "It was quite impossible for me to answer them all personally as I would have liked to do."[20] She also took charge of removing personal items from the Big House prior to turning it over to the government, dividing them among her children, whose frequent quarrels and needs for financial assistance distressed her.

Franklin had left the income from his estate, valued at about $1.4 million after taxes, in trust for her (curiously, he never changed his will that also left income to cover Missy LeHand's expenses, although, because LeHand had predeceased him, the money went to Eleanor). Using her own funds, Eleanor decided to buy Val-Kill and about 825 acres of surrounding farmland, woods, and buildings from Franklin's estate, since executors told her she could not rent the property under the will's terms.[21] She based her decision on the willingness of her son Elliott, then married to his third wife, actress Faye Emerson, to settle at Hyde Park and establish a mother-son farming operation. Eleanor reasoned that she wanted to keep Hyde Park land in the Roosevelt family because "I'm sure that is what Franklin wanted."[22]

Although he achieved an outstanding record as a pilot and rose to the rank of brigadier general in 1945, Elliott received adverse publicity during World War II when an enlisted man was bumped off a plane to make room for his dog. In 1946 Elliott published a book, *As He Saw It*, giving his father's plans for the postwar world. Eleanor, who wrote the introduction, defended the work, widely criticized as inaccurate.[23] Moving into Top Cottage, which Franklin had built on the estate to use as his own residence after leaving the White House, Elliott edited four volumes of Franklin's letters, published from 1946 to 1950, for which his mother wrote introductions. To the annoyance of her other children, Eleanor often favored Elliott, whose behavior remained unpredictable.[24]

In their rivalries, the Roosevelt children contended among themselves over which sons were to take precedence in following in their father's footsteps by seeking public office.[25] When Harold Ickes urged Eleanor herself to become a candidate for the U.S. Senate from New York State, she forcefully declined, writing him, "My children have labored for many years under the baffling necessity of considering their business of living as it affected their Father's position, and I want them to feel in the future that any running for public office will be done by them."[26] Yet, the public did not rule her out as a possible candidate. In a Gallup poll taken in December 1945, Eleanor's name appeared in a tie for fourth place as a potential presidential candidate, ranking behind two generals, Douglas MacArthur and Dwight D. Eisenhower, who stood in first and second place, respectively, and industrialist Henry Kaiser in third place. She tied with automotive magnate Henry Ford and financier Bernard Baruch.[27]

Two of her sons eventually did run for major offices, but neither succeeded to the extent he had hoped for, and each had a troubled domestic life. James (Jimmy), a California businessman who was married four times, ran unsuccessfully for governor of his state in 1950, in part because President Truman declined to endorse him. Four years later James won the first of six consecutive terms in the U.S. Congress, leaving in 1965 after an unsuccessful bid to become mayor of Los Angeles. His first book about his family, *Affectionately, F.D.R.*, brought a mixed review from Eleanor in a "My Day" column in which she objected to her son's criticism of her White House housekeeper, Henrietta Nesbitt.[28]

Franklin Jr., a lawyer and businessman who was married five times, was elected in 1949 to the first of three terms in Congress from New York City but had a poor record of attendance. He failed to get the party endorsement for the governorship in 1954. As a result Eleanor became extremely annoyed with the Tammany Hall political organization, which refused to back him for what was considered a steppingstone to the White House. Subsequently mother and son worked together in a New York City political reform movement in 1959 that led to the defeat of Tammany and its head, Carmine De Sapio.

As a private citizen in 1945, Eleanor remained continually in the public eye due in part to "My Day," which picked up subscribers immediately after Franklin's death, appearing in some ninety newspapers, and her monthly advice column, "If You Ask Me," in the *Ladies' Home Journal.* President Truman and other leaders were well aware of her political importance as the activist widow of a beloved president. For years Eleanor had won accolades as her husband's political partner. In 1942, for example, a British publication, *The Spectator*, had observed, "More than once it was apparent that the President's wife, far from being a parasite on her husband's popularity and prestige, was able to lend him, at low moments, some of the political capital she had accumulated."[29]

In spite of the strains in the Roosevelt marriage, Eleanor realized after Franklin's death that she had depended on his counsel, writing Lash, "I feel a bit bereft."[30] Nevertheless, she had no intention of giving up her own involvement in public affairs. Although deeply grieved by the presence of Lucy Rutherfurd at Warm Springs when Franklin died, Eleanor long had realized, as she wrote in her autobiography, that "you cannot live at all if you do not learn to adapt yourself to

In widow's garb, Eleanor speaks to the people of the United States over the CBS radio network on 19 August 1945, a day of prayer proclaimed by President Truman in thanksgiving for the cessation of World War II. Courtesy of the Franklin D. Roosevelt Library, Hyde Park, New York.

your life as it happens to be."[31] For the rest of her life she appeared proud to be known as "Mrs. Roosevelt," and she celebrated her husband's accomplishments and ideals. She wanted Franklin's name associated with the United Nations and tried unsuccessfully to have Hyde Park named as the site of the organization's headquarters.

Wearing widow's garb, Eleanor delivered a radio address on WNBC in commemoration of V-E Day, 8 May 1945, which marked the formal end of World War II in Europe. She appealed to her listeners to work for a permanent peace, declaring, "This was the main objective that my husband fought for."[32] Eleanor did not question President Truman's decision to drop atomic bombs on Japan in August 1945, but she argued in her column that atomic energy should be put under international control.

Shortly after Franklin's death Eleanor accepted a nomination to the board of the NAACP, where she argued that the Fair Employment Practices Committee should be made a permanent body to work for fair employment practices for all Americans. In the 1950s she displayed great personal courage in supporting the integrated Highlander Folk School in Tennessee, which trained civil rights leaders. Eleanor traveled there without police protection in 1958, despite warnings that her safety could not be guaranteed in the face of Ku Klux Klan threats. Not surprisingly, she backed the U.S. Supreme Court's *Brown v. Board of Education* decision in 1954, which outlawed racial segregation, and worked to commit the Democratic Party to integration. As a practical politician, however, she counseled a gradual approach to avoid splitting the party.

Truman's recognition of Eleanor's political appeal to African American voters led to her United Nations post. After her return to Hyde Park, Eleanor showed no hesitancy in communicating with the president in a conscious effort to influence his actions. Even though Truman sometimes resented her pressure, he realized he needed her prestige to hold together the New Deal coalition and he did not want to offend her. When she expressed surprise in "My Day" that the Russians had not announced V-E Day until almost twenty-four hours after Truman and Churchill had done so, Truman immediately wrote her an eight-page, longhand letter explaining the surrender arrangements so she would not think he was being unfair to the Russians.[33]

In December 1945 Truman told Secretary of State James Byrnes to find an appointment for Eleanor because he wanted her on his political team to maintain the support of African American voters.[34] When Byrnes recommended she be appointed a delegate to the United Nations, Truman moved swiftly to press her to accept. First declining on grounds that she had no experience in foreign affairs, she changed her mind after being urged to do so by Franklin Jr. and the faithful Tommy. Eleanor decided her presence would keep alive Franklin's high hopes for the new organization. Her confirmation sailed through the U.S. Senate with only one dissenting vote—that of the racist senator Theodore G. Bilbo of Mississippi. She now had an official platform from which to advance her own commitment to world peace, remaining in the post until Dwight D. Eisenhower, a Republican, was inaugurated as president in 1953.

At the age of sixty-one Eleanor joined a bipartisan, all-male U.S. delegation, which was skeptical of her abilities. Meeting without her, the delegation assigned her to Committee Three, which dealt with humanitarian, social, and cultural affairs, assuming this was a safe spot for a woman.[35] Little did they realize it would become one of the most volatile centers of United Nations activity and that the former first lady would show herself a shrewd and skillful diplomat. At the close of the London session, two Republicans on the delegation who had been hostile to her appointment, Senator Arthur H. Vandenberg and John Foster Dulles, who became secretary of state under Eisenhower, both applauded her performance.

Reading voluminous documents on her voyage across the Atlantic for the first meeting of the General Assembly in London in January 1946, Eleanor prepared herself for her new assignment. When issues regarding war refugees were referred to Committee Three, Eleanor debated the sharp-tongued Andrei Vishinsky of the Soviet Union. He wanted the refugees, of whom there were approximately a million from Eastern Europe living in displaced persons' camps, sent back to their homelands, regardless of whether they wanted to return. Appealing to Latin American countries, which represented a major voting bloc, Eleanor, who spoke without notes, argued that displaced persons should make their own decisions, and the committee agreed.[36]

Eleanor's work on Committee Three represented one of her three

Eleanor answers questions from journalists at the United Nations in Paris on 10 December 1948 following the adoption of the Declaration of Human Rights. Courtesy of the Franklin D. Roosevelt Library, Hyde Park, New York.

main achievements at the United Nations. In the beginning stages of the Cold War, she espoused the rights of refugees to refuse to return to their homelands. This stand countered the Soviet Union's insistence that refugees be forced to go back to countries that had been taken over by new Communist regimes. Her efforts on behalf of refugees led to her election in 1947 as chair of the U.N. Commission on Human Rights, which she considered "my most important task."[37]

As chair, she became the moving spirit behind the creation of the Universal Declaration of Human Rights, a document adopted by the United Nations General Assembly on 10 December 1948, without dissent, although eight countries, mainly from the Soviet bloc, abstained. After the adoption Eleanor, who had delivered an address in French at the Sorbonne University in Paris in support of the declaration, received a standing ovation, a tribute to her as the "first lady of the world."[38] The declaration remains the cornerstone for internationalization of moral and legal concepts governing human rights.[39]

To craft the declaration, for one and one-half years Eleanor, combining what appeared to be naïveté with cunning, drove the delegates, some said like a slave driver, to resolve ideological conflicts. These pitted the United States, with its stress on political freedom, against the Soviet Union, which emphasized social and economic rights. In debate the Soviets lambasted the Americans for denial of rights to African Americans, forcing Eleanor, known for her longtime advocacy of civil rights, to defend her country from their attacks.[40] As an official U.S. representative she faced the embarrassing position of having to refuse to bring an NAACP petition attacking racial discrimination in the United States before the world body. Even so, she remained on the NAACP board, which assumed she was operating under Department of State directives.[41]

Eleanor's belief in the United Nations, which she promoted endlessly in her writings, speeches, and travels, led her to criticize Truman for backing unilateral aid to Greece and Turkey in 1947. She feared that the United Nations, which she viewed as an instrument of collective security, would be weakened by this action. It was undertaken as part of the "Truman Doctrine," enunciated by the president as an effort by the United States to halt Communist takeovers in countries resisting attempted subjugation by armed minorities or outside pressures. She, however, favored Truman's endorsement of the Marshall Plan to give American aid to Europe.

Initially opposed to Zionism (the movement for a Jewish state), she reversed herself and voted for the U.N. partition of Palestine into Jewish and Arab states in 1947, pressuring Truman and Secretary of State George Marshall into implementation of the partition as a way of strengthening the United Nations. When the United States recognized the new state of Israel in 1948, without informing her or other members of the American United Nations delegation, she complained that the White House was ignoring the world organization. Restrained by her position as a delegate, she concealed her criticisms of Truman, whom she thought a bungler, from the public and offered to resign from her post, but the president persuaded her to continue.

Although she split with Henry Wallace, who ran for president on the Communist-linked Progressive Party ticket in 1948, she refused to endorse Truman to succeed himself until late in the campaign.[42] After Truman's surprise reelection, he reappointed her to the United Nations, where she supported his Korean War policies. In 1949 the president came to Eleanor's defense when Cardinal Francis J. Spellman, the principal spokesman for the American Catholic Church, attacked her for opposition to federal aid to parochial schools, as expressed in three "My Day" columns. The Cardinal subsequently apologized after sending Eleanor a letter calling her record "unworthy of an American mother," to which she replied, the "final judgment, my dear Cardinal Spellman, of the worthiness of all human beings is in the hands of God."[43]

Truman also backed Eleanor's trips, especially to Third World countries. As an official ambassador of goodwill, she traveled extensively both to commemorate the achievements of Franklin and see global conditions firsthand as a leading world figure. In 1948 she unveiled a statue of her husband in London as the guest of the king and queen and traveled to the Netherlands, where she received a doctor of laws degree from the University of Utrecht. Two years later, accompanied by her son Elliott and two grandchildren, she went to Norway to unveil another statue of Franklin and to visit Scandinavia.

After the end of the United Nations General Assembly in Paris in February 1952, she took a trip around the world, visiting the Arab countries of Lebanon, Syria, and Jordan, as well as refugee camps for Palestinians displaced from Israel, which she found "distressing beyond words."[44] In Israel, her next stop, she viewed desert reclamation projects as outstanding accomplishments, particularly contrasted with her perception of lack of development of Palestine areas. She then moved on to Pakistan and India, where she stayed for thirty days as the guest of Prime Minister Jawaharlal Nehru and Madame Vijaya Pandit, the head of the Indian delegation to the United Nations, before heading home via Indonesia and the Philippines. Her travels, which continued after she left the United Nations, helped solidify her international stature. In 1953 she published a book based on her trip to India, titled *India and the Awakening East*, which helped acquaint Americans with a part of the world about which many were not familiar.

As she encountered Soviet duplicity at the United Nations, Eleanor made it plain that she intended to fight communism in the United States, remembering how she had been led astray on the eve of World War II by Communist Party members in the American Youth Congress. She denounced Wallace's Communist backers and served as honorary chair of Americans for Democratic Action, an anti-Communist, independent political organization of liberals dedicated to preserving the ideals of the New Deal. Nevertheless, those termed "Red-baiters" viewed her stand on communism suspiciously, claiming that her passionate defense of civil rights and other liberal causes showed her involvement in so-called Red causes.

Certainly, Eleanor warned against the excesses of efforts to combat alleged Communist activity in the United States. She disliked Truman's loyalty program, which required investigations of the loyalty of government workers, and defended Alger Hiss, a State Department official found guilty of perjury in connection with spying for the Soviet Union. In particular, she criticized Republican senator Joseph R. McCarthy of Wisconsin, whose unsubstantiated charges of Communist influence in government gave rise to the derogatory term "McCarthyism." When a student asked her in 1952 what she thought of McCarthy, she called him the "greatest menace to freedom we have in this country." According to officials of Americans for Democratic Action, Eleanor's enormous prestige saved that organization from being investigated by McCarthy.[45]

A staunch defender of free speech, Eleanor took issue with the House Un-American Activities Committee (HUAC), particularly when it launched an investigation into alleged Communist activity in the mass media, including Hollywood film production, radio, and television. She distrusted Republican congressman Richard Nixon, who gained a seat on HUAC in 1947 and established himself as a Communist-hunter. Nixon employed Communist smear tactics to defeat Eleanor's good friend, Rep. Helen Gahagan Douglas, a Democratic liberal from California, for the U.S. Senate in 1950. To no avail Eleanor campaigned for Douglas and backed her in "My Day." Close readers of her column included FBI agents under J. Edgar Hoover, who kept a "My Day" file, apparently in an effort to illustrate that Eleanor let herself be duped by Communist sympathizers.[46] Hoover's agents also scanned her magazine advice column, "If You Ask Me," for evidence of her Communist leanings, clipping an answer to a 1953 question in which she agreed with a statement that HUAC was "ruining our reputation in the rest of the world."[47]

Considering Eleanor's disapproval of both McCarthy and Nixon, it was not surprising that the Republican administration of President Eisenhower and Vice President Nixon did not see fit to reappoint her as a delegate to the United Nations after taking office in 1953. During the presidential campaign of 1952, Eleanor, who supported the Democratic candidate Adlai Stevenson, berated Eisenhower for not having the courage to speak out publicly against McCarthy's excesses. After his inauguration Eisenhower quickly accepted the resignation that Eleanor, like other Democratic appointees, had submitted as a formality. Allegedly, Eisenhower also was angered by a mistaken report that Eleanor had called his wife, Mamie, an alcoholic.[48]

Unswerving in her commitment to the United Nations, which was under right-wing attack, Eleanor immediately became the chief volunteer of the American Association of the United Nations, a nonpartisan private organization dedicated to promoting the world organization. When the Democrats returned to the White House with the election in 1960 of President John F. Kennedy, who courted her support, Eleanor was reappointed to the United Nations. She served as a delegate to a special session in 1961 and was named a special advisor to the U.S. delegation the following year, but declining health limited her participation. Kennedy also appointed her as chair of the President's Commission on the Status of Women in 1961. Its final report, issued after her death in 1962, stopped short of calling for an Equal Rights Amendment, about which Eleanor herself was ambivalent, believing in recognition of gender differences.

After leaving the United Nations in 1953, Eleanor continued her career as a journalist, media personality, and revered stateswoman to the vast majority of the public, although anathema to some conservatives. She and her family remained the special target of venom from Westbrook Pegler, now writing for Hearst newspapers, who insinuated incorrectly that the Roosevelts had accumulated a huge fortune.[49] While Eleanor relinquished her right to a $5,000-a-year pension given other presidential widows, she needed more money than Franklin's estate provided for her personal expenses, charitable contributions, and aid to her children, especially Anna and Elliott. Disturbed generally by the knotty financial and marital affairs of her children, who quarreled endlessly among themselves, Eleanor particularly found upsetting the breakup of Anna's marriage to John Boettiger, who committed suicide in 1950.

In an effort to help Anna pay debts stemming from a failed newspaper venture with Boettiger in Arizona, Eleanor agreed in 1948 to join Anna in an afternoon radio talk show five days a week on the

American Broadcasting Company (ABC) network. Eleanor recorded her portion from Europe, where she was busy with the United Nations. While the program received critical acclaim—the *Hollywood Reporter* praised it as "the first network recognition of female intelligence in daytime programming"—ABC dropped it for lack of commercial sponsorship.[50] Eleanor's political views and serious conversation did not appeal to a wide range of sponsors.

Acting as Eleanor's agent and producer, her son Elliott was heavily involved in her broadcasting ventures, which included two shows in 1950 and 1951, a Sunday afternoon television show on the National Broadcasting Company (NBC), featuring her interviews with notable guests, and a midday radio talk show. These programs also left the air because of lack of continuous sponsorship, attributed chiefly to Eleanor's political views and predictability. Elliott, who acted as the announcer on the radio show, drew criticism for tasteless handling of commercials in which he told the audience that "mother uses" a particular kind of soap or brush.[51] The television program became controversial when NBC forced the cancellation of an appearance by singer Paul Robeson because of his Communist leanings. Ignoring her strong record on free speech, Eleanor failed to defend his right to appear.

Eleanor continued to be a regular guest on public affairs programs like *Meet the Press* and was interviewed by Edward R. Murrow on his popular *Person to Person* show. She spoke in French over the Voice of America, creating goodwill for the United States so successfully that she subsequently did broadcasts in German, Spanish, and Italian. Her fluency in languages, an asset at the United Nations, dated back to her boarding school days in England. In 1959 she agreed to do a commercial for margarine to show that she was able to appeal to sponsors, using her $35,000 fee for CARE packages to aid hungry children.[52] From 1959 to 1962 she moderated a public affairs documentary program, *Prospects for Mankind*, for National Educational Television, the predecessor of today's public television.

Elliott scored one impressive business achievement on behalf of his mother, arranging the sale of her White House memoir, *This I Remember*, to *McCall's*, then a leading woman's magazine, for $150,000 in 1949. He contacted *McCall's* after the editors of its rival, the *Ladies' Home Journal*, for which Eleanor had written for years, questioned the literary merit of the manuscript. *McCall's* also took Eleanor's "If You Ask Me" column away from the *Journal.* Fortunately for Eleanor and *McCall's*, the serialization of *This I Remember*, which relieved Eleanor's financial worries, proved an overwhelming success. Published in book form, it drew rave reviews and sold well, preparing the way for the last volume of her autobiography, *On My Own*, which appeared in 1958. Three years later Eleanor combined her first autobiographical work, *This Is My Story*, with the two later works to publish a single-volume *Autobiography of Eleanor Roosevelt.*

Unhappily, Elliott's farming venture at Hyde Park proved unsuccessful. In 1952 Eleanor was hurt when he sold Top Cottage without her knowledge and left Hyde Park. He departed after her youngest child, John Roosevelt, a businessman who had become a Republican, moved with his family to Stone Cottage, the building next to her Val-Kill cottage, and the two brothers bickered repeatedly. John eventually took over what remained of the farming operation. His residence at Stone Cottage allowed Eleanor to see a great deal of his four children, to whom she was a fond grandmother. With her own children, however, there were numerous financial and emotional strains. They were married a total of nineteen times, giving Eleanor twenty-two biological and five adopted grandchildren.

In her later years Eleanor depended for emotional support on David Gurewitsch, a handsome, urbane doctor, who was her personal physician, traveling companion, and closest friend from 1947 until the end of her life. He became her physician in 1945 at the recommendation of Trude Pratt Lash, whom Joe Lash had married in November 1944. The relationship between Eleanor and Gurewitsch grew in 1947 when they exchanged confidences while a plane taking them to Europe was fogged in at Shannon Airport.

At the time, Gurewitsch, the forty-five-year-old, Swiss-educated son of Russian Jewish parents, was traveling to Switzerland to seek treatment for tuberculosis, while Eleanor, then sixty-three, was headed to Geneva for a United Nations meeting. In subsequent correspondence with Gurewitsch, Eleanor expressed her affection and need for his personal counsel. She offered her emotional solace as Gurewitsch weathered a divorce and involvements with other women, including her old friend, journalist Martha Gellhorn, who had visited her at the White House. Like Hickok, Gellhorn had reported on Depression conditions for the New Deal.

During the next decade, Gurewitsch, an excellent photographer, often spent his vacations on extended trips abroad with Eleanor, taking countless pictures of their travels.[53] Accompanied by Maureen Corr, who became Eleanor's personal secretary in 1953 following the death of "Tommy" Thompson, Eleanor took extensive trips after she left the United Nations, using material gained from her travels for her column, magazine articles, and books. In 1953 after a five-week cultural exchange visit in Japan, Eleanor journeyed on to Turkey and Greece, where she met Gurewitsch, who joined her for a trip to Yugoslavia, where she interviewed President Josip Tito on his efforts to break away from the Soviet Union.

Two years later Gurewitsch traveled with her to Indonesia and Cambodia. In 1957 Eleanor accepted an invitation to tour Morocco as the guest of the sultan, taking along Gurewitsch and Elliott Roosevelt. Gurewitsch, who spoke Russian, stayed by her side when she interviewed Soviet premier Nikita S. Khrushchev in 1957, on the first of her two trips to the Soviet Union.

When Eleanor and Gurewitsch returned to the Soviet Union the following year, a new member had been added to their touring party, Edna Gurewitsch, an art historian, whom the doctor had married in February 1958. Eleanor had become despondent when Gurewitsch first announced his engagement, fearing the loss of his attention, but she remained eager to preserve her relationship with the doctor and persuaded the couple to be married in her New York apartment. The three bought a Manhattan townhouse together, frequently eating and going to the theater as a trio, although Eleanor maintained separate quarters from the couple.

Val-Kill continued to be her principal home where she offered unassuming hospitality to world leaders, including John F. Kennedy, Khrushchev, Nehru, Tito, and Haile Selassie of Ethiopia. She held annual picnics for students attending the nearby Wiltwyck School, the first interracial treatment center for troubled boys from New York City, as well as parties for foreign students and local groups. She faithfully attended St. James's Episcopal Church, frequently taking with her Lorena Hickok, who, almost destitute, had come to live in Hyde Park in 1955 to be near Eleanor.

In an effort to help Hickok financially, Eleanor collaborated with her on a book about women in politics, *Ladies of Courage*.[54] The two pointed to examples of successful women politicians on the local level, declaring that having children "should not deter them from holding office in their communities."[55] In the final chapter, they counseled, "If you are thirty-five or older, if your children are in school most of the day . . . , if you are beginning to experience that appalling sense of not being needed any more, politics can be a godsend to you, bringing new interests, activity, associations."[56] One wonders if Eleanor saw politics as her own salvation in her younger days.

As she aged, Eleanor was determined to continue her travels. In 1959 she took her grandchild, Nina, one of John's children, on a journey to Iran, where Anna's third husband, Dr. James Halsted, was helping set up a medical school. She also returned to Israel, for which her enthusiasm increased as the decade progressed. In 1960 she attended a meeting of the World Federation of United Nations Associations in Warsaw, Poland. In failing health, she made a last trip to Europe in February 1962, entertaining her companions, Corr and David and Edna Gurewitsch, with recollections of her 1905 honeymoon there.[57] She also stopped in Israel and visited her friend, Prime Minister David Ben-Gurion, for a final good-bye.

In 1960 Gurewitsch diagnosed Eleanor with aplastic anemia, a blood disease, and treated her with antibiotics. With her condition worsening in 1962, her family suggested other physicians, but she wanted only Gurewitsch. As her blood count fell, she was given steroids later believed to have reactivated an old tubercular infection that she had contracted while accompanying Franklin on a tour of World War I battlefields in France in 1919. She died at the age of seventy-eight at her home in New York City on 7 November 1962.

The body was taken to Hyde Park for an invitation-only funeral service on 10 November 1962 in St. James's Episcopal Church. President Kennedy, Vice President Lyndon B. Johnson, and former presidents Harry S Truman and Dwight D. Eisenhower attended, along with First Lady Jackie Kennedy, former first lady Bess Truman, and a future first lady, Lady Bird Johnson. Eleanor was buried next to Franklin in the rose garden of the Roosevelt estate.

The previous day a special memorial service had been held for

Eleanor meets with Prime Minister David Ben-Gurion during her last trip to Israel in February 1962. Courtesy of the Franklin D. Roosevelt Library, Hyde Park, New York.

her at the United Nations. Ambassador Adlai E. Stevenson spoke in tribute: "She would rather light candles than curse the darkness."[58] On 17 November an estimated 10,000 persons attended a memorial service for her at the Cathedral Church of St. John the Divine in New York City.

Eleanor left an estate valued at $340,000 before taxes. Actively pursuing a career up to the end of her life, she reported earnings of $135,552 ($75,874 after expenses) in 1961, the last full year of her life. Her tax records showed she made $7,794 from "My Day" (by then a three-day-a-week feature); $59,000 from other writing; $6,500 from Brandeis University, where she was a visiting lecturer; $33,499 from paid lectures; $8,430 from appearances on radio and television; and $20,000 from a proposed documentary series on Franklin.[59] From 1953 through 1961, her yearly taxable income averaged more than $97,000, of which 47 percent went to the high taxes of the period and about 25 percent to charitable contributions.[60]

Most of her estate was left in trust for the benefit of her daughter, Anna, during her lifetime. David Gurewitsch received $10,000. Varying amounts, not exceeding $2,000 per person, were left to personal employees, relatives, and friends, including Lorena Hickok, who received $1,000.[61] Eleanor's financial records testified to the effort that she put into her career as well as to the fact that she personally profited relatively little from her earnings, which were noteworthy for a woman of her day.[62]

CHAPTER 8

MODELING POLITICAL LEADERSHIP

"You gain strength, courage, and confidence by every experience in which you really stop to look fear in the face. . . . You must do the thing you think you cannot do."

Eleanor Roosevelt in *You Learn by Living* (1960)

"In the final analysis, a democratic government represents the sum total of the courage and the integrity of its individuals. It cannot be better than they are. . . . In the long run there is no more liberating, no more exhilarating experience than to determine one's position, state it bravely and then act boldly."

Eleanor Roosevelt in *Tomorrow Is Now*, published posthumously (1963)

In her final years Eleanor looked back on her life experience, which, while far different from that of most Americans, contained lessons of universal applicability, at least in her own mind. Glossing over the exceptional circumstances that lay behind her own career, she presented herself as a teacher and advisor to ordinary individuals. In *You Learn by Living* she offered everyday wisdom centered on making one's life useful to others. A year later she published *Your Teens and Mine*, written in collaboration with Helen Ferris, former editor of a book club for young readers.[1] In it she referred to her own adolescent shyness and urged girls to develop self-confidence.

Another coauthored book in 1962, *Eleanor Roosevelt's Book of Common Sense Etiquette*, instructed the unsophisticated in handling social situations.[2] Her last book, *Tomorrow Is Now*, published after her death, dealt with wider themes, mainly Cold War dangers on the international scene. It called on citizens to make their individual actions ensure continuation of a nation built on democratic values.

While none of these books were tied directly to her twelve years as first lady, they all drew from her performance in that nebulous role, in which she dramatized the position of the president's wife and elevated it to far greater symbolic importance than it had held previously. In her use of platitudes she spoke to average people, urging them to expand their horizons and see beyond selfish interests to the wider good. As she had discovered her own abilities by reaching out to others, she encouraged ordinary individuals to overcome adversity and work toward a more just world. Her message transcended the overt political realm, although she was identified clearly with the liberal wing of the Democratic Party.

Surely Eleanor recognized that she had conquered the fears of uselessness that she brought to the White House in 1933. From a nervous and diffident wife, she had emerged as first lady into a figure of national prominence who moved comfortably in the limelight, although her full development as a leader did not come until much later at the United Nations. According to Hickok, a pronounced change occurred after Eleanor's fiftieth birthday in 1934 when her self-confidence increased, and she and Hickok grew apart.[3]

Eleanor showed that a first lady could command attention and respect in support of high-minded principles such as democracy, justice for all, social betterment, and world peace. If her leadership faltered on specific tasks, such as her appointment in the Office of Civil Defense, she could be excused on grounds that she had given her best effort. Her energetic activities in the White House turned the office of first lady into a center of political influence, even though it remained unclear exactly what degree of influence.

In 1944 Virginia Pasley, a Washington journalist, wrote, "The truth about Mrs. Roosevelt is that she is a social service worker with all the faults and all the virtues of the genus—a 'good' woman . . .—an Americana type so rarely seen in sophisticated circles that cosmopolites simply can't believe their eyes and ears."[4] She noted that

Eleanor, while considered "tedious, irritating and sometimes comical" by the sophisticated, was commonly credited in the capital with creation of the National Youth Administration, along with a surplus food program for relief clients, the arts and crafts section of the WPA, and resettlement and community projects such as Arthurdale.[5]

While Eleanor believed throughout her life in charity as a personal act, her support for New Deal programs demonstrated her commitment to a modern concept of welfare administered by the state. By the end of her tenure as first lady, she had risen far beyond the class-based idea of noblesse oblige. She sought to redefine the obligations of citizens to their government and their government's responsibilities to them.[6]

Eleanor Roosevelt's activism as first lady has become a benchmark for measuring the actions of her successors. If a first lady involves herself in political and social causes, the mass media portrays her as following the nontraditional pattern set by Eleanor Roosevelt. Eleanor's emphasis on reaching out to the country at large has affected all the spouses who followed her into the White House, if only by providing a model for them to reject.

Eleanor turned the role of first lady into one of political celebrity.[7] She received a tremendous amount of public attention; in fact, she courted it, due to her own participation, as well as portrayal, in the news media. Unlike her predecessors she did not think it undignified to establish herself as a media personality. She utilized pathbreaking ventures such as sponsored radio commentaries and a daily newspaper column, as well as writing books and magazine articles, to make sure that she had a public voice, even though she was careful in what she said to conform to cultural limitations placed on women of her day. Her performance permanently altered the expectations for presidential wives who succeeded her.[8]

First ladies before Eleanor had become celebrities, too, furnishing material for news coverage of women, particularly wives of famous men, which accelerated after women won the right to vote in 1920. Increased use of printed photographs and newsreels, which stemmed from technological improvements in camera equipment during the early decades of the twentieth century, enhanced the actual visibility of presidents' wives in the public arena. Mass-circulation women's magazines found White House families enthralling fare for their readers, as did women's sections of newspapers.

Eleanor built on this curiosity and turned it to her own advantage. First ladies before her expected and received public attention in terms of limited social and domestic roles, although Lou Henry Hoover was eager to publicize the Girl Scout movement in which she was extensively involved. Eleanor carved out a different kind of role—one in which she pictured herself serving the public as a surrogate for her husband and his administration. She deliberately framed publicity for herself within the context of womanly concern for others.

Eleanor's interest in the unfortunate, her advocacy of civil rights, her numerous causes, including her efforts to do what she could to assist World War II refugees—all fit within a broad pattern of a stereotypical good woman of the early twentieth century aiding those who needed help. Franklin both benefitted and distanced himself from these activities, since Eleanor's insistence on having her own moneymaking career as a journalist and lecturer established her as a separate voice within the administration. Unlike her predecessors Eleanor used the White House as a "bully pulpit," the term made famous by her uncle Ted. She saw her press conferences for women reporters as a bridge between the White House and the general public. This represented a new concept for first ladies—to position themselves as pivotal instruments in an organized communications effort.

The presidents' wives who came after Eleanor received press coverage whether they wanted it or not. This stemmed partly from the organization of Eleanor's White House women's press corps that looked to the institution of the first lady as an ongoing source of news. Eleanor's immediate successor, Bess Truman, expressed determination not to meet with reporters, to their great disappointment. She refused to hold press conferences and shied away from public appearances except for the perfunctory. "The country was used to ER. I couldn't possibly be anything like her. I wasn't going down in any coal mines," she later quipped.[9]

While Franklin had used his wife's access to the media to his advantage, as when he insisted that she run a report in "My Day" on steel industry unemployment unfavorable to Republican industrialists, President Truman did not want his family in the spotlight. He wrote his sister, who asked if she should accept an invitation to a political meeting, "For goodness sake, refuse it. . . . I have kept Bess and Margaret [the Trumans' daughter] out of the political picture as much as I can and I am still trying to keep them from being talked about."[10] Eleanor, by contrast, saw "being talked about" as an opportunity to influence the public agenda, and Franklin, for the most part, saw her communication activities as assets to his administration.

Since Eleanor had turned the position of first lady into one of being a predictable staple of news, Washington women reporters determinedly sought news items from a hostile Bess Truman for the women's pages in metropolitan newspapers of the late 1940s and early 1950s. President Truman's press secretary, Charles Ross, did not think it politically expedient to refuse outright to accommodate them. This led to a series of non-news briefings in which women reporters sent questions to Mrs. Truman through her secretaries, who then transmitted the first lady's evasive answers to the journalists.

Because Bess Truman declined to voice any opinions, the reporters were reduced to grasping for tidbits of information on her personal preferences, posing mundane questions to which she relayed monosyllabic replies. For example, she was asked to name her favorite color ("blue"), her favorite style of clothing ("tailored"), whether she counted calories ("yes"), her dress size ("18"), and her shoe size ("6").[11] Even this unproductive exchange, however, reveals that first ladies after Eleanor were expected to produce news.

Like Bess Truman, her Republican successor, Mamie Eisenhower, wanted to distance herself from Eleanor's path. The Eisenhowers did not invite Eleanor to the White House during their eight-year tenure, and Mamie certainly did not applaud Eleanor's interest in communicating with the public. When asked if she would be interested in doing a column like Eleanor's, Mamie replied in a note to her secretary, "It sounds like a terrible chore, and smacks of [the] 'My Day' column, of which I have a perfect horror!"[12]

The elegant Jackie Kennedy, whose project to restore the White House enhanced her popularity and displayed her knowledge of culture, refused to enter the public political arena even to argue for government support of the arts. Although she lobbied privately, she refused to testify before Congress. "After all," she said, "I'm not Mrs.

Roosevelt."[13] Her comment, while dismissive, reflected the fact that Eleanor's successors could not forget about her performance. Although Jackie disliked members of the White House women's press corps, whom she referred to as "harpies," she benefitted greatly from the undeniable celebrity status that Eleanor first had brought to the position of first lady.[14] Far more than Eleanor, Jackie found it difficult to deal with intense public interest in herself and her family, especially since the public appetite for news about celebrities, particularly the glamorous Jackie herself, had markedly increased by the 1960s.

Subsequent first ladies, especially those representing the Democratic Party, were more eager to pattern themselves after Eleanor. Jackie's successor, Lady Bird Johnson, made a concerted effort to link her own White House activism on behalf of the environment, Head Start, and other programs with Eleanor's.[15] Speaking at the Eleanor Roosevelt Memorial Foundation dinner in 1964, Lady Bird said Eleanor's "conscience was her counselor," adding, "I met her first in print and admired her. I met her later in person and loved her."[16] Yet Lady Bird was a less outspoken individual than Eleanor and more interested in keeping a lower profile.

Elizabeth "Liz" Carpenter, her press secretary, explained the difference between the two women this way: "Mrs. Roosevelt was an instigator, an innovator, willing to air a cause even without her husband's endorsement. Mrs. Johnson was an implementer and translator of her husband and his purposes."[17] Carpenter, who assiduously courted the press on Lady Bird's behalf, also might have noted that Johnson was far more dependent on staff, particularly Carpenter herself, than Eleanor had been in publicizing her causes through the news media.

Republican Pat Nixon, like her husband, President Richard Nixon, did not enjoy positive press relations. The media dubbed her "plastic Pat" because of what appeared to be a pasted-on smile. Her cause in the White House, volunteerism, however, echoed Eleanor's efforts. Both she and Eleanor encouraged women to volunteer to improve society.

After Nixon's resignation in the wake of the Watergate political scandal, Betty Ford unexpectedly found herself first lady. She soon told the world that she had breast cancer at a time when some considered this a disease too shameful to discuss. In spite of their belonging to different political parties, Betty found Eleanor an inspiration. Betty commented that Eleanor "eventually became a role model for me because I liked her independence. . . . I really liked the idea that a woman was finally speaking out and expressing herself rather than just expressing the views of her husband."[18]

Betty and her Democratic successor, Rosalynn Carter, each tried to make the position of first lady the vital political symbol that it had been in Eleanor's day. When Betty held her first press conference, after letting it be known that she favored the Equal Rights Amendment, was pro-choice on abortion, had seen a psychiatrist, and used tranquilizers, *Newsweek* and several other publications compared her frank disclosures to Eleanor's willingness to offer opinions.[19]

Rosalynn became the first president's wife since Eleanor to testify before Congress, appearing before a U.S. Senate subcommittee to support recommendations included in a bill to improve mental health resources. In her autobiography she called attention to Eleanor as "the notable exception" to first ladies who limited themselves to being hostesses and private helpmates even though she was "severely criticized for her personal involvement in public affairs."[20] Herself criticized for acting as her husband's advisor and attending Cabinet meetings, Rosalynn expressed gratitude for Eleanor's example.

In describing her own approach to the role of first lady, Nancy Reagan pointed out that Eleanor had initiated an expectation for first ladies to "become not only more visible but more active as well."[21] Nancy used Eleanor's example of purchasing a new set of White House dishes as a precedent for her own decision to acquire new china, a move that resulted in unfavorable publicity.[22] Nancy hosted a White House lecture and luncheon in October 1984 to commemorate the centennial of Eleanor's birth. More importantly, in her speeches she frequently repeated a line attributed to Eleanor: "A woman is like a teabag. You never know how strong it is until it's in hot water."[23]

Neither Barbara Bush nor her daughter-in-law Laura Bush ever stated that she considered Eleanor a role model for her own performance as first lady, but exemplars as they were of the Republican Party, they still found themselves dealing with the shadow of Eleanor's presence. In personal style—what one author called a "matronly bearing of noblesse oblige"—Barbara was compared to Eleanor, even in terms of walking her dog outside the White House gates as Eleanor had done with hers. Barbara recalled in correspondence how her own mother, who previously had scorned Eleanor's activism, changed her mind and became a supporter after meeting Eleanor at the White House.[24]

While Laura Bush avoided comparisons with her predecessors, a journalist asked if she saw herself as a wartime first lady like Eleanor. The question came in the wake of the terrorist attacks of 11 September 2001, which led Laura Bush's husband, President George W. Bush, to declare a war on terror. Laura replied, "No," adding, "I don't really think of myself as first lady," perhaps a backhanded reference to Eleanor's definition of the role.[25]

Hillary Rodham Clinton, whose husband, Bill Clinton, was elected president in 1992, was by far the greatest emulator of Eleanor, whom she began to study during the campaign. She continued to model herself after Eleanor for the eight years the Clintons spent in the White House. The most controversial first lady since Eleanor, Hillary pursued political activism on various fronts, including equal rights for women, health care, global democracy, and education. Following Eleanor's example directly, she launched a chatty weekly newspaper column, "Talking It Over," in 1995, although it never came close to the popularity of Eleanor's "My Day" column and soon was dropped. Like Eleanor, she testified before Congress, attempting to push a health care plan she had chaired.

After the plan met defeat, Hillary held a series of "conversations" in the White House with Eleanor and Mahatma Gandhi led by a psychic philosopher. The sessions were revealed by Bob Woodward, the *Washington Post* journalist who had helped uncover President Nixon's involvement in Watergate. Hillary denied that they were séances, but they brought her ridicule in the media.[26] In her autobiography, she referred to these imaginary conversations as "a useful mental exercise to help analyze problems, provided you choose the right person to visualize."[27] She explained that "Eleanor Roosevelt was ideal . . . her spirit and commitment were indomitable, and she never let her critics slow her down."[28]

Hillary referred to Eleanor some fifteen separate times in her autobiography and told how she had added a bronze bust of Eleanor to the White House Roosevelt room that features portraits of her husband Franklin and uncle Ted.[29] She also supported a campaign to erect a bronze statue of Eleanor in New York's Riverside Park and presided at its unveiling in 1996. In a speech in 1998 at Georgetown University in Washington, D.C., Hillary described Eleanor's vision for human rights internationally and pledged herself to continue this work.[30]

While Michelle Obama has not gone on record giving her views about Eleanor, the names of the two women have been linked by others. In her biography of Obama, Elizabeth Lightfoot contends that the newest first lady has developed "her own form of rhinoceros hide," drawing on a comment from Eleanor: "Every woman in public life needs to develop skin as tough as rhinoceros hide."[31] Blogger Nathan Richter insists Michelle Obama is "shaping up to resemble another iconic counterpart," Eleanor Roosevelt, in part because both have the ability to connect with ordinary people.[32]

The news media also are quick to note when Obama's actions parallel Eleanor's. For example, when Obama planted a vegetable garden on the White House lawn, the *New York Times* pointed out that Eleanor had planted a victory garden there during World War II.[33] Similarly, when Obama became an honorary member of Alpha Kappa Alpha Sorority, a historically black organization, news accounts referred to the fact that Eleanor also had been made an honorary member.[34]

In the nation's collective memory Eleanor holds a well-recognized place. Far more than any other first lady, she has been commemorated in a variety of ways, ranging from postage stamps and streets named in her honor to dramatic reenactments of her life. The Franklin D. Roosevelt Memorial in Washington, D.C., includes a statue of Eleanor, making it the first presidential memorial to include a sculpture of a first lady. The Franklin D. Roosevelt Library and Museum at Hyde Park, New York, which houses her personal papers as well as a gallery illustrating her life, is the first presidential library to devote a special section to a first lady. Her Val-Kill cottage was designated a National Historical Site by the U.S. government in 1977. The site houses the Eleanor Roosevelt Center (ERVK), a private, nonprofit organization to provide educational programs furthering her ideals.

The Eleanor Roosevelt Memorial Foundation, set up after her

death to receive donations for projects in her memory, in 1987 became part of the Franklin and Eleanor Roosevelt Institute located at the Roosevelt Library. The institute gives grants for scholarship on the Roosevelt era. The Eleanor Roosevelt Papers Project, a research center associated with George Washington University and headed by Allida M. Black, currently is publishing scholarly, annotated, and multimedia editions of her papers, beginning with her work in human rights, and creating an electronic edition of her "My Day" columns.[35] It also offers curriculum guides for teachers based on documentary source material pertaining to Eleanor.

Nevertheless, historians are split on their assessment of Eleanor's performance as first lady. Lewis Gould, while crediting her with finding "new responsibilities for presidential wives," concluded that she had limited success "in channeling her prodigious energies into constructive and coherent programs of action." He attributed this to the fact that she played the role of "the celebrity as first lady."[36] Black took a different approach in discussing publication of the first volume of Eleanor's papers in 2007. She contended that Eleanor, who claimed she never changed Franklin's mind on any policy, simply "lied" when she denied she had power.[37] Susan Ware, editor of the most recent edition of the biographical encyclopedia *Notable American Women*, took a similar view: "Clearly Eleanor was a total political animal, but she wouldn't usually admit that. [She would say] 'Oh, I was just my husband's helpmate'—the historical records show otherwise."[38]

Undoubtedly she was more than that. Robert P. Watson, classifying first ladies in terms of their historical eras, placed Eleanor in the context of "aspiring spouses: developing new roles from 1901 to 1945."[39] By all measures she far overshadowed her predecessors, although they too tried to adjust their position to a society in which women were moving beyond the rigidity of the Victorian world. Watson pointed out that Eleanor "did more to change the institution of first lady than perhaps any other single person, event or historical period."[40]

Assessing the influence of presidential wives, a team of political scientists has compared the evolution of the roles of vice president and first ladies, pointing out that a vice president's power is closely related to his relationship with the president.[41] The same observation obviously can be made about first ladies. The team noted that Eleanor "shattered all conventions by traveling widely on her own."[42] It concluded that "she acted as FDR's vice president because of his paralysis. . . . No first lady since has been implicitly accorded such vice-presidential status."[43] The claim was bolstered by the fact that the *New York Times* index for 1933 showed that Eleanor had been mentioned 244 times compared to 40 for Vice President John Nance Garner.[44]

Still, Eleanor was a creature of times that called on women to take subordinate roles while holding to higher moral standards than men. To a degree this ideology of separate spheres sheltered her from being forced to take full responsibility for lapses in judgment, such as the appointment of her personal friends to the Office of Civil Defense. Eleanor herself clung to the fiction in public of being a traditional first lady, saying that she felt "a little like the prisoner of history in the White House, doing the things which the country expects this woman to do."[45]

In political terms, Eleanor's years at the White House showed how she put her own sense of morality into action. She had no qualms about making use of her position as Franklin's wife to attempt to influence policy both covertly and overtly. Because she often acted behind the scenes, no complete documentary record exists of what she did. If her marriage had evolved into a political, rather than a romantic, alliance, she still remained "Mrs. Roosevelt," with the privileges of a wife to counsel and give advice, even if her advice was not sought or taken. Perhaps she called herself a "helpmate" not to prevaricate, but because she truly saw herself as little more than that, pushing Franklin in a direction that she was sure he should go to promote social betterment.

To the horror of conservatives Eleanor strongly believed in the use of government programs for social ends, but unlike Franklin, she had no responsibility for shepherding programs through Congress and making sure that they worked. While Franklin listened to her as well as many others, he was known for making up his own mind. He did not necessarily do what she wanted. Therefore, perhaps she could honestly say that she had never changed his mind, or perhaps as a shrewd politician herself she preferred to minimize her own role because she thought it appropriate for a wife to do so in the context of the times.

To what degree she sought power for herself during her White House years is an open question. She saw that public fascination with the famous, including the president and his family, could be a means for her to engage in moneymaking activities that provided her an independent income. As Gould observes, she "turned the curiosity about her into a lever that brought offers of writing assignments [for] newspapers, magazines and books."[46] She also gave paid lectures. But she gave away much of what she earned. She wanted independence and recognition as a person in her own right, but she still clothed herself in the mantle of a traditional wife as far as her public persona was concerned. She refused to run for public office herself, although the most productive part of her career was in an official position at the United Nations.

For the most part Eleanor, insecure as a young woman and beset by unsatisfying family relationships, relished being in the public eye as first lady to affirm herself by reaching out to others. Her most notable contribution to the political scene may have been innate recognition that politics were becoming ever more dependent on the mass media. She apparently recognized that occupants of the White House would be increasingly judged by their ability to communicate with the public through both personal and media appearances.

Far ahead of her times in many ways, Eleanor recognized the public craze for celebrities and was able to draw on it for personal fulfillment. She saw presidential politics as a spectator sport and realized that the first lady was a vital member of the presidential team. Far more than a publicity seeker, as first lady she demonstrated passionate commitment to the Democratic Party and to her country as well as to causes in which she believed. She equated political leadership with the moral values later set forth in the Universal Declaration of Human Rights. Combining "vision and practicality," she was, according to Burns and Dunn, "the *woman* leader of the twentieth century."[47]

NOTES

PREFACE

1. James Roosevelt and Sidney Shalett, *Affectionately, F.D.R.: A Son's Story of a Lonely Man* (New York: Avon, 1959), 13.

2. Ibid.

INTRODUCTION

1. Eleanor Roosevelt to Harold Ickes, 26 May 1945, as cited in Joseph P. Lash, *Eleanor: The Years Alone* (New York: Norton, 1972), 28.

2. Bill Mauldin, editorial cartoon, "It's Her," *St. Louis Post-Dispatch*, 13 November 1962, reprinted in Jess Flemion and Colleen M. O'Connor, eds., *Eleanor Roosevelt: An American Journey* (San Diego: San Diego State University Press, 1987), 208.

3. Arthur M. Schlesinger Jr., *Journals: 1952–2000* (New York: Penguin, 2007), 179.

4. Ibid., 180.

5. Curtis Roosevelt, *Too Close to the Sun: Growing Up in the Shadow of My Grandparents, Franklin and Eleanor* (New York: Public Affairs, 2008), 22.

6. Ibid.

7. Ibid., 51.

8. See Joseph P. Lash, *Eleanor and Franklin: The Story of Their Relationship Based on Eleanor Roosevelt's Private Papers* (New York: Norton, 1971).

9. The connection between Hickok and Roosevelt first was explored in Doris Faber, *The Life of Lorena Hickok: E.R.'s Friend* (New York: Morrow, 1980). Blanche Cook, *Eleanor Roosevelt*, vols. 1 and 2 (New York: Viking, 1992 and 1999), situated Roosevelt in women's networks and examined her personal relationships with both her bodyguard, Earl Miller, and Hickok. Allida M. Black, *Casting Her Own Shadow: Eleanor Roosevelt and the Shaping of Postwar Liberalism* (New York: Columbia University Press, 1996), pictured her role as a civil libertarian. Mary Ann Glendon, *A World Made New: Eleanor Roosevelt and the Universal Declaration of Human Rights* (New York: Random House, 2001), interpreted Roosevelt's leadership at the United Nations.

10. Evan Thomas, "Hillary's Other Side, "*Newsweek*, 1 July 1996, p. 21.

11. Mrs. Franklin D. Roosevelt, "Women Must Learn to Play the Game as Men Do," *The Red Book Magazine* 50 (April 1928), 78–79, 141–142.

12. Lois Scharf, "Equal Rights Amendment," in Maurine H. Beasley, Holly C. Shulman, and Henry R. Beasley, eds., *The Eleanor Roosevelt Encyclopedia* (Westport, Conn.: Greenwood, 2001), 165.

13. Lois Scharf, "ER and Feminism," in Joan Hoff-Wilson and Marjorie Lightman, eds., *Without Precedent: The Life and Career of Eleanor Roosevelt* (Bloomington: Indiana University Press, 1984), 233.

14. Lewis L. Gould, "The Historical Legacy of Modern First Ladies," Afterword in Nancy Kegan Smith and Mary C. Ryan, eds., *Modern First Ladies: A Documentary Legacy* (Washington, D.C.: National Archives and Records Administration, 1989), 172.

15. See Maurine H. Beasley and Henry R. Beasley, "Eleanor Roosevelt as an Entrepreneur," *White House Studies* 4 (4 November 2004), 517–529.

CHAPTER 1. FINDING A PLACE

1. Eleanor Roosevelt, *The Autobiography of Eleanor Roosevelt* (New York: Harper & Brothers, 1961), 42.

2. Both Franklin and Eleanor Roosevelt were descendants of Claes Martenszen van Roosevelt, who arrived in New York about 1649. See complete genealogy by Linda E. Milano in Beasley, Shulman, and Beasley, *Eleanor Roosevelt Encyclopedia*, 205–209.

3. Joseph E. Persico, *Franklin and Lucy: President Roosevelt, Mrs. Rutherfurd and the Other Remarkable Women in His Life* (New York: Random House, 2008), 52.

4. Geoffrey C. Ward, *Before the Trumpet: Young Franklin Roosevelt, 1882–1905* (New York: Harper & Row, 1985), 313.

5. Roosevelt, *Autobiography*, 41.

6. Kati Marton, *Hidden Power: Presidential Marriages That Shaped Our Recent History* (New York: Pantheon, 2001), 50.

7. Ward, *Before the Trumpet*, 308.

8. Geoffrey C. Ward, *A First-Class Temperament: The Emergence of Franklin Roosevelt* (New York: Harper & Row, 1989), 412.

9. As quoted in Lash, *Eleanor and Franklin*, 138.

10. Ibid., 72.

11. Betty Boyd Caroli, *The Roosevelt Women* (New York: Basic, 1999), 253.

12. Roosevelt, *Autobiography*, 43.

13. Caroli, *Roosevelt Women*, 119.

14. Ibid., 133.

15. Roosevelt, *Autobiography*, 48.

16. Ibid.

17. Candace Fleming, *Our Eleanor: A Scrapbook Look at Eleanor Roosevelt's Remarkable Life* (New York: Atheneum, 2005), 22.

18. Ward, *Before the Trumpet*, 340.

19. Roosevelt, *Autobiography*, 50.

20. Joseph Lash interview with Alice Roosevelt Longworth, as quoted in David B. Roosevelt with Manuela Dunn Mascetti, *Grandmere: A Personal History of Eleanor Roosevelt* (New York: Warner Books, 2002), 34.

21. Stacy A. Cordery, *Alice: Alice Roosevelt Longworth, from White House Princess to Washington Power Broker* (New York: Viking, 2007), 383.

22. As quoted in Michel Teague, *Mrs. L.* (New York: Doubleday, 1981), 154.

23. Roosevelt, *Grandmere*, 86, 70.

24. Eleanor Roosevelt, "Wives of Great Men," *Liberty* 9 (1 October 1932), reprinted in Allida M. Black, ed., *What I Hope to Leave Behind: The Essential Essays of Eleanor Roosevelt* (Brooklyn, N.Y.: Carlson, 1995), 215–216.

25. Caroli, *Roosevelt Women*, 133.

26. James MacGregor Burns and Susan Dunn, *The Three Roosevelts: Patrician Leaders Who Transformed America* (New York: Atlantic Monthly Press, 2001), 574.

27. Quoted in Lash, *Eleanor and Franklin*, 252.

28. Ibid.

29. Roosevelt, *Autobiography*, 98.

30. Ibid., 4.

31. Blanche Wiesen Cook, *Eleanor Roosevelt*, vol. 1: *1884–1933* (New York: Viking, 1992), 39.

32. Roosevelt Family Papers Donated by the Children, hereafter referred to as RFPDC, folder—papers of Elliott Roosevelt Sr., 1870–1894, Elliott Roosevelt to Eleanor Roosevelt, 6 April 1893, Franklin D. Roosevelt Library, Hyde Park, N.Y., hereafter referred to as FDRL.

33. Roosevelt, *Autobiography*, 5.

34. Ibid., 9.

35. Lash, *Eleanor and Franklin*, 58.

36. Roosevelt, *Autobiography*, 3.

37. Ibid., 5.

38. Ibid., 6.

39. Eleanor Roosevelt, "Gracie Hall Roosevelt," in Beasley, Shulman, and Beasley, *Eleanor Roosevelt Encyclopedia*, 459.

40. Eleanor Roosevelt with Helen Ferris, *Your Teens and Mine* (Garden City, N.Y.: Doubleday, 1961), 37.

41. Roosevelt, *Autobiography*, 12–13.

42. Roosevelt, *Grandmere*, 34.

43. Eleanor Roosevelt, *This Is My Story* (New York: Harper & Brothers, 1937), 71.

44. Roosevelt, *Autobiography*, 37.

45. Ward, *Before the Trumpet*, 319.

46. Kathryn Kish Sklar, "National Consumers League," in Beasley, Shulman, and Beasley, *Eleanor Roosevelt Encyclopedia*, 364–365.

47. Roosevelt, *Autobiography*, 62.

48. Ibid., 60.

49. Lash, *Eleanor and Franklin*, 146.

50. As quoted in ibid., 162.

51. Joseph P. Lash, *Love, Eleanor: Eleanor Roosevelt and Her Friends* (New York: Norton, 1982), 56.

52. Roosevelt, *Autobiography*, 68.

53. Ibid.

54. Lash, *Eleanor and Franklin*, 220.

55. Persico, *Franklin and Lucy*, 90.

56. Ward, *First-Class Temperament*, 313.

57. Ibid., 108.

58. Cordery, *Alice*, 383.

59. Lash, *Eleanor and Franklin*, 215.

60. Lash, *Love, Eleanor*, 67.

61. "How to Save in Big Homes," *New York Times*, 17 July 1917.

62. RFPDC, correspondence: Franklin Delano Roosevelt, 1888–1945; folder, Franklin D. Roosevelt to Eleanor Roosevelt, 1915–1918, hereafter referred to as FDR to ER, 18 July 1917, FDRL.

63. RFPDC, correspondence: Eleanor Roosevelt, 1917; folder—ER to FDR, 20 July 1917, FDRL.

64. Persico, *Franklin and Lucy*, 125.

65. Ibid., 348–352.

CHAPTER 2. LAUNCHING A CAREER

1. Keith W. Olson, "Wilson Era Sunday Evening Suppers," in Beasley, Shulman, and Beasley, *Eleanor Roosevelt Encyclopedia*, 565–567.

2. Roosevelt, *Autobiography*, 92.

3. Ibid., 93.

4. Lash, *Eleanor and Franklin*, 219.

5. Roosevelt, *Autobiography*, 97.

6. Ibid., 93.

7. Lash, *Eleanor and Franklin*, 231.

8. Ibid., 237.

9. Jane Brissett, "Health," in Beasley, Shulman, and Beasley, *Eleanor Roosevelt Encyclopedia*, 230–232.

10. Persico, *Franklin and Lucy*, 131.

11. As quoted in Cook, *Eleanor Roosevelt*, vol. 1, 235.

12. Lorena Hickok, *Reluctant First Lady* (New York: Dodd, Mead, 1962), 91–92.

13. Lash, *Eleanor and Franklin*, 252.

14. Ibid., 253.

15. Lewis L. Gould, *Grand Old Party* (New York: Random House, 2003), 218.

16. Lois W. Banner, *Women in Modern America: A Brief History*, 2nd ed. (New York: Harcourt Brace Jovanovich, 1984), 147.

17. For full discussion of Eleanor Roosevelt's involvement with the League of Women Voters, see Hilda R. Watrous, *In League with Eleanor: Eleanor Roosevelt and the League of Women Voters, 1921–1962* (New York: Foundation for Citizen Education of League of Women Voters of New York State, 1984).

18. Ibid., 3–6.

19. Jean Edward Smith, *FDR* (New York: Random House, 2007), xii.

20. Lash, *Love, Eleanor*, 71.

21. Roosevelt, *Autobiography*, 117.

22. Ibid., 118–119.

23. Ibid., 120.

24. Fleming, *Our Eleanor*, 25; Roosevelt, *Autobiography*, 59–60.

25. Mrs. Franklin D. Roosevelt, "The American Peace Award," *Ladies' Home Journal* 40 (October 1923), 4.

26. Frank Freidel, *Franklin D. Roosevelt: The Ordeal* (Boston: Little, Brown, 1954), 127–129.

27. See Charles De Benedetti, "American Peace Award of 1924," *The Pennsylvania Magazine of History and Biography* 98 (April 1974), 224–249.

28. Cook, *Eleanor Roosevelt*, vol. 1, 345.

29. Roosevelt, *Autobiography*, 121.

30. Ibid., 124.

31. Smith, *FDR*, 213.

32. Persico, *Franklin and Lucy*, 177.

33. Ibid., 176.

34. Ibid., 163–166.

35. Smith, *FDR*, 213.

36. Persico, *Franklin and Lucy*, 177.

37. Kenneth S. Davis, *Invincible Summer: An Intimate Portrait of the Roosevelts* (New York: Atheneum, 1974), 21.

38. Mrs. Franklin D. Roosevelt, "Why I Am a Democrat," *Junior League Bulletin*, November 1923, 18–19.

39. Lash, *Eleanor and Franklin*, 280.

40. Ibid.

41. Cook, *Eleanor Roosevelt*, vol. 1, 325.

42. Ibid., 334.

43. Jan Pottker, *Sara and Eleanor: The Story of Sara Delano Roosevelt and Her Daughter-in-Law, Eleanor Roosevelt* (New York: St. Martin's Press, 2004), 231.

44. Elizabeth Israels Perry, "Training for Public Life: Eleanor Roosevelt and Women's Political Networks in New York in the 1920s," in Hoff-Wilson and Lightman, *Without Precedent*, 38.

45. As cited in Lash, *Eleanor and Franklin*, 289.

46. Cook, *Eleanor Roosevelt*, vol. 1, 349–350.

47. Ibid., 350.

48. Roosevelt, *Autobiography*, 125.

49. Ibid., 143.

50. Cordery, *Alice*, 313.

51. Henry Morgenthau III, "Elinor F. Morgenthau," in Beasley, Shulman, and Beasley, *Eleanor Roosevelt Encyclopedia*, 344.

52. Cook, *Eleanor Roosevelt*, vol. 1, 339–340.

53. Roosevelt, *Autobiography*, 122.

54. Mrs. Franklin D. Roosevelt, "Women Must Learn to Play the Game as Men Do," *The Red Book Magazine* 50 (April 1928), 141.

55. Ibid., 70.

56. Ibid., 70–71.

57. Ibid.

58. As cited in Lash, *Eleanor and Franklin*, 311.

59. See Mrs. Franklin D. Roosevelt, "What I Want Most out of Life," *Success Magazine*, May 1927, 16–17, 70.

60. Ibid.

61. As cited in Lash, *Eleanor and Franklin*, 301.

62. S. J. Woolf, "A Woman Speaks Her Political Mind," *New York Times Magazine*, 8 April 1928, p. 3.

63. Cook, *Eleanor Roosevelt*, vol. 1, 371.

64. As cited in ibid., 346.

65. Ibid., 372–373.

66. Lash, *Eleanor and Franklin*, 314.

67. Eleanor Roosevelt, *This I Remember* (New York: Harper & Brothers, 1949), 41.

68. Lash, *Eleanor and Franklin*, 317.

69. Roosevelt, *This I Remember*, 46.

70. Cook, *Eleanor Roosevelt*, vol. 1, 375.

71. As cited in ibid., 376.

72. As cited in Lash, *Eleanor and Franklin*, 319.

73. As cited in Cook, *Eleanor Roosevelt*, vol. 1, 379.

74. Geoffrey Ward, "Franklin D. Roosevelt," in Beasley, Shulman, and Beasley, *Eleanor Roosevelt Encyclopedia*, 455.

75. Cook, *Eleanor Roosevelt*, vol. 1, 384.

76. Emma Bugbee, "Keeping Up with Mrs. Roosevelt a Joy, Not a Job, Secretary Says," clipping, *New York Herald-Tribune*, 18 December 1939, Malvina Thompson Papers, in personal possession of Eleanor Zartman, Bethesda, Md.

77. Susan Ware, "Mary Williams (Molly) Dewson," in Beasley, Shulman, and Beasley, *Eleanor Roosevelt Encyclopedia*, 133.

78. Lash, *Eleanor and Franklin*, 323.

79. Ibid.

80. Ibid., 325.

81. Interview with Frances A. Perkins, vol. 3, part 1, Oral History Collection, Columbia University, New York, N.Y., 22.

82. Roosevelt, *This I Remember*, 56.

83. Persico, *Franklin and Lucy*, 194.

84. Ibid., 193.

85. Mrs. Franklin D. Roosevelt, "Ten Rules for Success in Marriage," *Pictorial Review* 33 (December 1931), 4.

86. Roosevelt, *This I Remember*, 349.

CHAPTER 3. MERGING THE PERSONAL AND THE POLITICAL

1. Roosevelt, *This I Remember*, 69.

2. Lash, *Eleanor and Franklin*, 351.

3. Kenneth S. Davis, *FDR: The New York Years 1928–1933* (New York: Random House, 1979), 339.

4. Lash, *Eleanor and Franklin*, 352.

5. Susan Ware, "ER and Democratic Politics: Women in the Postsuffrage Era," in Hoff-Wilson and Lightman, *Without Precedent*, 51.

6. Mrs. Franklin D. Roosevelt, "What Do Ten Million Women Want?" *Home* (March 1932), 19–21, 86.

7. Ibid.

8. As quoted by Susan Faludi, "Second-Place Citizens," *New York Times*, 26 August 2008, A19.

9. Mrs. Franklin D. Roosevelt, "What Is a Wife's Job Today? An Interview with M. K. Wisehart," *Good Housekeeping* 91 (August 1930), 34–35, 166, 169–173.

10. Ibid.

11. Ibid.

12. As cited in Lash, *Eleanor and Franklin*, 346.

13. Roosevelt, *This I Remember*, 73.

14. Ibid.

15. Roosevelt, "Ten Rules for Success in Marriage," 4.

16. Ibid.

17. "Todhunter School," in Beasley, Shulman, and Beasley, *Eleanor Roosevelt Encyclopedia*, 517.

18. "Finances, Personal," in Beasley, Shulman, and Beasley, *Eleanor Roosevelt Encyclopedia*, 181.

19. Donald A. Ritchie, *Electing FDR: The New Deal Campaign of 1932* (Lawrence: University Press of Kansas, 2007), 140.

20. As quoted in ibid.

21. Roosevelt, *Autobiography*, 135.

22. Eleanor Roosevelt Papers, hereafter referred to as ERP, Business and Financial Material: folder, income tax matters, 1933, FDRL.

23. Maurine Beasley and Paul Belgrade, "Eleanor Roosevelt: First Lady as Radio Pioneer," *Journalism History* 11 (Autumn/Winter 1984), 42.

24. Beth Haller, "Babies—Just Babies," in Beasley, Shulman, and Beasley, *Eleanor Roosevelt Encyclopedia*, 44.

25. "Just Babies," *Time* (20 July 1932), 24.

26. Mollie Somerville, *Eleanor Roosevelt: As I Knew Her* (McLean, Va.: EPM Publications, 1996), 81–83.

27. Ibid., 81–82.

28. ERP, Speech and Article File, folder—memo, "Suggested Topics for Articles for Baby Magazine," FDRL.

29. As cited in Lash, *Eleanor and Franklin*, 373.

30. Lorena Hickok Papers, hereafter referred to as LHP, folder—ER–Hickok correspondence, 11 April 1933, FDRL.

31. As cited in Cook, *Eleanor Roosevelt*, vol. 1, 399.

32. Roosevelt, *This I Remember*, 74.

33. ERP, Speech and Article File, "What I Hope to Leave Behind!" typescript for *Pictorial Review* article, April 1933, p. 3, FDRL.

34. Davis, *FDR: The New York Years*, 330.

35. Ibid., 331.

36. Blanche W. Cook, "Earl Miller," in Beasley, Shulman, and Beasley, *Eleanor Roosevelt Encyclopedia*, 339–343.

37. Elliott Roosevelt and James Brough, *An Untold Story: The Roosevelts of Hyde Park* (New York: Putnam's, 1973), 276.

38. James Roosevelt with Bill Libby, *My Parents: A Differing View* (Chicago: Playboy, 1976), 110.

39. Frances Perkins, *The Roosevelt I Knew* (New York: Viking, 1946), 69.

40. Ibid.

41. Ibid.

42. Roosevelt, *This I Remember*, 69.

43. Roosevelt, "Ten Rules for Success in Marriage," 4.

44. Roosevelt, *Autobiography*, 158.

45. Cook, *Eleanor Roosevelt*, vol. 1, 205.

46. Nancy Beck Young, *Lou Henry Hoover: Activist First Lady* (Lawrence: University Press of Kansas, 2004), 141.

47. Betty Boyd Caroli, *First Ladies*, expanded ed. (New York: Oxford, 1995), 182–183.

48. Louis Liebovich, "Lou Henry Hoover," in Beasley, Shulman, and Beasley, *Eleanor Roosevelt Encyclopedia*, 245–246.

49. Young, *Lou Henry Hoover*, 144.

50. Caroli, *First Ladies*, 183.

51. Roosevelt, *This I Remember*, 76.

52. See Mrs. Franklin D. Roosevelt, *When You Grow Up to Vote* (Boston: Houghton Mifflin, 1932).

53. See *Hunting Big Game in the Eighties: The Letters of Elliott Roosevelt, Sportsman, Edited by His Daughter* (New York: Scribner's, 1932); see also review in *New York Times*, 12 March 1933, p. 10.

54. Lash, *Eleanor and Franklin*, 382.

55. Mrs. Franklin D. Roosevelt, *It's Up to the Women* (New York: Frederick Stokes, 1933), 145.

56. Ibid., 192.

57. Ibid., 212–213.

58. Lash, *Eleanor and Franklin*, 381.

59. Suzanne La Follette, "To the Ladies," *Saturday Review of Literature* 10 (11 November 1933), 253.

60. Mary R. Beard, "Mrs. Roosevelt as Guide and Philosopher," *New York Herald Tribune Books* (5 November 1933), 7.

61. Hickok, *Reluctant First Lady*, iii.

62. Doris Faber, *The Life of Lorena Hickok: E.R.'s Friend* (New York: William Morrow, 1980), 13–23.

63. Ibid., 24–69.

64. Hickok, *Reluctant First Lady*, 10.

65. Agnes Hooper Gottlieb, "Lorena A. Hickok," in Beasley, Shulman, and Beasley, *Eleanor Roosevelt Encyclopedia*, 232–233.

66. The letters, which total some 23,000, are among materials that make up the Lorena Hickok Papers contained in eighteen boxes, FDRL.

67. Gottlieb, "Lorena A. Hickok," in Beasley, Shulman, and Beasley, *Eleanor Roosevelt Encyclopedia*, 235.

68. LHP, folder, Associated Press news copy, 9 November 1932, FDRL.

69. LHP, folder, Hickok to Malvina Thompson, 23 July 1949, FDRL.

70. Hickok, *Reluctant First Lady*, 96.

71. Roosevelt, *This I Remember*, 78.

72. Blanche Wiesen Cook, *Eleanor Roosevelt*, vol. 2: *1933–1938* (New York: Viking, 1999), 26–27.

73. Hickok, *Reluctant First Lady*, 103.

74. Beasley, *Eleanor Roosevelt and the Media*, 35.

75. Roosevelt, *Autobiography*, 177.

76. Bess Furman, *Washington By-Line: The Personal History of a Newspaperwoman* (New York: Knopf, 1949), 151.

77. Roosevelt, *This I Remember*, 112.

78. Ibid., 113.

79. Alfred B. Rollins Jr., *Roosevelt and Howe* (New York: Knopf, 1962), 387.

80. Ibid., 388; see also Lash, *Eleanor and Franklin*, 367.

81. Phyllis Lee Levin, *Abigail Adams* (New York: St. Martin's Griffin, 2001), 388.

82. As cited in Lash, *Eleanor and Franklin*, 369.

83. Ibid.

84. Robert E. Sherwood, *Roosevelt and Hopkins: An Intimate History* (New York: Harper & Brothers, 1948), 205.

85. Ibid.

86. Ibid.

87. *The White House: An Historic Guide* (Washington, D.C.: White House Historical Association, 2001), 144.

88. Ibid., 90.

89. Cook, *Eleanor Roosevelt*, vol. 2, 33.

90. J. B. West with Mary Lynn Kotz, *Upstairs at the White House: My Life with the First Ladies* (New York: Warner Communications, 1974), 20; see also Persico, *Franklin and Lucy*, 208.

91. Lash, *Eleanor and Franklin*, 370.

92. Cook, *Eleanor Roosevelt*, vol. 2, 33.

93. Lash, *Eleanor and Franklin*, 370–371.

94. As cited in Lash, *Love, Eleanor*, 222.

95. Lillian Rogers Parks in collaboration with Frances Spatz Leighton, *The Roosevelts: A Family in Turmoil* (Englewood Cliffs, N.J.: Prentice-Hall, 1981), 5.

96. Persico, *Franklin and Lucy*, 220.

97. Parks, *Roosevelts*, 177.

98. As cited in Persico, *Franklin and Lucy*, 224.

99. Roosevelt, *This I Remember*, 87.

100. Betty C. Monkman, "First Lady, Ceremonial Role," in Beasley, Shulman, and Beasley, *Eleanor Roosevelt Encyclopedia*, 193.

101. Ibid.

102. Ibid.

103. Cook, *Eleanor Roosevelt*, 372.

104. Irwin Hood (Ike) Hoover, *Forty-Two Years in the White House* (Boston: Houghton Mifflin, 1934), 226.

105. West, *Upstairs at the White House*, 15.

106. Lash, *Franklin and Eleanor*, 372.

107. Marilyn Elizabeth Perry, "Victoria Henrietta Kugler Nesbitt," in Beasley, Shulman, and Beasley, *Eleanor Roosevelt Encyclopedia*, 372.

108. Cook, *Eleanor Roosevelt*, vol. 2, 57.

109. Eleanor Roosevelt to Katherine Buckley, as cited in Cook, *Eleanor Roosevelt*, vol. 2, 58.

110. Margaret Truman, *The President's House* (New York: Ballantine, 2003), 144, 189.

111. Ibid., 189–190.

112. Parks, *Roosevelts*, xii.

113. Ibid., 16.

114. Ibid., 18.

115. Henrietta Nesbitt, *White House Diary* (Garden City, N.Y.: Doubleday, 1949), 79.

116. Roosevelt, *It's Up to the Women*, 65–80.

117. Furman, *Washington By-Line*, 157.

118. Perry, "Victoria Henrietta Kugler Nesbitt," 373.

119. Nesbitt, *White House Diary*, 63.

120. Ibid., 186.

121. Cook, *Eleanor Roosevelt*, vol. 2, 55–56.

122. Alonzo Fields, *My 21 Years in the White House* (New York: Coward-McCann, 1961), 53.

123. Ibid., 50–51.

124. West, *Upstairs at the White House*, 11.

125. Ibid., 18.

126. Parks, *Roosevelts*, 70.

127. Cook, *Eleanor Roosevelt*, vol. 2, 55.

128. West, *Upstairs at the White House*, 17.

129. Cook, *Eleanor Roosevelt*, vol. 2, 37.

130. West, *Upstairs at the White House*, 19.

131. Sherwood, *Roosevelt and Hopkins*, 215.

132. Ibid., 20.

133. Ibid.

134. Lash, *Eleanor and Franklin*, 388.

135. Richard Lowitt, "Henry Lloyd Hopkins," in Beasley, Shulman, and Beasley, *Eleanor Roosevelt Encyclopedia*, 246–247.

136. Lash, *Eleanor and Franklin*, 503.

137. Ibid., 504.

138. James B. McPherson, "James Roosevelt," in Beasley, Shulman, and Beasley, *Eleanor Roosevelt Encyclopedia*, 460.

139. Leonard Schlup, "Harold L. Ickes," in Beasley, Shulman, and Beasley, *Eleanor Roosevelt Encyclopedia*, 268.

140. Ibid., 218.

141. William E. Leuchtenburg, *Franklin D. Roosevelt and the New Deal: 1932–1940* (New York: Harper Colophon, 1963), 125.

142. Harold Ickes, *The Secret Diary of Harold Ickes*, vol. 1 (New York: Simon & Schuster, 1953), 252–253.

143. David M. Kennedy, *Freedom from Fear: The American People in Depression and War, 1929–1945* (New York: Oxford, 1999), 379.

144. Mollie Somerville, "White House Social Office," in Beasley, Shulman, and Beasley, *Eleanor Roosevelt Encyclopedia*, 558.

145. Fields, *My 21 Years in the White House*, 61–62.

146. Ibid., 56.

147. Ickes, *Secret Diary of Harold Ickes*, vol. 1, 249.

148. Somerville, "White House Social Office," 559.

149. Fields, *My 21 Years in the White House*, 61–62.

150. Ibid., 63.

151. Roosevelt, *This I Remember*, 88.

152. Ibid., 89.

153. Ibid., 90.

154. Ickes, *Secret Diary of Harold Ickes*, vol. 1, 163.

155. Elise K. Kirk, *Music at the White House: A History of the American Spirit* (Urbana: University of Illinois Press, 1986), 229.

156. Ibid.

157. Roosevelt, *This I Remember*, 83.

158. Ibid. See also Somerville, *Eleanor Roosevelt*, 62–63.

159. Richard Grid Powers, "Federal Bureau of Investigation," in Beasley, Shulman, and Beasley, *Eleanor Roosevelt Encyclopedia*, 174.

160. Bugbee, "Keeping Up with Mrs. Roosevelt a Joy, Not a Job."

161. Interview with Hope Ridings Miller by Maurine Beasley, Washington, D.C., 3 May 1979, as cited in Beasley, *Eleanor Roosevelt and the Media*, 104.

162. Bugbee, "Keeping Up with Mrs. Roosevelt a Joy, Not a Job."

163. Ickes, *Secret Diary of Harold Ickes*, vol. 1, 239.

164. Tracy A. Johnstone, "Malvina Thompson (Scheider)," in Beasley, Shulman, and Beasley, *Eleanor Roosevelt Encyclopedia*, 512–515.

165. Parks, *Roosevelts*, 67.

166. Geoffrey Ward, *Closest Companion: The Unknown Story of the Intimate Friendship between Franklin Roosevelt and Margaret Suckley* (Boston: Houghton Mifflin, 1995), 218.

167. Faber, *Life of Lorena Hickok*, 92–93.

168. Cathy D. Knepper, ed., *Dear Mrs. Roosevelt: Letters to Eleanor Roosevelt through Depression and War* (New York: Carroll & Graf, 2004), xxi. Knepper has

edited a selection of the letters divided into four categories: The Great Depression, The New Deal, The War Years, and The Home Front.

169. Somerville, *Eleanor Roosevelt*, 25.

170. Ibid., 60; see also Lash, *Eleanor and Franklin*, 372.

171. The letters are included in about 490 cubic feet of the papers of Anna Eleanor Roosevelt, which total some two million pages, FDRL. The bulk of the letters are contained in "Series 70: Correspondence with Government Departments, and Series 100: Personal Letters."

172. As cited in Frances M. Seeber, "'I Want You to Write to Me,' The Papers of Anna Eleanor Roosevelt," in Smith and Ryan, *Modern First Ladies: Their Documentary Legacy*, 61.

173. Ibid., 63.

174. Ibid., 62–63.

175. ERP, Speech and Article File, "Mail of a President's Wife," unpublished article, 1939, p. 1; also "My Mail," unpublished article; and "Mrs. Eleanor Roosevelt's Own Radio Program," 1940, FDRL.

176. Lash, *Eleanor and Franklin*, 373.

177. Mrs. Franklin D. Roosevelt, "I Want You to Write to Me," *Woman's Home Companion* (August 1933), 4.

178. Lash, *Eleanor and Franklin*, 373.

179. Robert Cohen, ed., *Dear Mrs. Roosevelt: Letters from Children of the Great Depression* (Chapel Hill: University of North Carolina Press, 2002), 237.

180. Ibid.

181. Ibid., 240.

182. John A. Salmond, "National Youth Administration," in Beasley, Shulman, and Beasley, *Eleanor Roosevelt Encyclopedia*, 367.

183. Bess Furman typescript of notes on Eleanor Roosevelt's press conference, 6 March 1933, Box 51, Bess Furman Papers, Manuscript Division Library of Congress, Washington, D.C., hereafter referred to as BFP, MDLC.

184. Roosevelt, *This I Remember*, 102.

185. Susan Ware, *Partner and I: Molly Dewson, Feminism, and New Deal Politics* (New Haven, Conn.: Yale University Press, 1987), 176.

186. Ibid., 184.

187. Ibid., 187.

188. As cited in Cook, *Eleanor Roosevelt,* vol. 2, 69.

189. ERP, Series 100: folder, Dewson 1933 (July–December); ER–Dewson correspondence, 21 August 1933, FDRL.

190. ER–Dewson correspondence, 30 August 1933, FDRL.

191. Ware, *Partner and I*, 190.

192. Ibid., 191.

193. Martha H. Swain, "Great Depression," in Beasley, Shulman, and Beasley, *Eleanor Roosevelt Encyclopedia*, 211.

194. Martha Swain, "White House Conferences," in Beasley, Shulman, and Beasley, *Eleanor Roosevelt Encyclopedia*, 558.

195. Lisa R. Barry, "Eleanor Roosevelt: A Rhetorical Reconstruction of First Ladydom," in Molly Meijer Wertheimer, ed., *Inventing a Voice: The Rhetoric of American First Ladies of the Twentieth Century* (Lanham, Md.: Rowman & Littlefield, 2004), 182.

196. As cited in Robert P. Watson, ed., *Life in the White House: A Social History of the First Family and the President's House* (Albany: State University of New York Press, 2004), 143–144.

197. Perkins, *The Roosevelt I Knew*, 166–167.

198. Lois Scharf, "Anna Eleanor Roosevelt," in James S. Olson, ed., *Historical Dictionary of the New Deal* (Westport, Conn.: Greenwood Press, 1985), 428.

199. Perkins, *The Roosevelt I Knew*, 173.

200. Ibid., 69–70.

201. Ibid., 70.

202. Leuchtenburg, *Franklin Roosevelt and the New Deal*, 192.

CHAPTER 4. CLAIMING THE PUBLIC STAGE

1. Roosevelt, *This I Remember*, 103.

2. Ibid.

3. Ibid., 102.

4. Ibid.; Bess Furman typescript, 6 March 1933, Box 76, BFP, MDLC.

5. Roosevelt, *This I Remember*, 102.

6. Kelly A. J. Powers, "Travels," in Beasley, Shulman, and Beasley, *Eleanor Roosevelt Encyclopedia*, 518–520.

7. "Finances, Personal," in Beasley, Shulman, and Beasley, *Eleanor Roosevelt Encyclopedia*, 181.

8. Ibid., 182.

9. Ibid.

10. Ibid.

11. Ibid., 181.

12. Ruby A. Black, United Press dispatches from Washington, 16 January 1935 and 11 January 1936, Box 16, Ruby A. Black Papers, Manuscript Division, Library

of Congress, Washington, D.C., hereafter referred to as RABP, MDLC; see also Beasley, *Eleanor Roosevelt and the Media*, 74.

13. Lash, *Eleanor and Franklin*, 418.

14. Eleanor Roosevelt to Edward G. Skdahl, 21 May 1934, as quoted in "Mrs. Roosevelt Feels Overpaid," clipping, *New York Times*, Box 51, BFP, MDLC.

15. ERP, Speech and Article File, script for Simmons broadcast, 18 September 1934, p. 9, FDRL.

16. ERP, Speech and Article File, script for Simmons broadcast, 9 July 1934, p. 9, ERP.

17. ERP, Speech and Article File, script for Simmons broadcast, 25 September 1934, p. 5, ERP.

18. ERP, Speech and Article File, script for Selby Shoe Co. broadcast, 22 March 1935, pp. 1–2, RABP, MDLC.

19. Ibid.

20. Ibid., 3.

21. "Finances, Personal," in Beasley, Shulman, and Beasley, *Eleanor Roosevelt Encyclopedia*, 182.

22. Kirstin Downey, *The Woman behind the New Deal: The Life of Frances Perkins, FDR's Secretary of Labor and His Moral Conscience* (New York: Nan Talese/Doubleday, 2009), 390.

23. Furman diary, entry for 14 May 1934, Box 1, BFP, MDLC.

24. Roosevelt and Brough, *Untold Story*, 68.

25. LHP, folder, ER–Hickok correspondence, ER to Hickok, 31 May 1933, FDRL.

26. See Daniel J. Boorstin, "From News Gathering to News Making: A Flood of Pseudo-Events," in his *The Image: A Guide to Pseudo-Events in America* (New York: Atheneum, 1978), 7–44.

27. Roosevelt, *This I Remember*, 102.

28. As cited in Beasley, *Eleanor Roosevelt and the Media*, 43.

29. Roosevelt, *This I Remember*, 103.

30. Ibid.

31. Ann Cottrell Free, "Press Conferences," in Beasley, Shulman, and Beasley, *Eleanor Roosevelt Encyclopedia*, 413.

32. Ibid., 414.

33. Caroli, *Roosevelt Women*, 133–136.

34. Ibid., 137.

35. Ibid., 128.

36. Beasley, *Eleanor Roosevelt and the Media*, 41. See also Betty H. Winfield,

"Mrs. Roosevelt's Press Conference Association: The First Lady Shines a Light," *Journalism History* 8 (Summer 1981), 54.

37. ERP, Topical File, folder—ER Press Conferences, 1933–1944, memo, Stephen Early to ER, 9 March 1933, FDRL.

38. Dorothy Roe Lewis, "A First Lady as an Inside Source," *New York Times*, 13 March 1981, p. A31.

39. As cited in Beasley, *Eleanor Roosevelt and the Media*, 42.

40. Ross, *Ladies of the Press*, 510. Strayer's shorthand notes are transcribed in part by William D. Mohr in Maurine H. Beasley, ed., *The White House Press Conferences of Eleanor Roosevelt* (New York: Garland, 1983).

41. ERP, Topical File, folder—ER Press Conferences, 1933–1944, Martha Strayer to Eleanor Roosevelt [30 March 1933], FDRL.

42. Ross, *Ladies of the Press*, 539–542.

43. LHP, Hickok correspondence, LH to Malvina Thompson, 23 July 1949, FDRL.

44. LHP, ER–Hickok correspondence, ER to LH, 3 April 1933, FDRL.

45. Faber, *Life of Lorena Hickok*, 360.

46. Richard Lowitt and Maurine Beasley, eds., *One Third of a Nation: Lorena Hickok Reports the Great Depression* (Urbana: University of Illinois Press, 1981), x.

47. Hickok, *Reluctant First Lady*, 173.

48. Ibid., 176.

49. Roosevelt, *This I Remember*, 350–351.

50. Furman, *Washington By-Line*, 200.

51. *Time*, 19 February 1934, as quoted in Faber, *Life of Lorena Hickok*, 158–159.

52. Cook, *Eleanor Roosevelt*, vol. 2, 169–171.

53. Ibid., 173–174.

54. Roosevelt, *This I Remember*, 104.

55. Furman, *Washington By-Line*, 153.

56. E. A. Kelly, "Distorting the News," *American Mercury*, March 1935, p. 313.

57. See Ruby A. Black, *Eleanor Roosevelt: A Biography* (New York: Duell, Sloan and Pearce, 1940).

58. Ruby A. Black, "Covering Mrs. Roosevelt," *Matrix* 18 (April 1933), 1.

59. Beasley, *Eleanor Roosevelt and the Media*, 48.

60. Beasley, *White House Press Conferences of Eleanor Roosevelt*, 339–342.

61. Free, "Press Conferences," in Beasley, Shulman, and Beasley, *Eleanor Roosevelt Encyclopedia*, 415.

62. Mrs. Roosevelt's Press Conference Association Papers, folder—minutes, standing committee, Mrs. Roosevelt's Press Conference, 1942, FDRL.

63. Free, "Press Conferences," in Beasley, Shulman, and Beasley, *Eleanor Roosevelt Encyclopedia*, 416.

64. James T. Howard, "Males Squirm at First Lady's Parley," clipping, *PM*, 28 September 1943, Box 16, RABP, MDLC.

65. Bess Furman, *Washington By-Line* (New York: Knopf, 1949), 153.

66. As quoted in Beasley, *Eleanor Roosevelt and the Media*, 48.

67. See Merrilee Cox, "Mrs. R and the Press Girls," unpublished paper, University of Maryland College of Journalism, College Park, Md., Fall 2008.

68. ERP, Topical File, Thompson transcript of Eleanor Roosevelt's Press Conference, 27 February 1935, FDRL.

69. Cox, "Mrs. R. and the Press Girls."

70. Ishbel Ross, *Ladies of the Press* (New York: Harper's, 1936), 309.

71. "First Lady: Press Conferences Help Pet Projects and F.D.R.," *Newsweek*, 17 April 1937, p. 24.

72. Black, "Dinner Table Talk in Washington," unidentified, undated clipping, Box 16, RABP, MDLC.

73. David Welky, *Everything Was Better in America* (Urbana: University of Illinois Press, 2008), 20.

74. Associated Press news copy, as quoted in Furman, *Washington By-Line*, 194.

75. John Tebbel and Sarah Mills Watts, *The Press and the Presidency: From George Washington to Ronald Reagan* (New York: Oxford, 1985), 437.

76. Ibid., 438.

77. Ibid.

78. LHP, ER–Hickok correspondence, 24 September 1937, FDRL.

79. "News Media," in Otis L. Graham Jr. and Meghan Robinson Wander, eds., *Franklin D. Roosevelt: His Life and Times: An Encyclopedic View* (New York: Da Capo, n.d.), reprint of 1985 edition, 293.

80. Tebbel and Watts, *Press and the Presidency*, 438.

81. As quoted in Beasley, *Eleanor Roosevelt and the Media*, 66.

82. Drew Pearson and Robert S. Allen, "Washington Merry-Go-Round," 14 May 1938, clipping, unidentified newspaper, Box 27, May Craig Papers, MDLC.

83. ERP, Speech and Article File, Thompson transcription, Eleanor Roosevelt's press conference, 23 April 1934, FDRL.

84. Furman typescript of notes on Eleanor Roosevelt's press conference, 30 April 1934, Box 76, BFP, MDLC.

85. Ibid., typescript of notes for 6 March 1933.

86. William H. Chafe, *The American Woman: Her Changing Social, Economic, and Political Roles, 1920–1970* (New York: Oxford, 1972), 55.

87. "Curb on Women Hit by Mrs. Roosevelt," *New York Times*, 11 April 1933, p. 21.

88. ERP Scrapbooks, "Horse Throws Mrs. Roosevelt into Mud Hole," clipping, *New York Herald Tribune*, 13 April 1933, Box T-121, FDRL.

89. Cook, *Eleanor Roosevelt*, vol. 2, 56.

90. Furman, *Washington By-Line*, 165–166.

91. Brooke Kroeger, *Fannie* (New York: Times Books, 1999), 256.

92. Furman, *Washington By-Line*, 188–189.

93. Ibid., 190.

94. Cook, *Eleanor Roosevelt*, vol. 2, 56.

95. As pictured in Beasley, *Eleanor Roosevelt and the Media*, 50.

96. As quoted in Beasley, *Eleanor Roosevelt and the Media*, 56.

97. Ibid.

98. Typescript, unpublished book on Eleanor Roosevelt's press conferences, Box 2, Martha Strayer Papers, University of Wyoming, referred to hereafter as MSP, UW.

99. Edith P. Mayo, "Clothing," in Beasley, Shulman, and Beasley, *Eleanor Roosevelt Encyclopedia*, 99.

100. Jean Collins, *She Was There: Stories of Pioneering Women Journalists* (New York: Messner, 1980), 40.

101. As quoted in Beasley, *Eleanor Roosevelt and the Media*, 55–56.

102. Hickok, *Reluctant First Lady*, 86

103. Lash, *Eleanor and Franklin*, 341.

104. Personal interview by Maurine Beasley with Max Desfor, 27 June 2008, Silver Spring, Md.

105. Mayo, "Clothes," in Beasley, Shulman, and Beasley, *Eleanor Roosevelt Encyclopedia*, 99.

106. "Women's Forest Work Camps May Be Set Up," clipping, *New York Times*, 24 May 1933, Winifred Mallon scrapbook, Box 154, BFP, MDLC.

107. Ware, *Beyond Suffrage*, 7.

108. Roosevelt to Furman, 15 April 1933, Box 32, BFP, MDLC.

109. Free, "Press Conferences," in Beasley, Shulman, and Beasley, *Eleanor Roosevelt Encyclopedia*, 413.

110. Lash, *Eleanor and Franklin*, 362.

111. Eleanor Roosevelt statement to the press, 3 April 1933, Box 76, BFP, MDLC.

112. ERP, Series 100: White House correspondence, 1933–1945, folder—personal letters, 1933, Martha Strayer to ER, 15 October 1933, FDRL.

113. See Winfield, "Mrs. Roosevelt's Press Conference Association," 54–58.

114. Stephen T. Early Papers, correspondence, Early to ER, 10 February 1941, FDRL.

115. Ibid.

116. Donald A. Ritchie, *Reporting from Washington: The History of the Washington Press Corps* (New York: Oxford University Press, 2005), 28–33.

117. Strayer typescript of notes on Eleanor Roosevelt's press conference, 15 May 1936, Box 2, MSP, UW.

118. Linda Lotridge Levin, *The Making of FDR: The Story of Stephen T. Early, America's First Modern Press Secretary* (Amherst, N.Y.: Prometheus Books, 2008), 148.

119. James R. Kearney, *Anna Eleanor Roosevelt: The Evolution of a Reformer* (Boston: Houghton Mifflin, 1968), 72–73.

120. Furman diaries, entries for 25 March 1935, 27 May 1935, and 10 February 1936, Box 1, BFP, MDLC.

121. William H. Chafe, *Private Lives/Public Consequences: Personality and Politics in Modern America* (Cambridge: Harvard University Press, 2005), 34.

122. President's Secretary's File, folder—subject file, Eleanor Roosevelt, 1936–1942, memo to the President, Mr. Farley, Mr. Michelson, Mr. High, Mr. Early, Miss Dewson, 16 July 1936, FDRL.

123. Furman, *Washington By-Line*, 253.

124. John B. Roberts, *Rating the First Ladies* (New York: Citadel, 2003), 242–244.

125. Lash, *Love, Eleanor*, 243–244.

126. Lash, *Eleanor and Franklin*, 522.

127. Welky, *Everything Was Better in America*, 58.

128. Frank Freidel, Foreword, in Beasley, *White House Press Conferences of Eleanor Roosevelt*, x.

129. William D. Mohr transcription of Strayer notes, in Beasley, *White House Press Conferences of Eleanor Roosevelt*, 287–288.

130. Bess Furman diary, entry for 25 March 1934, Box 1, BFP, MDLC.

131. Furman typescript, 4 May 1939, Box 78, BFP, MDLC.

132. Ibid.

133. Lash, *Love, Eleanor*, 245.

134. LHP, ER–Hickok correspondence, ER to LH, 31 July 1935, FDRL.

135. ERP, "My Day," 30 December 1935, FDRL.

136. Lash, *Eleanor and Franklin*, 425–426.

137. ERP, "My Day," 1 January 1936, FDRL.

138. ERP, "My Day" correspondence, Monte F. Bourjaily to ER, 27 December 1935, FDRL.

139. Mohr transcription of Strayer shorthand notes, 16 January 1936, in Beasley, *White House Press Conferences of Eleanor Roosevelt*, 36; Roosevelt, *This I Remember*, 178.

140. Beasley, *Eleanor Roosevelt and the Media*, 86.

141. ERP, "My Day," 4 December 1937, FDRL.

142. ERP, "My Day," 6 March 1937, FDRL.

143. As cited in Beasley, *Eleanor Roosevelt and the Media*, 97.

144. Mohr transcription of Strayer shorthand notes, 17 September 1939, in Beasley, *White House Press Conferences of Eleanor Roosevelt*, 128.

145. ERP, "My Day" correspondence, George Carlin to ER, 10 April 1937, enclosing memo from JC [unidentified editor], 8 April 1937, FDRL.

146. ERP, "My Day" correspondence, ER to George Carlin, 16 April 1937, FDRL.

147. ERP, "My Day," 7 January 1936, FDRL.

148. LHP, ER–Hickok correspondence, ER to LH, 16 January 1936, FDRL.

149. ERP, "My Day," 20 August 1936, Box 3170, FDRL.

150. Margaret Marshall, "Columnists on Parade," *Nation* 137 (26 February 1938), 14–15.

151. See Henry Morgenthau III, "Crashing F.D.R.'s Party," *New York Times*, 1 December 2009, p. A35.

152. Tebbel and Watts, *Press and the Presidency*, 440.

153. Beth Haller, "American Newspaper Guild," in Beasley, Shulman, and Beasley, *Eleanor Roosevelt Encyclopedia*, 9.

154. Furman diary, entry for 15 February 1938, Box 1, BFP, MDLC.

155. ERP, "My Day," 23 September 1936, FDRL.

156. LHP, ER–Hickok correspondence, ER to LH, 27 July 1936, FDRL.

157. LHP, ER–Hickok correspondence, LH to ER, 31 July 1936, FDRL.

158. LHP, ER–Hickok correspondence, LH to ER, 16 October 1938, FDRL.

159. Beasley, *Eleanor Roosevelt and the Media*, 109.

160. Rebecca West, "Finds Mrs. Roosevelt 'Timid,'" *Philadelphia Bulletin*, 2 February 1937.

161. Beasley, *Eleanor Roosevelt and the Media*, 109.

162. ERP, "My Day," 11 February 1938, FDRL; Mohr transcription of Eleanor Roosevelt press conference, 14 February 1938, in Beasley, *White House Press Conferences of Eleanor Roosevelt*, 49.

163. Mohr transcription of Eleanor Roosevelt's press conference, 17 January 1939, in Beasley, *White House Press Conferences of Eleanor Roosevelt*, 73–74.

164. Ibid., 74.

165. Bess Furman and Lucile Furman, "Discover Your Home Town," *Democratic Digest*, March 1940, pp. 18–19, 37.

166. ERP, "My Day," 13 February 1937, FDRL.

167. ERP, "My Day," 30 March 1937, FDRL.

168. ERP, "My Day," 25 June 1938, FDRL.

169. ERP, "My Day," 1 February 1936, FDRL.

170. Roberts, *Rating the First Ladies*, 244.

171. Ibid., 244–245.

172. Roosevelt and Brough, *Untold Story*, 268.

173. ERP, "My Day," 14 December 1936, FDRL.

174. ERP, "My Day," 23 January 1937, FDRL.

175. ERP, "My Day," 18 January 1937, FDRL.

176. Burns and Dunn, *Three Roosevelts*, 100.

177. Mark H. Leff, "Revisioning U.S. Political History," *American Historical Review* 100, no. 3 (June 1995), 850–851.

178. "My Day," 16 April 1938, as quoted in Rochelle Chadakoff, ed., *Eleanor Roosevelt's* My Day*: Her Acclaimed Columns, 1936–1945* (New York: Pharos Books, 1989), 85.

179. "My Day," 2 October 1938, in ibid., 100–101.

180. Leff, "Revisioning U.S. Political History," 851.

181. "My Day," 12 August 1938, as published in Chadakoff, *Eleanor Roosevelt's* My Day, 95.

182. Ibid.

183. Allida Black, "(Anna) Eleanor Roosevelt," in Lewis L. Gould, ed., *American First Ladies: Their Lives and Their Legacy* (New York: Garland, 1996), 433.

184. ERP, "My Day," 11 May 1936, FDRL.

185. LHP, ER–Hickok correspondence, ER to LH, 12 June 1936, FDRL.

186. Mohr transcription of Strayer shorthand notes, 27 September 1939, in Beasley, *White House Press Conferences of Eleanor Roosevelt*, 128.

187. Arthur Krock, *New York Times*, 10 August 1939, p. 18.

188. See Excerpts Press Conference 570 in *The Public Papers and Addresses of Franklin D. Roosevelt*, vol. 8 (New York: Macmillan, 1949), 432–433.

189. ERP, "My Day," 8 August 1939, FDRL. See also Krock, ibid., and "'My Day' Dominant Influence," *Saturday Evening Post*, 9 September 1939, p. 24.

190. ERP, "My Day," 12 June 1939, FDRL.

191. ERP, "My Day," 14 June 1939, FDRL.

192. George Carlin to ER, 17 August 1940, as quoted in Lash, *Eleanor and Franklin*, 429.

193. Chadakoff, *Eleanor Roosevelt's* My Day, 113.

194. See Allida M. Black, "Championing a Champion: Eleanor Roosevelt and the Marian Anderson 'Freedom Concert,'" *Presidential Studies Quarterly* 20 (Fall 1990), 719–736.

195. Linda Reed, "Southern Conference Movement: The Southern Conference for Human Welfare and the Southern Conference Educational Fund," in Beasley, Shulman, and Beasley, *Eleanor Roosevelt Encyclopedia*, 486.

196. Lash, *Eleanor and Franklin*, 526.

197. Reed, "Southern Conference Movement," in Beasley, Shulman, and Beasley, *Eleanor Roosevelt Encyclopedia*, 486.

198. Scott A. Sandage, "Marian Anderson," in Beasley, Shulman, and Beasley, *Eleanor Roosevelt Encyclopedia*, 23.

199. Lash, *Eleanor and Franklin*, 526–527.

200. Sandage, "Marian Anderson," 24.

201. Black, *Casting Her Own Shadow*, 43.

202. Lash, *Eleanor and Franklin*, 526.

CHAPTER 5. REACHING THE DISPOSSESSED

1. As cited in Chafe, *Private Lives/Public Consequences*, 35.

2. Abigail McCarthy, "Democratic Party," in Beasley, Shulman, and Beasley, *Eleanor Roosevelt Encyclopedia*, 129.

3. Ibid.

4. Eleanor Roosevelt press conference, 15 May 1933, Martha Strayer typescript, Box 2, MSP, UW.

5. Ibid.

6. Burns and Dunn, *Three Roosevelts*, 389.

7. Kelley A. J. Powers, "Travels," in Beasley, Shulman, and Beasley, *Eleanor Roosevelt Encyclopedia*, 520.

8. Ibid.

9. Burns and Dunn, *The Three Roosevelts*, 389.

10. Ware, "ER and Democratic Politics," in Hoff-Wilson and Lightman, *Without Precedent*, 53.

11. The reports were published in Lowitt and Beasley, *One Third of a Nation*.

12. LHP, ER–Hickok correspondence, ER to LH, 12 November 1933, FDRL.

13. Harry L. Hopkins Papers, Hopkins–Hickok correspondence, LH to Hopkins, 11 April 1934, FDRL.

14. LHP, ER–Hickok correspondence, ER to LH, 25 June 1934, FDRL.

15. Joanna Schneider Zangrando and Robert L. Zangrando, "ER and Black Civil Rights," in Hoff-Wilson and Lightman, *Without Precedent*, 92–93.

16. Leonard Ray Teel, "Antilynching Movement," in Beasley, Shulman, and Beasley, *Eleanor Roosevelt Encyclopedia*, 28.

17. Lash, *Eleanor and Franklin*, 516.

18. Zangrando and Zangrando, "ER and Black Civil Rights," in Hoff-Wilson and Lightman, *Without Precedent*, 100.

19. Cook, *Eleanor Roosevelt*, vol. 1, 6.

20. Lash, *Eleanor and Franklin*, 522.

21. Ibid.

22. Lowitt and Beasley, xxxii.

23. Zangrando and Zangrando, "ER and Black Civil Rights," in Hoff-Wilson and Lightman, *Without Precedent*, 100.

24. As quoted in Lash, *Eleanor and Franklin*, 525.

25. Zangrando and Zangrando, "ER and Black Civil Rights," in Hoff-Wilson and Lightman, *Without Precedent*, 100–101.

26. Caryn Neumann, "Eleanor Clubs," in Beasley, Shulman, and Beasley, *Eleanor Roosevelt Encyclopedia*, 157.

27. Roosevelt, *This I Remember*, 126–127.

28. Ibid., 127.

29. Bryan Ward, "Arthurdale," in Beasley, Shulman, and Beasley, *Eleanor Roosevelt Encyclopedia*, 33.

30. Ibid., 32.

31. Lash, *Eleanor and Franklin*, 396.

32. Letter from Clarence Pickett to Elizabeth Marsh cited by Holly Cowan in a master's thesis submitted to the Columbia University Department of History, 1968, and reprinted in Lash, *Eleanor and Franklin*, 396.

33. Ibid., 400.

34. Ibid., 398.

35. Ibid., 397–398.

36. Hickok, *Reluctant First Lady*, 140.

37. Ward, "Arthurdale," in Beasley, Shulman, and Beasley, *Eleanor Roosevelt Encyclopedia*, 32.

38. Ibid.

39. Ickes, *Secret Diary of Harold L. Ickes*, vol. 1, 207.

40. Lash, *Eleanor and Franklin*, 400.

41. RFPDC, correspondence, Eleanor Roosevelt to Sara D. Roosevelt, ER to Sara D. Roosevelt, 14 January 1918, FDRL.

42. Henry Morgenthau III, "Elinor Morgenthau," in Beasley, Shulman, and Beasley, *Eleanor Roosevelt Encyclopedia*, 344.

43. Ibid., 347.

44. Ibid., 345.

45. Ibid., 348.

46. Jordan A. Schwarz, *The Speculator: Bernard M. Baruch in Washington, 1917–1965* (Chapel Hill: University of North Carolina Press, 1981), 308.

47. Cited in ibid., 309.

48. Ibid., 309, 311.

49. Mildred Gilman, "Homesteaders Wildly Cheer for First Lady," *Washington Herald*, 8 June 1934.

50. Ward, "Arthurdale," in Beasley, Shulman, and Beasley, *Eleanor Roosevelt Encyclopedia*, 35.

51. Ibid.

52. Personal communication from Helen L. Cawley to Maurine H. Beasley, 2 May 1983.

53. Cook, *Eleanor Roosevelt*, vol. 2, 147–148.

54. Ward, "Arthurdale," in Beasley, Shulman, and Beasley, *Eleanor Roosevelt Encyclopedia*, 31.

55. Cook, *Eleanor Roosevelt*, vol. 2, 148.

56. Burns and Dunn, *Three Roosevelts*, 275.

57. Cook, *Eleanor Roosevelt*, vol. 2, 157.

58. J. Kirkpatrick Flack, "District of Columbia," in Beasley, Shulman, and Beasley, *Eleanor Roosevelt Encyclopedia*, 138.

59. Ibid., 137.

60. As cited in Cook, *Eleanor Roosevelt*, vol. 2, 157.

61. Flack, "District of Columbia," in Beasley, Shulman, and Beasley, *Eleanor Roosevelt Encyclopedia*, 138.

62. Beasley, *White House Press Conferences of Eleanor Roosevelt*, 49.

63. Lash, *Eleanor and Franklin*, 461.

64. Black, *Eleanor Roosevelt*, 302.

65. *Washington Star*, 6 May 1940, as cited in Flack, "District of Columbia," in Beasley, Shulman, and Beasley, *Eleanor Roosevelt Encyclopedia*, 140.

66. Roosevelt, *This I Remember*, 162.

67. See Eleanor Roosevelt, "Can a Woman Ever Be President of the United States?" *Cosmopolitan* (October 1935), 22–23, 120–121.

68. LHP, ER–Hickok correspondence, ER to LH, 6 August 1935, FDRL.

69. LHP, ER–Hickok correspondence, ER to LH, 30 July 1935, with typescript of "Can a Woman Be Elected President of the United States," p. 13, FDRL.

70. Ibid., 14, 15.

71. Cook, *Eleanor Roosevelt,* vol. 2, 276.

72. LHP, typescript, "Can a Woman Be Elected President?" 3.

73. Furman typescript, Eleanor Roosevelt press conference, 27 February 1939, Box 78, BFP, MDLC.

74. Roosevelt, *It's Up to the Women*, 202.

75. Cook, *Eleanor Roosevelt*, vol. 2, 354.

76. LHP, ER–Hickok correspondence, ER to LH, 2 May 1935, FDRL. See also Cook, *Eleanor Roosevelt*, vol. 2, 257–259.

77. Mary Evans Seeley, *Season's Greetings from the White House* (New York: Mastermedia, 1996), 29–31. See also Eleanor Roosevelt, *Eleanor Roosevelt's Christmas Book* (New York: Dodd, Mead, 1963).

78. Roosevelt, *This I Remember*, 159.

79. Cook, *Eleanor Roosevelt*, vol. 2, 282.

80. Lois Scharf, *Eleanor Roosevelt: First Lady of American Liberalism* (Boston: Twayne, 1987), 93–94.

81. Ibid., 94.

82. Ibid., 75.

83. Ware, *Beyond Suffrage*, 6–7.

84. Ibid., 8–10, 146.

85. Ibid., 51–52.

86. Lash, *Eleanor and Franklin*, 383.

87. Perkins, *The Roosevelt I Knew*, 32.

88. Ware, *Beyond Suffrage*, 89.

89. Julieanne Phillips, "Frances Perkins," in Beasley, Shulman, and Beasley, *Eleanor Roosevelt Encyclopedia*, 401.

90. Katherine Lenroot to Malvina Thompson Scheider, 7 April 1938, as cited in Lash, *Eleanor and Franklin*, 459.

91. Other members of the women's network included Lucille Foster McMillin, civil service commissioner from 1933 to 1949, and Emily Guffey Miller, vice-chair of the Democratic National Committee, who was the sister of a powerful

senator, Joseph Guffey of Pennsylvania. She and Eleanor did not see eye to eye; Miller favored the Equal Rights Amendment while Eleanor did not.

92. Cook, *Eleanor Roosevelt*, vol. 2, 68.

93. Ibid., 69.

94. Mary Anderson, as told to Mary N. Winslow, *Woman at Work: The Autobiography of Mary Anderson* (Minneapolis: University of Minnesota Press, 1951), 178.

95. As quoted in Ware, *Beyond Suffrage*, 116.

96. Ware, *Beyond Suffrage*, 79.

97. As cited in ibid.

98. See Martha H. Swain, "ER and Ellen Woodward: A Partnership for Women's Relief and Security," in Hoff-Wilson and Lightman, *Without Precedent*, 135–152.

99. Martha H. Swain, "White House Conferences," in Beasley, Shulman, and Beasley, *Eleanor Roosevelt Encyclopedia*, 558.

100. "Mrs. Roosevelt Hits Low Pay for Women Enrolled as Skilled Relief Workers," *New York Times*, 5 December 1933, Mallon scrapbooks, Box 154, BFP, MDLC.

101. Swain, "ER and Ellen Woodward," in Hoff-Wilson and Lightman, *Without Precedent*, 146.

102. Cook, *Eleanor Roosevelt*, vol. 2, 275–276.

103. Swain, "ER and Ellen Woodward," in Hoff-Wilson and Lightman, *Without Precedent*, 146.

104. As cited in Scharf, *Eleanor Roosevelt*, 92.

105. June Hopkins, "Hallie Flanagan," in Beasley, Shulman, and Beasley, *Eleanor Roosevelt Encyclopedia*, 194.

106. Swain, "ER and Ellen Woodward," in Hoff-Wilson and Lightman, *Without Precedent*, 147.

107. Ibid.

108. Randolph Boehm and Linda Reed, "Mary McLeod Bethune," in Beasley, Shulman, and Beasley, *Eleanor Roosevelt Encyclopedia*, 51.

109. Reminiscence prepared for the 1958 convention of Americans for Democratic Action, cited in Lash, *Eleanor and Franklin*, 457–458.

110. Chafe, *Private Lives/Public Consequences*, 35.

111. As cited in Lash, *Eleanor and Franklin*, 536.

112. See discussion of CCC camps in Lash, *Franklin and Eleanor*, 539–540.

113. June Hopkins, "Hilda Worthington Smith," in Beasley, Shulman, and Beasley, *Eleanor Roosevelt Encyclopedia*, 481.

114. Ibid.

115. As cited in Robert Cohen, "Youth," in Beasley, Shulman, and Beasley, *Eleanor Roosevelt Encyclopedia*, 591.

116. Roosevelt, *This I Remember*, 165.

117. Winifred D. Wandersee, "ER and American Youth: Politics and Personality in a Bureaucratic Age," in Hoff-Wilson and Lightman, *Without Precedent*, 68.

118. Ibid., 69.

119. Scharf, *Eleanor Roosevelt*, 114.

120. Elaine Smith, "Mary McLeod Bethune," in Sicherman and Green, eds., *Notable American Women*, 76–80.

121. "Mary McLeod Bethune," in Graham and Wander, *Franklin D. Roosevelt: His Life and Times*, 26.

122. Boehm and Reed, "Mary McLeod Bethune," in Beasley, Shulman, and Beasley, *Eleanor Roosevelt Encyclopedia*, 80.

123. "Black Cabinet," in Graham and Wander, *Franklin D. Roosevelt: His Life and Times*, 39.

124. Boehm and Reed, "Mary McLeod Bethune," in Beasley, Shulman, and Beasley, *Eleanor Roosevelt Encyclopedia*, 48.

125. Lash, *Eleanor and Franklin*, 526.

126. Ibid.

127. Cook, *Eleanor Roosevelt*, vol. 2, 161.

128. Patricia Bell-Scott, "Anna Pauline ('Pauli') Murray," in Beasley, Shulman, and Beasley, *Eleanor Roosevelt Encyclopedia*, 352.

129. Lash, *Eleanor and Franklin*, 524.

130. As quoted in Cook, *Eleanor Roosevelt*, vol. 1, 441.

131. Roosevelt press conference, 10 October 1939, in Beasley, *White House Press Conferences of Eleanor Roosevelt*, 131.

132. Cook, *Eleanor Roosevelt*, vol. 2, 511.

133. Ibid., 504.

134. Scharf, *Eleanor Roosevelt*, 115.

135. Wandersee, "ER and American Youth: Politics and Personality in a Bureaucratic Age," in Hoff-Wilson and Lightman, *Without Precedent*, 76.

136. Ibid.

137. Roosevelt, *This I Remember*, 202.

138. Scharf, *Eleanor Roosevelt*, 116.

139. Chafe, *Private Lives/Public Consequences*, 52.

140. As cited in ibid.

141. Joseph Lash, *A Friend's Memoir* (Garden City, N.Y.: Doubleday, 1964), 140–141.

142. Veronica A. Wilson, "Joseph P. Lash," in Beasley, Shulman, and Beasley, *Eleanor Roosevelt Encyclopedia*, 306.

143. Telephone interview by Maurine Beasley with India Edwards, 27 April 1983.

144. Faber, *Life of Lorena Hickok*, 282–283.

145. Lash, *Eleanor and Franklin*, 605.

146. As cited in ibid., 606.

147. Eileen Eagan, "American Youth Congress," in Beasley, Shulman, and Beasley, *Eleanor Roosevelt Encyclopedia*, 18.

148. Roosevelt, *This I Remember*, 204.

149. Ibid.

150. Ibid, 205.

CHAPTER 6. BACKING THE WAR EFFORT

1. LHP, ER–Hickok correspondence, ER to LH, 21 July 1939, FDRL.

2. George Gallup, "Mrs. Roosevelt More Popular Than President, Survey Finds," *Washington Post*, 15 January 1939, Section 3, p. 1.

3. "Oracle," *Time*, 17 April 1939, 22.

4. *New York World-Telegram*, 2 December 1939, as quoted in Kearney, *Anna Eleanor Roosevelt*, 32.

5. Dorothy Thompson, "On the Record," *New York Herald Tribune*, 16 February 1940, as quoted in Kearney, *Anna Eleanor Roosevelt*, 51–52.

6. Albert L. Warner, "Roosevelt Ousts Doris Stevens and Stirs a Women's Tempest," clipping, unidentified newspaper, 16 February 1939, Mallon scrapbooks, Box 156, BFP, MDLC.

7. Furman typescript, notes on Mrs. Roosevelt's press conference, 7 February 1939, Box 78, BFP, MDLC.

8. Ibid.

9. Ibid.

10. Mohr transcripton of Roosevelt press conference, 17 January 1939, in Beasley, *White House Press Conferences of Eleanor Roosevelt*, 72.

11. Furman typescript, notes on Mrs. Roosevelt's press conference, 7 February 1939, Box 78, BFP, MDLC.

12. ERP, "My Day," 6 April 1938, FDRL.

13. Furman typescript, notes on Mrs. Roosevelt's press conference, 7 February 1939, Box 78, BFP, MDLC.

14. Truman, *President's House*, 215.

15. ERP, "My Day" correspondence, George Carlin to ER, 23 May 1939, FDRL.

16. ERP, "My Day," 26 May 1939, FDRL.

17. Furman typescript, Mrs. Roosevelt's press conference, 7 February 1939.

18. Roosevelt, *This I Remember*, 190.

19. Ibid., 198.

20. Mohr transcription, Eleanor Roosevelt press conference, 27 September 1939, in Beasley, *White House Press Conferences of Eleanor Roosevelt*, 127.

21. "Peace Crusade Begun Here by Mrs. Roosevelt," unidentified newspaper clipping, 7 April 1937, quoted in Beasley, *Eleanor Roosevelt and the Media*, 124.

22. Ruby A. Black, United Press dispatch from Washington, 27 September 1939, Box 6, RABP, MDLC.

23. Louis Howe Personal Papers, folder—Anna Eleanor Roosevelt, 1935–1944; ER to Grace Howe, 5 October 1938, FDRL.

24. Roosevelt, *It's Up to the Women*, 237.

25. As quoted in Blanche W. Cook, "'Turn Toward Peace': ER and Foreign Affairs," in Hoff-Wilson and Lightman, *Without Precedent*, 109.

26. Ibid.

27. As quoted in ibid., 113.

28. Ibid., 114.

29. See Eleanor Roosevelt, *This Troubled World* (New York: Kinsey, 1938).

30. Katherine Woods, "Mrs. Roosevelt's Views on Peace," *New York Times Book Review*, 2 January 1938, p. 3.

31. Carl Joseph Bon Tempo, "Refugees," in Beasley, Shulman, and Beasley, *Eleanor Roosevelt Encyclopedia*, 432.

32. Furman typescript, Eleanor Roosevelt press conference, 13 February 1939, Box 78, BFP, MDLC.

33. Ibid.

34. Bon Tempo, "Refugees," 433.

35. Michael Berenbaum, "Holocaust," in Beasley, Shulman, and Beasley, *Eleanor Roosevelt Encyclopedia*, 239.

36. Ibid.

37. Cook, *Eleanor Roosevelt*, vol. 2, 329.

38. Ibid., 305.

39. Leonard Dinnerstein, "Jews," in Graham and Wander, *Franklin D. Roosevelt: His Life and Times*, 217.

40. Doris Kearns Goodwin, *No Ordinary Time: Franklin and Eleanor Roosevelt: The Home Front* (New York: Simon & Schuster, 1994), 102.

41. Cook, *Eleanor Roosevelt*, vol. 2, 312.

42. As cited in Cook, "Turn toward Peace," in Hoff-Wilson and Lightman, *Without Precedent*, 115.

43. Eleanor Roosevelt to Varian Fry, 8 July 1940, as cited in Michael Berenbaum, "Varian Fry," in Beasley, Shulman, and Beasley, *Eleanor Roosevelt Encyclopedia*, 199.

44. Holly Cowan Shulman, "Sumner Welles," in Beasley, Shulman, and Beasley, *Eleanor Roosevelt Encyclopedia*, 556.

45. Lash, *Eleanor and Franklin*, 637.

46. As quoted in ibid.

47. Berenbaum, "Varian Fry," in Beasley, Shulman, and Beasley, *Eleanor Roosevelt Encyclopedia*, 199.

48. Eleanor Roosevelt to Eileen Fry, 13 May 1941, as cited in ibid., 200.

49. Goodwin, *No Ordinary Time*, 103.

50. Berenbaum, "Holocaust," in Beasley, Shulman, and Beasley, *Eleanor Roosevelt Encyclopedia*, 240.

51. Deborah E. Lipstadt, *Beyond Belief* (New York: Free Press, 1986), 201.

52. As cited in ibid., 241.

53. ERP, "My Day," 14 August 1943, FDRL.

54. Ibid.

55. Lipstadt, *Beyond Belief*, 227.

56. Berenbaum, "Holocaust," in Beasley, Shulman, and Beasley, *Eleanor Roosevelt Encyclopedia*, 240.

57. Roosevelt, *This I Remember*, 212.

58. As quoted in Goodwin, *No Ordinary Time*, 18.

59. As quoted in ibid., 89.

60. As quoted in Richard S. Kirkendall, "Henry A. Wallace," in Graham and Wander, *Franklin D. Roosevelt: His Life and Times*, 442.

61. Roosevelt, *This I Remember*, 215.

62. Ibid., 217.

63. Ibid.

64. As quoted in Goodwin, *No Ordinary Time*, 133.

65. Roosevelt, *This I Remember*, 218.

66. As quoted in Lash, *Eleanor and Franklin*, 612.

67. Furman typescript, Eleanor Roosevelt's press conference, 22 May 1939, Box 78, BFP, MDLC.

68. As quoted in Lash, *Eleanor and Franklin*, 613.

69. As quoted in Goodwin, *No Ordinary Time*, 140.

70. Mohr transcription, Eleanor Roosevelt's press conference, 10 October 1939, in Beasley, *White House Press Conferences of Eleanor Roosevelt*, 136, 133.

71. ERP, "My Day," 2 November 1940, FDRL.

72. As quoted in Goodwin, *No Ordinary Time*, 187.

73. ERP, "My Day," 2 November 1940, FDRL.

74. Mohr transcription, Eleanor Roosevelt press conference, 13 May 1941, in Beasley, *White House Press Conferences of Eleanor Roosevelt*, 199.

75. Eleanor [Roosevelt] to Isabella [Greenway], 22 August 1940, in Kristie Miller and Robert H. McGinnis, eds., *A Volume of Friendship: The Letters of Eleanor Roosevelt and Isabella Greenway, 1904–1953* (Tucson: Arizona Historical Society, 2009), 261–262.

76. Questions submitted to Mrs. Roosevelt attached to Black, to Roosevelt, 15 March 1940, and replies, Roosevelt and Thompson to Black, Thompson to Black, 2 July 1940, and Black to Thompson, 5 July 1940, Box 2, RABP, MDLC.

77. Roosevelt, *This I Remember*, 219.

78. Westbrook Pegler, "Fair Enough," *New York World-Telegram*, 17 March 1938, as cited in Lash, *Eleanor and Franklin*, 428.

79. Pegler, "Fair Enough," *New York World-Telegram*, 6 August 1940, as quoted in *Editor and Publisher*, 10 August 1940, p. 5.

80. ERP, "My Day," 9 August 1940 and 16 September 1940, FDRL.

81. Lash, *Eleanor and Franklin*, 630; Roosevelt, *This I Remember*, 219.

82. Howard W. Allen, "Elections in the Roosevelt Era," in Graham and Wander, *Franklin D. Roosevelt: His Life and Times*, 120.

83. Lash, *Eleanor and Franklin*, 631.

84. Truman, *President's House*, 144.

85. Ibid.

86. Ibid.

87. Eleanor Roosevelt, "If You Ask Me: Defense and Girls," *Ladies' Home Journal* 58 (May 1941), 25, 54.

88. Roosevelt, *This I Remember*, 232.

89. As quoted in Lash, *Eleanor and Franklin*, 642.

90. Roosevelt, *This I Remember*, 230–231.

91. As quoted in Beasley, *Eleanor Roosevelt and the Media*, 141.

92. ERP, "My Day," 7 September 1941, FDRL.

93. Lash, *Eleanor and Franklin*, 643.

94. As quoted in Pottker, *Sara and Eleanor*, 337.

95. Ward, *Closest Companion*, 148.

96. Ibid., 159.

97. Ibid., 143.

98. Roosevelt, "Gracie Hall Roosevelt," in Beasley, Shulman, and Beasley, *Eleanor Roosevelt Encyclopedia*, 459.

99. "First Lady Is Tardy for New Job," *Washington Times-Herald*, 30 September 1941.

100. Ruby Black, United Press dispatch from Washington, D.C., 15 September 1941, in Beasley, *Eleanor Roosevelt and the Media*, 141.

101. Roosevelt, *This I Remember*, 230.

102. Ibid., 231.

103. ERP, Speech and Article File, script of Eleanor Roosevelt's Pan-American Coffee Bureau radio program, 7 December 1941, FDRL.

104. Lash, *Eleanor and Franklin*, 647.

105. Roosevelt, *This I Remember*, 234.

106. Lash, *Eleanor and Franklin*, 648.

107. ERP, "My Day," 16 December 1941, FDRL.

108. ERP, "My Day," 21 December 1941, FDRL.

109. Roosevelt, *This I Remember*, 243.

110. ERP, scrapbook, "Amidst Crowded Days" by A. Cypen Lubitsh, Walter Lippman, clipping, *New York Herald Tribune*, 16 December 1941, FDRL.

111. Mohr transcription of Eleanor Roosevelt press conference, 12 January 1942, in Beasley, *White House Press Conferences of Eleanor Roosevelt*, 250.

112. ERP, "My Day," 16 December 1941, FDRL.

113. Donald A. Ritchie, "Office of Civil Defense," in Beasley, Shulman, and Beasley, *Eleanor Roosevelt Encyclopedia*, 389.

114. *Time*, 16 February 1942, p. 49.

115. Mohr transcription of Eleanor Roosevelt press conference, 9 February 1942, in Beasley, *White House Press Conferences of Eleanor Roosevelt*, 268.

116. Mohr transcription of Eleanor Roosevelt press conference, 5 January 1942, in ibid., 238.

117. Mohr transcription of Eleanor Roosevelt press conference, 12 January 1942, in ibid., 248.

118. Roosevelt, *This I Remember*, 240.

119. Ibid., 250.

120. ERP, Speech and Article File, script of Mrs. Roosevelt's Pan-America Coffee Bureau radio program, 22 February 1942, FDRL.

121. ERP, "My Day," 23 February 1942, FDRL.

122. Westbrook Pegler, "Fair Enough," *Washington Post*, 14 July 1942.

123. *Time*, 2 March 1942, p. 2.

124. "Mrs. Roosevelt Resigns," *New York Times*, 21 February 1942.

125. Beasley, *Eleanor Roosevelt and the Media*, 151.

126. David Witwer, "Westbrook Pegler, Eleanor Roosevelt, and the FBI," *Journalism History* 34, no. 4 (Winter 2009), 195.

127. Ibid., 199.

128. Ibid., 200.

129. Quoted in Black, *Casting Her Own Shadow*, 143.

130. Script of Eleanor Roosevelt Pan-American Coffee Bureau radio program, 15 February 1942, 3, 4, RABP, MDLC.

131. ERP, Japanese American Internment Artificial Collection, Series 100 correspondence, folder Ea to Ei, ER to Flora Rose, 16 June 1942, FDRL.

132. ERP, Japanese American Internment Artificial Collection, Series 70 correspondence, Letter signed by Malvina Thompson to Clara Hinze, 22 May 1942, FDRL

133. ERP, "My Day," 27 April 1943, FDRL.

134. Black, *Casting Her Own Shadow*, 146.

135. Pauli Murray, *The Autobiography of a Black Activist, Feminist, Lawyer, Priest, and Poet* (Knoxville: University of Tennessee Press, 1987), 190.

136. Ibid.

137. As quoted in Goodwin, *No Ordinary Time*, 351.

138. Murray, *Autobiography of a Black Activist*, 173.

139. Goodwin, *No Ordinary Time*, 489.

140. Ibid., 370.

141. For a full description of the "Eleanor Club" investigation, see Eleanor Roosevelt, FBI File, Microfilm Roll 1-0405, FDRL.

142. "Colored Guests Rumor of Value to Nazis, Mrs. Roosevelt Says," *Washington Star*, 17 December 1942.

143. As quoted in Black, *Casting Her Own Shadow*, 89.

144. Eleanor Roosevelt, *The Moral Basis of Democracy* (New York: Howell, Soskin, 1940), 43.

145. Nick Broughton, "Books in a World at War," *Peace Action of the National Council for Prevention of War* 7 (December 1940), 7.

146. See Leon Bryce Block, "Speaking of Books," *Living Age* 359 (November 1940), 286–288.

147. Eleanor Roosevelt, "Race, Religion and Prejudice," *New Republic* 106 (11 May 1942), 630.

148. See Eleanor Roosevelt, "If I Were a Negro," *Negro Digest* 1 (October 1943), 8–9.

149. Ibid.

150. Ibid.

151. Black, *Casting Her Own Shadow*, 91.

152. As quoted in ibid., 92.

153. See "Los Angeles Zoot Suit Riots," http://www.laalmanac.com/history/hi07t.htm, retrieved 31 August 2009.

154. See "Zoot Suits Riots," *The American Experience*, http://www.pbs.org/wgbh/amex/zoot/eng_peopleevents/e_riots.html, retrieved 31 August 2009.

155. "Mrs. Roosevelt Says Racial Friction Was Basis of Coast/Zoot-Suit Rioting," clipping, *PM*, 17 June 1943, Eleanor Roosevelt, FBI File, Microfilm Roll 1-0400, FDRL.

156. Roosevelt, *This I Remember*, 265.

157. As quoted in Lash, *Eleanor and Franklin*, 668.

158. Goodwin, *No Ordinary Time*, 383.

159. ERP, "My Day," 5 November 1942, ERP.

160. Joan London, "American Red Cross," in Beasley, Shulman, and Beasley, *Eleanor Roosevelt Encyclopedia*, 12.

161. Goodwin, *No Ordinary Time*, 422.

162. *Chicago Defender*, 10 April 1943, quoted in Bryant Simon, "World War II," in Beasley, Shulman, and Beasley, *Eleanor Roosevelt Encyclopedia*, 588.

163. As quoted in Black, *Casting Her Own Shadow*, 92.

164. As quoted in Simon, "World War II," in Beasley, Shulman, and Beasley, *Eleanor Roosevelt Encyclopedia*, 589.

165. Roosevelt, *This I Remember*, 306.

166. For Lash's explanation and the official investigative file, see Lash, *Love, Eleanor*, 458–493.

167. As quoted in Joseph Lash, *A World of Love: Eleanor Roosevelt and Her Friends* (Garden City, N.Y.: Doubleday, 1984), 71.

168. Goodwin, *No Ordinary Time*, 468–469.

169. London, "American Red Cross," in Beasley, Shulman, and Beasley, *Eleanor Roosevelt Encyclopedia*, 13.

170. *Time*, 22 May 1944, p. 43.

171. As quoted in J. William T. Youngs, *Eleanor Roosevelt: A Personal and Public Life*, 3rd ed. (New York: Pearson Longman, 2006), 230.

172. Eleanor Roosevelt, "How to Take Criticism," *Ladies' Home Journal* 61 (November 1944), 155.

173. Lash, *Eleanor and Franklin*, 693.

174. George Carlin to Eleanor Roosevelt, 27 November 1943, Box 4873, ERP.

175. Mohr transcription of Strayer notes on Eleanor Roosevelt's press conference, 12 January 1942 and 14 May 1942, in Beasley, *White House Press Conferences of Eleanor Roosevelt*, 250, 298.

176. Mohr transcription of Strayer notes for 29 April 1942, ibid., 287.

177. Ann Cottrell Free, "Mrs. Roosevelt Assails Stories about Waacs," *New York Herald Tribune*, 8 June 1943.

178. Transcript of Mrs. Roosevelt's press conference, 24 February 1943, Box 2997, ERP, FDRL.

179. As quoted in Beasley, *Eleanor Reosevelt and the Media*, 138.

180. "Mrs. Dewey's Press Conference," clipping, *Washington Times-Herald*, 1 July 1944, RABP, MDLC.

181. Lash, *Love, Eleanor*, 38.

182. Eleanor Roosevelt to Catherine D. Stallworth, 26 August 1944, Series 100, ERP, FDRL.

183. "Is It a Grievous Mistake That We Are Americans?" and "Mrs. F.D.R.'s Letter Called Bid for Southern Vote," *Baltimore Afro-American*, 16 September 1944, p. 4.

184. See Ruth Montgomery, *Hail to the Chief* (New York: Coward McCann, 1976), 16–17. See also Beasley, *Eleanor Roosevelt and the Media*, 161–162.

185. Montgomery, *Hail to the Chief*, 16–17.

186. *New York Times* news copy marked "First Lady," 11 October 1944, Box 51 BFP, MDLC.

187. Eulalie McDowell, "When Stranger Places Are Discovered, Mrs. Roosevelt Will Show Up in Them," clipping, *Washington Daily News*, 19 January 1945, RABP, MDLC.

188. "President Looks Much Better, Mrs. Roosevelt Tells Press," clipping, *Washington Times-Herald*, 2 May 1944, RABP, MDLC.

189. Lash, *Eleanor and Franklin*, 697.

190. Michael S. Sweeney, *Secrets of Victory* (Chapel Hill: University of North Carolina Press, 2001), 182–183.

191. As quoted in Lash, *Eleanor and Franklin*, 708.

192. As quoted in Lash, *World of Love*, 139.

193. Ted Morgan, *FDR: A Biography* (New York: Simon & Schuster, 1985), 675.

194. Ibid., 676–677.

195. Smith, *FDR*, 402.

CHAPTER 7. VISIONARY FOR THE WORLD

1. Furman typescript of Eleanor Roosevelt press conference, 12 April 1945, Box 79, BFP, MDLC.

2. Beasley, *White House Press Conferences of Eleanor Roosevelt*, 335–336.

3. As quoted in Goodwin, *No Ordinary Time*, 604.

4. Ibid.

5. Roosevelt, *This I Remember*, 345.

6. Ibid.

7. Bernard Asbell, "Death of FDR," in Graham and Wander, *Franklin D. Roosevelt: His Life and Times*, 91.

8. Roosevelt, *This I Remember*, 346.

9. Ibid.

10. Ibid., 349.

11. Ibid.

12. Ibid., 350.

13. ERP, "My Day," 16 April 1945, FDRL.

14. ERP, "My Day," 18 April 1945, FDRL.

15. Goodwin, *No Ordinary Time*, 617.

16. As quoted in ibid.

17. *Newsweek*, 30 April 1945, p. 44.

18. Roosevelt, *This I Remember*, 351.

19. Tracey A. Johnstone, "Opinion Polls," in Beasley, Shulman, and Beasley, *Eleanor Roosevelt Encyclopedia*, 391.

20. Roosevelt, *This I Remember*, 348.

21. Lash, *Eleanor: The Years Alone*, 13.

22. As quoted in ibid.

23. Leonard Schlup, "Elliott Roosevelt," in Beasley, Shulman, and Beasley, *Eleanor Roosevelt Encyclopedia*, 449.

24. Bernard Asbell, ed., *Mother and Daughter: The Letters of Eleanor and Anna Roosevelt* (New York: Coward, McCann & Geoghegan, 1982), 225.

25. Lash, *Eleanor: The Years Alone*, 16.

26. Eleanor Roosevelt to Harold Ickes, 21 May 1945, as quoted in Lash, ibid., 18.

27. Tracey A. Johnstone, "Opinion Polls," in Beasley, Shulman, and Beasley, *Eleanor Roosevelt Encyclopedia*, 394.

28. ERP, "My Day," 19 November 1959, FDRL.

29. Johnstone, "Opinion Polls," 393.

30. Lash, *World of Love*, 188.

31. Roosevelt, *This I Remember*, 349.

32. Lash, *Eleanor: The Years Alone*, 13.

33. Ibid., 19.

34. Ibid., 26–27.

35. Eleanor Roosevelt, *On My Own* (New York: Harper, 1958), 41–44.

36. Glendon, *A World Made New*, 29–30.

37. Ibid., 33; see also Roosevelt, *On My Own*, 71.

38. Scharf, *Eleanor Roosevelt*, 148.

39. Jason Berger, "Universal Declaration of Human Rights," in Beasley, Shulman, and Beasley, *Eleanor Roosevelt Encyclopedia*, 539–540.

40. Jean Harvey Baker, "United Nations," in Beasley, Shulman, and Beasley, *Eleanor Roosevelt Encyclopedia*, 536.

41. Patricia Sullivan, "National Association for the Advancement of Colored People," in Beasley, Shulman, and Beasley, *Eleanor Roosevelt Encyclopedia*, 361.

42. Richard S. Kirkendall, "Harry S Truman," in Beasley, Shulman, and Beasley, *Eleanor Roosevelt Encyclopedia*, 526.

43. As quoted in Lash, *Eleanor: The Years Alone*, 152–153.

44. Roosevelt, *Autobiography*, 326.

45. Black, *Casting Her Own Shadow*, 168, 169.

46. Anna Kasten Nelson and Sara E. Wilson, "Cold War," in Beasley, Shulman, and Beasley, *Eleanor Roosevelt Encyclopedia*, 102.

47. Eleanor Roosevelt, "If You Ask Me," *McCall's*, July 1953, http://www.gwu.edu/~erpapers/documents/displaydoc.cfm?_t=columns&_docid=iyam059818, retrieved 21 April 2010.

48. Lash, *Eleanor: The Years Alone*, 211.

49. Beasley, *Eleanor Roosevelt and the Media*, 171.

50. As quoted in ibid., 172.

51. Lash, *Eleanor: The Years Alone*, 180.

52. Douglas Gomery, "Television," in Beasley, Shulman, and Beasley, *Eleanor Roosevelt Encyclopedia*, 511–512.

53. See A. David Gurewitsch, *Eleanor Roosevelt: Her Day* (New York: Interchange Foundation, 1973).

54. See Eleanor Roosevelt and Lorena A. Hickok, *Ladies of Courage* (New York: Putnam, 1954).

55. Ibid., 76.

56. Ibid., 306–307.

57. Lash, *Eleanor: The Years Alone*, 318.

58. Mieke van Thoor, "Death of Eleanor Roosevelt," in Beasley, Shulman, and Beasley, *Eleanor Roosevelt Encyclopedia*, 122–123.

59. "Personal Finances," in Beasley, Shulman, and Beasley, *Eleanor Roosevelt Encyclopedia*, 183–184.

60. Ibid., 183.

61. Ibid.

62. Ibid., 184.

CHAPTER 8. MODELING POLITICAL LEADERSHIP

1. See Eleanor Roosevelt with Helen Ferris, *Your Teens and Mine* (Garden City, N.Y.: Doubleday, 1961).

2. See Eleanor Roosevelt with Robert O. Ballou, *Eleanor Roosevelt's Book of Common Sense Etiquette* (New York: Macmillan, 1962).

3. Faber, *Life of Lorena Hickok*, 281–282.

4. Virginia Pasley, "First Lady to the Common Man," *American Mercury* (March 1944), 275.

5. Ibid., 283.

6. Allida Black, ed., *The Eleanor Roosevelt Papers:* Vol. 1, *The Human Rights Years, 1945–1948* (Detroit, Mich.: Thomson Gale, 2007), xxxv.

7. Lisa M. Burns, *First Ladies and the Fourth Estate: Press Framing of Presidential Wives* (DeKalb: Northern Illinois University Press, 2008), 77–78.

8. Lewis L. Gould, "First Ladies," *American Scholar* 55 (1986), 531.

9. Carl Sferrazza Anthony, *First Ladies: The Saga of the Presidents' Wives and Their Power*, vol. 1 (New York: Morrow, 1990), 517.

10. Harry S Truman to Mary Jane Truman, 16 January 1946, as quoted in Margaret Truman, *Harry S Truman* (New York: Morrow, 1973), 304.

11. Summary of questions answered by Mrs. Truman, n.d., Box 32, Edith B. Helm Papers, MDLC.

12. Ibid., 569.

13. Anthony, *First Ladies: The Saga of the Presidents' Wives and Their Power*, vol. 2 (New York: Morrow, 1991), 39.

14. Quoted in Winzola McLendon and Scottie Smith, *Don't Quote Me: Washington Newswomen and the Power Society* (New York: Dutton, 1970), 71–72.

15. Anthony, "Connections with First Ladies," in Beasley, Shulman, and Beasley, *Eleanor Roosevelt Encyclopedia*, 187.

16. As quoted in Anthony, *First Ladies*, vol. 2, 114.

17. Liz Carpenter, *Ruffles and Flourishes: The Warm and Tender Story of a Simple Girl Who Found Adventure in the White House* (Garden City, N.Y.: Doubleday, 1970), 57.

18. As quoted in Anthony, *First Ladies*, vol. 2, 222.

19. Ibid.

20. Rosalynn Carter, *First Lady from Plains* (Boston: Houghton Mifflin, 1984), 292.

21. Nancy Reagan with William Novak, *My Turn: The Memoirs of Nancy Reagan* (New York: Random House, 1989), 57.

22. Ibid., 28–29.

23. As quoted in Anthony, "Connections with First Ladies," in Beasley, Shulman, and Beasley, *Eleanor Roosevelt Encyclopedia*, 188.

24. Anthony, *First Ladies*, vol. 2, 423.

25. Ann Gerhart, *The Perfect Wife: The Life and Choices of Laura Bush* (New York: Simon & Schuster, 2004), 173.

26. Maurine H. Beasley, *First Ladies and the Press: The Unfinished Partnership of the Media Age* (Evanston, Ill.: Northwestern University Press, 2005), 221.

27. Hillary Rodham Clinton, *Living History* (New York: Simon & Schuster, 2003), 258.

28. Ibid., 258–259.

29. Ibid., 147–148.

30. Anthony, "Connections with First Ladies," in Beasley, Shulman, and Beasley, *Eleanor Roosevelt Encyclopedia*, 189.

31. As quoted in Elizabeth Lightfoot, *Michelle Obama: First Lady of Hope* (Guilford, Conn.: Lyons Press, 2009), 87.

32. Nathan Richter, "Michelle Obama and the Third Roosevelt," 10 March 2009, http://www.theglobalist.com/StoryId.aspx?StoryId=7588, retrieved 16 August 2009.

33. Marian Burros, "Obamas to Plant Vegetable Garden at White House," http://www.nytimes.com/2009/03/20/dining/20garden.html?_r=1&hp, retrieved 16 August 2009.

34. Austin Bogues, "Sorority Celebrates Michelle Obama's Acceptance," http://thecaucus.blogs.nytimes.com/2008/07/14/sorority-celebrates-michelle-obamas-accept, retrieved 16 August 2009.

35. See Allida Black, *Eleanor Roosevelt Papers:* Vol. 1, *The Human Rights Years, 1945–48.*

36. Lewis Gould, "First Ladies," 532.

37. As quoted in Julia Baird, "The Savvy, Salty Political Saint," *Newsweek* (24 December 2007), 55.

38. As quoted in ibid.

39. Robert P. Watson, *The Presidents' Wives: Reassessing the Office of First Lady* (Boulder, Colo.: Lynne Rienner, 2000), 54.

40. Ibid.

41. Karen O'Connor, Bernadette Nye, and Laura Van Assendelft, "Wives in the White House: The Political Influence of First Ladies," *Presidential Studies Quarterly* 26 (Summer 1996), 835–853.

42. Ibid., 845.

43. Ibid., 842.

44. Ibid., 841.

45. Betty Houchin Winfield, "The Legacy of Eleanor Roosevelt," *Presidential Studies Quarterly* 20 (Fall 1990), 703.

46. Gould, "First Ladies," 532.

47. Burns and Dunn, *Three Roosevelts*, 574–575.

BIBLIOGRAPHIC ESSAY

More has been written by and about Eleanor Roosevelt than any other first lady, yet there is no source that lists and annotates all of this material. John A. Edens has prepared a 500-page bibliography, *Eleanor Roosevelt: A Comprehensive Bibliography* (Westport, Conn., 1994) that annotates more than 3,700 sources by or about her, but it does not include references to her "My Day" column. Internet resources offer a vast array of material pertaining to Roosevelt, yet they are not all-encompassing. A Google search produces 200,000 separate items, many highly repetitious, which deal with her accomplishments, biography, timeline, quotations, correspondence, homes, and FBI file, among other topics.

In the wealth of information readily available about Eleanor Roosevelt, her transformative influence on the role of the first lady, while clearly recognized, has been almost eclipsed in recent historical study by both her subsequent career at the United Nations and the drama of her extraordinary marriage and personal life. To focus on her contributions as first lady, I have relied on both published sources and unpublished sources. I have drawn on memoirs by Eleanor herself as well as those of family members, White House employees, and journalists who covered her, along with biographies, encyclopedias, and scholarly analyses of New Deal programs.

My aim has been to cite Eleanor's own words whenever possible, by quoting from her extensive body of work. I have consulted entries in *The Eleanor Roosevelt Encyclopedia* (Westport, Conn., 2001), edited by Holly C. Shulman, Henry R. Beasley, and me, finding particularly useful an entry on "Biographies," by Nancy Marie Robertson. Another reference book, *Franklin D. Roosevelt: His Life and Times* (Boston, 1985), edited by Otis L. Graham Jr. and Meghan Robinson Wander, has given quick access to key facts.

The starting point for this research, however, has been the Eleanor Roosevelt Papers at the Franklin D. Roosevelt Library in Hyde Park, New York. The library contains some two million pages documenting Eleanor's extensive correspondence, in which she often was addressed as "Mrs. President." It gives a picture of her importance as a symbol of caring for ordinary Americans during the Great Depression and World War II and illustrates her contacts with government agencies. For an overview, see Frances Seeber, "'I Want You to Write to Me': The Papers of Anna Eleanor Roosevelt," in Nancy Kegan Smith and Mary C. Ryan, eds., *Modern First Ladies: Their Documentary Legacy* (Washington, D.C., 1989). As Seeber explains, the two most important files at Hyde Park from the White House years are "Series 70: Correspondence with Government Departments" and "Series 100: Personal Letters." The library also has a complete set of Eleanor's "My Day" columns and manuscripts of many of her writings and speeches.

To a substantial degree these materials have been mined by historians. Some 200 letters sent to her by impoverished young people have been published in Robert Cohen, ed., *Dear Mrs. Roosevelt: Letters from Children of the Great Depression* (Chapel Hill, N.C., 2002). The letters also are featured on a website, "Dear Mrs. Roosevelt," http.//newdeal.feri.org/eleanor/index.htm. Another work, Cathy D. Knepper, ed., *Dear Mrs. Roosevelt: Letters to Eleanor Roosevelt through Depression and War* (New York, 2004), contains some 150 letters from citizens seeking help and voicing their concerns. Some 270 letters, mainly from the Roosevelt Library and written chiefly to public figures after Eleanor left the White House, are featured in Leonard C. Schlup and Donald W. Whisenhunt, eds., *It Seems to Me: Selected Letters of Eleanor Roosevelt* (Lexington, Ky., 2001). Letters between her and her daughter appear in Bernard Asbell, ed., *Mother & Daughter: The Letters of Eleanor and Anna Roosevelt* (New York, 1982).

While Eleanor's correspondence provides tantalizing glimpses of her as first lady, it is insufficient for addressing her total performance at the White House. In an introduction to the Smith and Ryan book, Lewis L. Gould, editor of *American First Ladies: Their Lives and Their Legacy* (New York, 1996), points to the need for more research into the life of Eleanor Roosevelt. Gould, who has done more than any other historian to establish first ladies as a subject of genuine historical investigation, notes that "despite the shelves of books on Mrs. Roosevelt, many phases of her own rich life have yet to be fully investigated" (vii).

This work does not purport to uncover new findings about Eleanor. Instead, it investigates by synthesizing sources. It attempts to show how Eleanor redefined duties performed by the president's spouse and turned what had been an amorphous position into a powerful political role. This effort requires delving into her private life; obviously the job of first lady is based on a personal relationship.

Eleanor's own publications during the 1930s and 1940s give insight into her thinking about herself, her family, the role of women in general, and liberal democracy. These include her books *Hunting Big Game in the Eighties: The Letters of Elliott Roosevelt, Sportsman, Edited by His Daughter* (New York, 1932); *It's Up to the Women* (New York, 1933); *This Is My Story* (New York, 1937), the first volume of her autobiography; *My Days* (New York, 1938), a collection of selected "My Day" columns from 1936 to 1938; *This Troubled World* (New York, 1938); and *The Moral Basis of Democracy* (New York, 1940). The second volume of her autobiography, *This I Remember* (New York, 1949), covers both the period of her involvement in New York State politics in the 1920s and her years in the White House; it has been particularly valuable for this work.

One hundred twenty-six of Eleanor's most significant articles and speeches, many written and given during her period as first lady, are collected in Allida M. Black, ed., *What I Hope to Leave Behind: The Essential Essays of Eleanor Roosevelt* (Brooklyn, N.Y., 1995). A sampling of her "My Day" columns from 1936 to 1962 appears in a three-volume set, *Eleanor Roosevelt's My Day* (New York, 1989–1991). Rochelle Chadakoff edited volume 1, which includes the White House years. Partial transcripts of Eleanor's press conferences are contained in *The White House Press Conferences of Eleanor Roosevelt* (New York, 1983), which I edited. In *Eleanor Roosevelt and the Media: A Public Quest for Self-Fulfillment* (Urbana, Ill., 1987), I elaborated on Eleanor's media career.

Over the years that I have been studying Eleanor, I have interviewed journalists who knew her, and incorporated some of their comments in this book. I also have used the papers of Bess Furman and Ruby Black in the Manuscript Division of the Library of Congress, Washington, D.C., and the Martha Strayer Papers at the University of Wyoming, Laramie. Furman's memoir, *Washington By-Line: The Personal History of a Newspaperwoman* (New York, 1949), glorified Eleanor's press conferences and friendships with women reporters. Media-related materials, however, while outlining Eleanor's growth as a public communicator, encompass only part of the role of the first lady.

In researching this book I have tried to familiarize myself with biographies that look at Eleanor and her relationship with Franklin from different standpoints. The initial work on her, *Eleanor Roosevelt: A Biography* (New York, 1940), was written by Ruby Black, a journalist and personal friend who lauded the first lady as a pathbreaking figure interested in the downtrodden. The second, Alfred Steinberg, *Mrs. R: The Life of Eleanor Roosevelt* (New York, 1958), like Black's book, lacked citations and praises Eleanor, but concluded her emotions overrode her intellect. These books, which pictured her dedication to good works, set the stage for subsequent biographies.

Historians of Franklin's presidency have been generally less admiring. They have portrayed Eleanor as a subordinate and occasionally troublesome political partner, although they have granted that she played a worthwhile role by reaching out to deprived groups. Works such as Arthur M. Schlesinger Jr., *The Politics of*

Upheaval (Boston, 1960); James MacGregor Burns, *Roosevelt: The Soldier of Freedom, 1940–1945* (New York, 1970); Ted Morgan, *FDR: A Biography* (New York, 1985); Kenneth S. Davis, *FDR into the Storm: 1937–1940* (New York, 1993); and William E. Leuchtenburg, *The FDR Years* (New York, 1995), took this approach. Doris Kearns Goodwin's Pulitzer prizewinning book, *No Ordinary Time: Franklin and Eleanor Roosevelt: The Home Front in World War II* (New York, 1994), also described Eleanor as Franklin's liberal conscience.

Burns and Susan Dunn broadened appraisal of Eleanor in *The Three Roosevelts: Patrician Leaders Who Transformed America* (New York, 2001), suggesting that Eleanor's leadership abilities surpassed those of both Theodore and Franklin Roosevelt. They based that assessment mainly on her post–White House career. The private and public lives of both Franklin and Eleanor in the prepresidential years were explored in Geoffrey C. Ward, *A First-Class Temperament: The Emergence of Franklin Roosevelt* (New York, 1989). It generates background for understanding the Roosevelt marriage and Eleanor's eventual development as first lady. Ward's *Closest Companion: The Unknown Story of the Intimate Friendship between Franklin Roosevelt and Margaret Suckley* (Boston, 1995), which is based on diaries and letters kept by Suckley, Franklin's distant cousin, from 1933 to 1945, viewed Eleanor as first lady through Suckley's discreetly critical gaze.

A more recent biographical study of Franklin is Jean Edward Smith, *FDR* (New York, 2007), which refers to the emotional distance in the Roosevelt partnership. Conrad Black, *Franklin Delano Roosevelt: Champion of Freedom* (New York, 2003), saw Eleanor as insensitive to Franklin and taken in by left-wing causes.

The most influential full-scale biography of Eleanor for years has been Joseph P. Lash, *Eleanor and Franklin: The Story of Their Relationship Based on Eleanor Roosevelt's Private Papers* (New York, 1971), which won both a Pulitzer Prize and a National Book Award. Eleanor's close friend, as well as the first researcher to be allowed to use her papers, Lash emphasized her unhappy childhood. He presented her desire to do good as compensation for personal unhappiness stemming from Franklin's affair with Lucy Mercer Rutherfurd. His comprehensive narrative recounted Eleanor's White House career in exhaustive detail. It has been an integral part of this study.

Lash also wrote *Eleanor: The Years Alone* (New York: 1972), the first detailed look at her activities after Franklin's death. Moving beyond Lash's work, Jason Berger, *A New Deal for the World: Eleanor Roosevelt and American Foreign Policy* (New York, 1981), traced Eleanor's views throughout her life on America's place in the world. Although not the focus of this work, Eleanor's remarkable perfor -

mance at the United Nations, distilled in Mary Ann Glendon, *A World Made New: Eleanor Roosevelt and the Universal Declaration of Human Rights* (New York, 2001), drew on her experiences as first lady and consequently bears some relationship to this project. Allida M. Black, ed., *The Eleanor Roosevelt Papers: The Human Rights Years, 1945–1948* (New York, 2007), the first of a five-volume series being produced at George Washington University, Washington, D.C., expands knowledge of Eleanor's post–White House influence as a public figure.

In *Franklin and Lucy: President Roosevelt, Mrs. Rutherfurd, and the Other Remarkable Women in His Life* (New York, 2008), Joseph E. Persico followed a theme much like Lash's in considering Eleanor's career as first lady. He contended that Franklin's infidelity led to a repressed Eleanor's transformation into political leadership. Persico also examines the impact of Franklin's relationships with other women, including his dominating mother, Sara Delano Roosevelt, on the Roosevelt marriage. A more positive interpretation of Sara's influence on Eleanor was highlighted in Jan Pottker, *Sara and Eleanor: The Story of Sara Delano Roosevelt and Her Daughter-in-Law, Eleanor Roosevelt* (New York, 2004). Both of these works aimed to connect the public and private lives of Franklin and Eleanor.

In a similar mode, memoirs by the Roosevelt children recounted numerous anecdotes about Eleanor and Franklin. They tended to be more uncomplimentary to Eleanor than to Franklin, revealing strains in the White House and other family settings. Among them are James Roosevelt and Sidney Shalett, *Affectionately, F.D.R.* (New York, 1959); Elliott Roosevelt and James Brough, *A Rendezvous with Destiny: The Roosevelts of the White House* (New York, 1975); and James Roosevelt with Bill Libby, *My Parents: A Differing View* (Chicago, 1976). David B. Roosevelt with Manuela Dunn-Mascetti, in *Grandmere: A Personal History of Eleanor Roosevelt* (New York, 2002), and Curtis Roosevelt, in *Too Close to the Sun: Growing Up in the Shadow of My Grandparents, Franklin and Eleanor* (New York, 2008), wrote from the nostalgic perspective of grandchildren. Stacy A. Cordery, *Alice: Alice Roosevelt Longworth, from White House Princess to Washington Power Broker* (New York, 2007), a biography of Eleanor's first cousin, told of the tension between the Hyde Park and Oyster Bay Roosevelts.

Historians oriented to women's history have seen Eleanor quite differently from other biographers. They challenge Lash by picturing her as an independent career woman who should be judged more for her own achievements and less for her contributions to a political partnership. My work endeavors to incorporate their findings while acknowledging strengths that exist in previous interpretations. Susan Ware, *Beyond Suffrage: Women in the New Deal* (Cambridge, 1981), placed Eleanor at the center of a group of women reformers with roots in the

Progressive era. Various women's networks and their influence on Eleanor's political interests were examined in Joan Hoff-Wilson and Marjorie Lightman, eds., *Without Precedent: The Life and Career of Eleanor Roosevelt* (Bloomington, Ind., 1984), published as a centennial tribute to her. It offers a valuable backdrop for Eleanor's White House years.

William Chafe analyzed the interaction of Eleanor's public and private life in "The Personal and Political: Two Case Studies," in Linda K. Kerber, Alice Kessler-Harris, and Kathryn Kish Sklar, *U.S. History as Women's History: New Feminist Essays* (Chapel Hill, N.C., 1995). J. William T. Young, *Eleanor Roosevelt: A Personal and Public Life* (New York, 1985), devoted considerable attention to her childhood and adolescence. Betty Boyd Caroli set Eleanor in the context of bold women within her own family in *The Roosevelt Women* (New York, 1998).

The feminist reinterpretation of Eleanor's life was highlighted in Blanche Cook's two-volume biography, *Eleanor Roosevelt, 1884–1933* and *Eleanor Roosevelt, 1933–1938* (New York, 1992, 1999). These books picture her as a passionate individual whose political power and personal influence have been minimized by historians confining her to the sidelines of Franklin's presidency. Cook now is working on a volume that is expected to yield greater insights into Eleanor's White House career after 1938. Another feminist work, Allida M. Black's *Casting Her Own Shadow: Eleanor Roosevelt and the Shaping of Postwar Liberalism* (New York, 1996), revealed Eleanor's influence on issues of civil rights and civil liberty, particularly after Franklin's death.

The issue of whether Eleanor should be considered a feminist or a reformer marks other studies of her. Lois Scharf, *Eleanor Roosevelt: First Lady of American Liberalism* (Boston, 1987), contended that Eleanor cannot be considered a feminist because her political philosophy did not rest on issues of gender. Scharf viewed Eleanor as a reformer, as did her first two academic biographers, Tamara Hareven, *Eleanor Roosevelt: An American Conscience* (Chicago, 1968), and James Kearney, *Anna Eleanor Roosevelt: The Evolution of a Reformer* (Boston, 1968). Hareven concentrated on psychological factors prompting Eleanor's career, while Kearney discussed her public life up to 1941, including her advocacy for African Americans, but found her an impractical idealist. Susan Hartmann, in Jess Flemion and Colleen M. O'Connor, eds., *Eleanor Roosevelt: An American Journey* (San Diego, 1987), called Eleanor a feminist because she inspired other women.

As part of her reinterpretation, Cook takes up the subject of Eleanor's sexuality, exploring the possibility of a lesbian relationship with Hickok. This first came to light with publication of Doris Faber's *The Life of Lorena Hickok: E.R.'s Friend* (New York, 1980), written after Hickok's papers were opened at the Roosevelt Library and revealed a possible romance between the two. Their private correspondence has been edited by Rodger Streitmatter in *Empty without You: The Intimate Letters of Eleanor Roosevelt and Lorena Hickok* (New York, 1998).

After publication of the Faber book, Lash, who disputed the contents of the Hickok letters as being sexual in nature, published two collections of Eleanor's letters to various friends. They are *Love, Eleanor: Eleanor Roosevelt and Her Friends* (Garden City, N.Y., 1982) and A *World of Love: Eleanor Roosevelt and Her Friends* (Garden City, N.Y., 1984). While these letters contain affectionate phrases, they do not appear to display the same depth of feeling as the Hickok correspondence.

The question of Eleanor's sexuality is tangential to the purpose of this work, yet pertinent. Hickok lived at the White House while Eleanor was first lady and offered her emotional support during her first years there. Evidence of their closeness can be seen in Hickok, *Reluctant First Lady* (New York, 1962), which gives a vivid account of Eleanor's fears about becoming first lady. A book that Richard Lowitt and I edited, *One Third of a Nation: Lorena Hickok Reports the Great Depression* (Urbana, Ill., 1981), shows how Hickok, in her capacity as a federal investigator of relief conditions, brought firsthand accounts of Depression misery to both Eleanor and Franklin and influenced relief administration.

Books by members of the Roosevelt administration offer firsthand accounts of Eleanor's involvement in the New Deal. Those of special utility for this study are Frances Perkins, *The Roosevelt I Knew* (New York, 1946), which depicts a working relationship between Eleanor and Franklin, and Harold L. Ickes, *The Secret Diary of Harold L. Ickes*, 3 vols. (New York, 1953–1954). Volume 1 accuses Eleanor of overspending on the Arthurdale project to relocate unemployed miners and being lax in details of White House management. Pauli Murray, *The Autobiography of a Black Activist, Feminist, Lawyer, Priest, and Poet* (Knoxville, Tenn., 1987), details a remarkable friendship between Eleanor and Murray, a young African American woman, who influenced Eleanor's commitment to civil rights.

Memoirs of the staff add another dimension to understanding Eleanor's performance as mistress of the White House. Eleanor's social secretary, Edith Benham Helm, in *The Captains and the Kings* (New York, 1954), commented carefully on colorful details of social activities. More biting was Henrietta Nesbitt's *White House Diary* (Garden City, N.Y., 1949), in which she defended herself from accusations of poor management. Two secretaries gave admiring recollections of Eleanor in Mollie Somerville, *Eleanor Roosevelt as I Knew Her* (McLean, Va., 1996), and Ruth K. McClure, ed., *Eleanor Roosevelt, an Eager Spirit: Selected Letters of Dorothy Dow, 1933–1945* (New York, 1984). The head butler offered his account of Eleanor as a hostess in Alonzo Fields, *My 21 Years in the White House* (New York, 1961).

Unusual aspects of Roosevelt family life emerged from a book written by J. B. West, chief White House usher, with Mary Lynn Kotz, *Upstairs at the White House: My Life with the First Ladies* (New York, 1973). A maid told of her experiences with the Roosevelts in two books, Lillian Rogers Parks with Frances Spatz Leighton, *My Thirty Years Backstairs at the White House* (New York, 1961), and *The Roosevelts: A Family in Turmoil* (Englewood Cliffs, N.J., 1981). Margaret Truman criticized Eleanor's performance in *First Ladies: An Intimate Group Portrait of White House Wives* (New York, 1995).

In total, all the works referenced in this essay, plus numerous others cited in this study, show that a consensus has yet to be reached on Eleanor Roosevelt as first lady. What impact did she have on her husband's administration and how did she operate as a politician herself? How did she transform the position of first lady? What was the relationship between the personal and the political in her own life? What impact did she have as a role model for other women? This book attempts to unravel at least some of the enigmatic aspects of Eleanor Roosevelt's White House career.

INDEX